BOOKS BY RICHARD E. RUBENSTEIN

REBELS IN EDEN:
MASS POLITICAL VIOLENCE IN THE UNITED STATES

LEFT TURN:
ORIGINS OF THE NEXT AMERICAN REVOLUTION

LEFT TURN

ORIGINS OF THE NEXT AMERICAN REVOLUTION

LEFT TURN

ORIGINS OF THE NEXT AMERICAN REVOLUTION

RICHARD E. RUBENSTEIN

Little, Brown and Company / Boston / Toronto

FIRST EDITION

T10/73

Library of Congress Cataloging in Publication Data

Rubenstein, Richard E
   Left turn.

   Includes bibliographical references.
   1. United States--Politics and government.
2. Liberalism--United States--History. 3. Political
science--History--United States. 4. Social classes--
United States--History. I. Title.
JK271.R89   320.9'73   73-5902
ISBN 0-316-76083-8

*Published simultaneously in Canada
by Little, Brown & Company (Canada) Limited*

PRINTED IN THE UNITED STATES OF AMERICA

To the Memory of My Father,
HAROLD S. RUBENSTEIN
(1908–1972)

ACKNOWLEDGMENTS

The usual list of scholarly acknowledgments will not appear in this space. This was a relatively solitary work, done without benefit of government funds, institutional grants, or research assistants. Perhaps out of pigheadedness, I did not circulate the manuscript to many of my fellow-academicians, and I suspect that it has, therefore, both the virtues and the faults of a one-man job. I do owe profound debts of gratitude, however, to the following:

My colleagues and students at Roosevelt University, Chicago, who were the first audience for most of the ideas expressed herein, and who were not afraid to offer loud and effective criticism. I am particularly grateful to William Pelz, Edward Phillips, Howard Primer, Thaddeus Tecza, Frank Untermyer, and Judith Wittner for their suggestions;

My friends in the Socialist Workers Party, who have helped me link ideas to practice;

Richard Curtis and Roger Donald, who gave aid and comfort when it was most needed;

Ruth Muller who, with her usual good will, helped prepare the manuscript for publication;

Eqbal Ahmad, Judith Corvin, Victor Cook, Julie Diamond, Dr. Jerome Katz, and Michael Schwartz, all of whose friendship and counsel I treasure; and

My wife, Libby, and my sons, Alec and Matthew, for their unfailing love and encouragement.

This book is dedicated to my father, who loved politics, and frequently disagreed with mine. Only death could terminate our dialogue.

RICHARD E. RUBENSTEIN

PREFACE

My purpose in writing this extended essay is to demonstrate that there is both a necessity and a potential for revolution in America. By "revolution" I do not mean the coup-cum-bloodbath of conservative mythology or the election of a liberal reformer, the metaphorical "revolutions" in marketing or taste, or the adventures of rural guerrillas. I mean a rapid, drastic alteration of the political system which will destroy the economic basis for big business' domination of American social and political life and which will bring the working class majority to power.

The demonstration proceeds through three stages: Part I, focusing on American political history, describes the exhaustion of the tradition of liberal reform, emphasizing the role played by liberal coalitions in adapting the political system to the demands of change. Part II seeks to develop an analytic understanding of the relationship between coalition government and class conflict in America. Part III analyzes contemporary changes in class structure and political forms, and attempts to outline the nature and direction of the coming upheaval. The burden of my argument is that the American system of bourgeois coalition government has lost the capacity to absorb and redirect social change, and that, as a result, a new system is even now in the making. What will it look like? That question will not be answered by theorists writing books, but by people struggling for power. Part III suggests, however, that our options are narrowing down. Americans will soon be compelled to decide whether to move decisively Right or Left — whether to support an American-style fascism or a new type of socialism.

Most of those who write or comment upon American history are conscious or unconscious evolutionists; that is, they adopt a stance which assumes that political change is progressive, that it generally takes place in small increments, and that, even when the pace of change accelerates, the most significant adoptions are made peacefully, following the accepted norms of "the system." Recently, under the impact of the assassinations and disorders of the 1960's, evolutionists have been compelled to modify their views somewhat. It is now generally accepted that America has had to swallow large doses of political violence, that assassinations, riots, racial violence, labor-management warfare, and "official violence" have played an important part in American history. But the rediscovery of domestic violence has not overthrown the prevailing evolutionist view since, as many analysts have pointed out, group violence in the United States was usually not revolutionary.* Racial and ethnic riots, farmer insurrections and bloody strikes, gang wars and lynchings, were the results of group struggles for access to political power, wealth, and social status. Through violent revolt, groups without property or power sought those minimal systemic adjustments which would guarantee them a stake in America. In turn, groups a generation or two removed from poverty used coercion to counter threats to their newly won status. The existence of a continuing relationship between political violence and political change is demonstra-

---

* See, for example, Hugh D. Graham and Ted R. Gurr, eds., *Violence in America: Historical and Comparative Perspectives* (New York, Bantam Books, 1969); Richard E. Rubenstein, *Rebels in Eden: Mass Political Violence in the United States*, (Boston, Little, Brown, 1970).

ble, but does not alone overthrow the major premise of evolutionary theory: that periodic surges of liberal reform, carried out peacefully and incrementally, have consistently obviated the necessity for revolution in America.

Carried forward into the present, evolutionism promises significant political change without revolution. Its message to activists is: curb your impatience, get organized, work diligently within the pressure group or political party of your choice, and the system will be reformed as it was under Jefferson, Jackson, Lincoln, and Roosevelt. The tradition of liberal reform is alive and well in America. But is it? Before attempting to answer this question for our own time, it is necessary to define that tradition historically and analytically — or, rather, to redefine it, since it is so poorly understood. This requires, in turn, a reexamination of the nature of American political development.

CONTENTS

PART 1

THE EXHAUSTION OF LIBERAL POLITICS

. . . I do not assert that men living in democratic communities are naturally stationary; I think, on the contrary, that a perpetual stir prevails in the bosom of those societies, and that rest is unknown there; but I think that men bestir themselves within certain limits, beyond which they hardly ever go. They are forever varying, altering, and restoring secondary matters; but they carefully abstain from touching what is fundamental. They love change, but they dread revolutions.
— ALEXIS DE TOCQUEVILLE,
Democracy in America, 1840

The accepted view of American political development remains progressive and Manichean. For all our sophistication, we still picture American history as a series of struggles between the forces of darkness and light, with the forces of light gaining ground in each successive battle. Democracy, it seems, has frequently been menaced both from "above," for example, by Tory aristocrats and southern slaveholders, and from "below," by violent mobs and political fanatics. Yet each challenge produces the necessary response. Flying the banners of liberty, equality, and democracy, "the people" rally behind a series of heroic leaders, each of whom brings the banner-slogan nearer to realization by defeating an elitist enemy in a fair fight.

The first liberal hero, Thomas Jefferson, invents a political party through which farmers and workers can make their voices heard, commits the nation to French revolutionary ideals, and buries New England Federalism. Next, Andrew Jackson completes the Jeffersonian revolution by opening up the political process to mass participation, strengthening executive power, and bringing to bay the "Monster Bank" of the United States. Slavery and secessionism threaten to destroy the Union and terminate the dream, but a new party and a new democratic champion arise — the Republican Lincoln, who frees the slaves and wins the Civil War. For a long time thereafter, politics takes a back seat to economic development, but when big business threatens to become antidemocratic and antiliberal the people rise again, first behind Woodrow Wilson and then behind Franklin Roosevelt, to put the would-be autocrats in their place. The Progressive movement permits the people to vote for United States senators, gives the vote to women, legislates wage-and-hour laws, and exposes corrupt political machines. Its successor, the New Deal, carries the fight to a near finish, championing the cause of the farmer and the union man, writing welfare-state proposals into law, and creating a federal bureaucracy to implement them. Latter-day New Dealers move even farther along the road by extending federal government protection to minority groups and declaring an end to poverty in the United States; they defend American ideals abroad as well by fighting the spread of international communism. Problems remain, of course, but a new surge of liberal reform cannot be far off. Somewhere a new Leader awaits the people's call.

Of course, this is a child's history of the United States. One may object that no one really believes it without qualification, least of all scholars specializing in American history and government. But that is precisely the point: with appropriate qualifications and reservations, its core ideas are accepted by almost everyone, from liberal scholars who await the second coming of F.D.R. to conservatives who admire the restraint and traditionalism of the famous liberals. What accounts for the longevity of this tradition, even among scholars, in the face of contrary evidence?

There are three methods of handling facts which appear to challenge a belief: (1) admit them but show that they do not challenge the belief; (2) admit them without changing the belief; or (3) deny them. All three methods are now employed to defend the liberal faith against other perspectives. For example, we know that Jefferson was a slaveholder and (in his *Notes on Virginia*) a theoretical racist[1]; that Jackson owned slaves, and spent much of his life either fighting Indians or deporting them illegally from the South[2]; that Lincoln did not believe in either social *or political* equality for Negroes[3]; that Woodrow Wilson reintroduced racial segregation into the federal government establishment[4]; and that F.D.R. did little to advance the cause of civil rights for black people either in the North or in the South.[5] Could there be a connection between liberalism and racism? No — of course not. And so the facts do not lead the analyst to explore this convoluted relationship; they lead to explanations, qualifications, and denials. *Explanation*: The political interests of black people could not be recognized until blacks moved into northern cities and became an organized pressure group. *Qualification*: Historically, some liberal leaders have been racists, but this is a perversion of liberalism. Now that mistake is being corrected. *Denial*: Liberals have always been antiracist at heart; Roosevelt, for example, *did* advance the cause of civil rights by negotiating with A. Philip Randolph about job discrimination in defense industries.

Clearly, although there seems to be a relationship between liberalism and racism, it is not easy to define. This is also true if we consider the relationship between liberal reform movements and war. Thomas Jefferson, an admitted expansionist, fought an undeclared naval war against the Barbary States and instituted an embargo on trade with Great Britain, paving the way for the disastrous war on Canada and England waged by his "Warhawk" disciples.[6] Andrew Jackson gained national prominence through military exploits against the British, Indians, and Spanish Floridians (the last an unauthorized expedition to round up runaway slaves). His followers were militant expansionists, and his most ardent disciple, James K. Polk ("Young Hickory"), threatened England with war over

Oregon and manufactured a disgraceful war of conquest against Mexico.[7] Lincoln, of course, was a wartime President, his heroic role in the Civil War marred somewhat by his suspension of the writ of habeas corpus, his attempts to destroy the Democratic opposition in the North, and his postwar sympathy for southern white supremacists.[8] Woodrow Wilson, elected on a peace platform in 1916, led the nation into World War I in 1917, failed to protect German-Americans against continuous persecution, and launched the vindictive campaign against leftist antiwar dissenters which culminated in the infamous Red Scare of 1919–1924.[9] Franklin Roosevelt, an apostle of "preparedness" since the 1920's, mobilized the nation for World War II. Immediately after Pearl Harbor, he ordered the removal and internship in concentration camps of virtually the entire Japanese-American population of the West Coast.[10] His successors, Presidents Truman, Kennedy, and Johnson, led the nation into the Korean and Indochinese wars.

The charge made frequently by Republicans that the Democrats are the "war party," evokes a predictable set of responses. *Explanation*: If reform leaders have sometimes involved the nation in war, this is not because they are militarists, but because they are internationalists who are willing to fight for their ideals. *Qualification*: Some liberals *have* been militarists, but militarists are more often "conservative"; in any event, the error is now being corrected. *Denial*: Each historical situation is different. The apparent link between liberalism and militarism is a coincidence of history, nothing more. Again, these self-contradictory and equivocal responses lead nowhere. On the one hand, we are not convinced that liberals are inherently militaristic, or that the Democrats are a war party; on the other, the evidence suggests that there *is* a connection which the stock responses are designed to obfuscate. Those who believe in the progressive evolution of American politics through liberal reform are compelled to respond to such evidence somewhat as Aristotelian scientists responded to the findings of Copernicus and Galileo. By explaining and qualifying ancient theories, and by denying that Galileo's telescope worked, they could still prove that the sun revolved around the earth — until a simpler and more comprehensive theory won men's minds.

A third question may clarify the point further:

What is the relationship between the liberal coalition and big business? At first glance, one would suppose it to be antagonistic, for, according to tradition, the great "democrats" have represented the "little man" in frequent battles against great concentrations of wealth and power. Did not Jefferson lay low the merchant princes of New England and Jackson the Bank of the United States? Didn't Lincoln destroy the slave aristocracy, Wilson the robber-baron trusts, and Roosevelt the "economic royalists"? Alas, the facts do not corroborate this Jack-the-Giant-Killer image. Once in office, Jefferson and his followers adopted Alexander Hamilton's system of funding debt and raising revenue. By 1816, "Jefferson's party had taken over the whole complex of Federalist policies — manufactures, bank, tariffs, army, navy, and all."[11] Jackson opposed the "Monster Bank" in the name of the "little man," but proved as friendly to business (including the banks) as any Whig. He suppressed the southern rebellion against the protective tariff, opposed government restrictions on business activity, and favored expansion of the southern slave empire to the south and west.[12] Lincoln *was* a Whig, and remained one on matters of economics despite his conversion to Republicanism. Had he lived, he probably would not have been surprised to see his party become the creature of the big business oligarchy, gradually surrendering its idealistic principles of the 1850's to embrace those of the Vanderbilts and the Goulds.

At the very least, one would suppose, Wilson's New

Freedom and Roosevelt's New Deal would be immune to this sort of criticism — but it is precisely in these cases that the contrast between liberal-democratic rhetoric and actual devotion to the interests of the great corporations becomes most apparent. Although Theodore Roosevelt, Wilson, and F.D.R. preached against monopoly and restraint of trade, neither made more than token efforts to prevent the (seemingly irresistible) trend towards industrial concentration — the swallowing up of small businesses by giant monopolies. Both Progressives and New Dealers advocated government regulation of business, but neither challenged the power of the great corporations to nullify regulatory schemes and corrupt the regulators. Both spoke movingly of the need to reduce the gap between rich and poor and to defeat poverty; neither effected a substantial redistribution of income or eliminated that "other America" described by outraged reformers from Jacob Riis to Michael Harrington. Progressives, New Dealers and their liberal successors solicited and received heavy financial support from the big business community, whose members were duly rewarded with public contracts, defense business, tariff protection, tax breaks, foreign policy favors, and great chunks of the public domain.[13] In 1964, President Lyndon Johnson, who believed himself the new Roosevelt, declared another "war on poverty." By 1968, it was apparent that the war was over, and that poverty had won. Similarly, the Progressives, New Dealers and New Frontiersmen promised an end to corruption in government — the elimination of graft, vote-stealing, and favoritism to preferred economic interests. By the time the scandals of the Truman administration were revealed, the New Deal had been thoroughly corrupted both by "honest" businessmen and by gangsters allied with big-city political machines.

What explains the apparent inconsistencies between

liberal-reformist preachment and practice? Why have the "great democrats" so often preached brotherhood and practiced racism, promised peace and delivered war, threatened big business and protected the big businessman? Clearly, the discrepancy between principles and practice is not a function of intention. Jefferson *wanted* to eliminate slavery but found that he could not; Roosevelt *wanted* to eliminate poverty but failed nonetheless. A capitalist democracy's contradictions are not merely ideological but structural — and since the existence of these contradictions is not admitted, larger doses of liberalism succeed only in intensifying them. It is not a question of hypocrisy.

The charge of "hypocrisy" was raised during the 1960's by middle-class students who objected to the wide gap separating their parents' high-flown principles from their personal practices. Hannah Arendt has pointed out that this charge has been hurled by revolutionaries ever since Robespierre attempted to found "the Republic of Virtue."[14] I wish to stress that a principal function of any ruling class ideology is to *prevent* subjective "hypocrisy" by institutionalizing it — to separate principle from practice, but in such a way that its adherents (even the rulers themselves) are unaware of the disparity. Consider, for example, the person who proclaims his opposition to the war in Indochina but invests in "defense" industry stock. Is he a hypocrite? Probably not. He is a conscious hypocrite only if he perceives a logical connection between his private economic activity and his public political stance. But why should he? His liberal ideology rigorously separates the public sphere from the private sphere, just as it erects a wall between politics and economics. (The result could be called "unconscious hypocrisy" if that were not a contradiction in terms.) The investor believes that the war is a political mistake unrelated to the economic order; and he is conditioned to believe that something will be done about it by citizens and officeholders acting in their public capacities, while private persons and companies go about their (unrelated) private business. ("If I liquidate my investments," he might say, "the effect will be nil; but if I retain my wealth, I can use it to work against the war.") In short, the contradiction is not merely, if at all, in the mind of the subject. It is generated by the imperatives of bourgeois rule, which require that a costly, losing war be liquidated, that industry be kept powerful enough to defend its imperial interests, and that investors maintain their class position without suffering perpetual *crises de conscience*. The business of America, Calvin Coolidge stated, is business. As a corollary, one might add: the private business of American citizens is private; it is "none of your business."

Historical analysis may help us to understand, at least in political terms, how a praxis which was revolutionary in the 1770's became in the twentieth century a means of preserving the status quo for the most powerful ruling class in world history. The point is not merely to offer a critical analysis of liberal-democratic ideology, but to describe the relationship between that ideology and American social structure. To anticipate, I believe that the analysis will support the following propositions:

(1) The social function of American liberalism has been to make possible the unification of two great (and conflicting) economic classes: an enlarged petty bourgeoisie or small-propertied class and the big business class with its allies in government, the military establishment, and the professions.

(2) The political institutions developed to embody liberal ideology and to implement this unification are the American-style political party and, more important, the governing coalition.

(3) These ideological and institutional arrangements, which are of the essence of American liberal democracy, have insured the exclusion of the underclass (unskilled labor, the poor, nonwhites) from the political system, and have guaranteed the continuation in the world's richest nation of poverty, racism, corruption, expansionism, and war.

(4) At the present time, because of basic changes in the American social structure, these arrangements are collapsing. The result, outlines of which may already be perceived, is change of a new qualitative order — that is, revolutionary change.

■■

The history of the early Republic shadows forth patterns of political organization and change which, like photographic negatives, become "fixed" in the acid bath of later industrialization. Analysis reveals that, since the American Revolution, this nation has been governed by a succession of coalitions, few in number, which have generally come to power after periods of intense civil disorder, and which have held power for long periods of time, becoming steadily more elitist, warlike, and repressive in the process. The rhythm of this process is inexplicable according to commonly accepted "evolutionary" and "revolutionary" theories of change. "Evolution" does not explain the apparent necessity for violence and disorder during periods of coalitional breakdown and reorganization, nor is the assumption of progress ("the evolution of democracy") warranted. "Revolution" is inaccurate as a description of traditional American styles of political violence, and does not account for the remarkable continuity of our political institutions. New conceptual tools will be necessary to help us understand the life cycle of the American governing coalition.

The process of coalition-formation, to begin with, is almost always a violent one. The American Revolution, for example, was preceded by two stormy decades of group revolt — a long series of uncoordinated, frequently conflicting uprisings by Indian tribes along the frontier, tenant farmers in Maryland and New Jersey, independent debtor farmers in Massachusetts, Pennsylvania, and the Carolinas, poor workers in Rhode Island, merchants in New England, large planters in Virginia, and urban artisans in several major cities.[15] These revolts were not, at first, "revolutionary": they were "each group for itself and against every other group" mobilizations, with farmers arrayed against Indians and colonial merchants, merchants disobeying the British authorities but pressing small farmers and gentlemen planters for payment of debts, poor workers rioting for debt relief and against colonial legislatures, and those same legislatures challenging the power of British-appointed governors. The true crisis of authority began with the passage of the Stamp Act of 1765, which was as much a focus for dissident energies then as the Indochinese war was for the American Left of the 1960's. The succeeding ten years, marked by spreading civil disobedience, vain petitions to king and Parliament, violent mass demonstrations, and increasingly repressive parliamentary legislation, resulted, finally, in arms stockpiling and fighting in the countryside. Throughout this period one can trace the gradual development of a Patriot coalition, including some, but not all, of the groups formerly in isolated revolt, but cutting across class lines and sectional boundaries. The Loyalist opposition, equally diverse, included alienated backcountry farmers and rebellious Indians as well as Tory "aristocrats," while a neutral Centrist group, originally very large, saw itself steadily diminished by polarization.[16]

This revolutionary ferment is illustrative of several persistent patterns in the history of American disorder and reform. First, the initial resort of individual groups to violent rebellion is usually the result of their inability to achieve essentially reformist goals within the existing political system. These groups do not become interested in revolution until it appears that their very right to exist as effective political entities depends on a radical alteration of the political system. (Even then, as the pattern of Loyalist recruitment makes clear, some alienated groups may be "polarized" onto the counterrevolutionary side.) Second, the alliances formed among groups during the early crisis period are *not* organized on the basis of economic class solidarity. They cut across class lines, and unless the crisis is extremely deep and prolonged, (as during the depression of the 1930's) solidary class-based alliances do not materialize. Both coalitions, revolutionary and counterrevolutionary, seek to represent a cross-section of "the nation," an alliance of lower-middle-class with upper-middle- and upper-class groups. (The very poor, who constitute a racial or ethnic caste, are excluded from "the nation.")

For this reason, the organizing principle of such coalitions is *the national principle*: the coalition claims to represent the entire nation, with the exception of the "invisible" underclass and the opposition elite. The result of successful coalitions among dissident groups organized on a national basis is a tacit compromise. To oversimplify, the new coalition adopts the political rhetoric, and to some extent the political program, of those groups which provide its mass base — principally small-propertied groups representing skilled workers, family farmers, small businessmen and lower level professionals — while its economics are dictated by upper-class coalition members representing the worlds of banking and finance, commerce, industry, and large-scale agriculture. If small-propertied groups are angry with the banks (as they usually are), the coalition will announce an "antibank" program which singles out a few scapegoats for punishment or "regulation" while leaving the fundamental structure of private banking undisturbed. If they are antiwar (as they usually are), the coalition will implement an "antiwar" program which promises to end the current fighting without damaging the industrial interest in death-for-profit (cf. "peace-through-preparedness" and "Vietnamization"). As a result, political change is restricted to those reforms which purport to recognize the interests of dissident groups without interfering with what business leaders consider to be "normal" economic development. Radical reform is gutted at its inception by the national character of the reform coalition.

This, it seems to me, helps to explain the transformation of the revolutionaries of 1776 into the constitutionalists of 1789, as well as subsequent transformations of liberal reform coalitions into conservative, business-dominated coalitions. The American Revolutionary coalition, like its successors, rested on a mass base of men of small property — the independent farmers and workers who seemed the living proof of Jefferson's equalitarian political theory. Its political rhetoric reflected what we should now call lower-middle-class demands — demands for the dissolution of "artificial" barriers to the free acquisition of land and economic opportunity, political representation and social acceptability. Characteristically, lower-middle-class politics demands *both* upward mobility *and* protection from the underclass at the bottom of the social structure. "All men are created equal" means that the small farmer or urban worker is ultimately just as capable of self-government as the shipping magnate or cattle baron. But the phrase implies a series of exclusions: in 1776, "men" did not include black slaves or red Indians whose self-government would threaten to end the dream of endless land and opportunity for poorer whites.[17] Then and since, the perceived "threat from below" to the white workingman provided the principal motive for an alliance between those of small property and those of great wealth. Then and since, the superior party to this alliance was the big business class, which assumed the power of political and economic innovation in exchange for political recognition and protection of selected white out-groups.

The first product of this arrangement, the United States Constitution, was expressly based upon the philosophy of "mixed government" espoused by Aristotle and Polybius, Montaigne and Locke. Reflecting the desires of the framers for political stability and security of property, it "balanced" the powers of political institutions which, they believed, would reflect competing class interests. In the all-important Legislature, the House of Representatives would represent the white small-propertied class, while the Senate represented the "more permanent" great-propertied interests of the community. The President (like all monarchs, naturally conservative) would embody the national will in international affairs, and the judiciary, devoted to the law, would remain above politics, protecting vested property rights against the passions of the "mob." Class interests, then, were to be expressed through institutions whose interaction was planned in advance; no other group interests, not even those of political parties, were recognized by the Constitution.[18]

Political life in the United States was thus defined institutionally as a potentially endless series of controlled interclass compromises. Economic matters were left outside the constitutional scheme — except that, by guaranteeing the sanctity of contracts and vesting in the federal government the right to regulate interstate commerce, coin money, impose duties, etc., the Constitution linked the central government with the only economic class whose interests were truly national — the commercial bourgeoisie. The "vital interests" of slaveholders were also recognized in the twenty-year ban on congressional action against the slave trade, and the "three-fifths compromise," which assured the South that three-fifths of its slaves and

Indians would be counted for purposes of apportioning federal representatives, even while they were denied citizenship. The interests of the white poor and lower middle class were considered to be sufficiently protected by the popular election of representatives and a Bill of Rights reluctantly granted to protect against government overreaching. Interestingly, the freedoms guaranteed by the Bill of Rights were negative and procedural, defining areas of private life which the federal government was forbidden to enter, or affirming to ex-colonists the traditional "rights of Englishmen." We shall see that benefits granted to the "junior partners" of American governing coalitions are often negative or procedural, while the upper classes retain the power to make substantive political or economic innovations.

Ratification of the Constitution, however, did not avert the social disorder feared by the framers. The Federalists who took office in 1791 moved under Alexander Hamilton's leadership to cement the government-business alliance foreshadowed by the Constitution. But their favoritism towards the banking and commercial interests of the Northeast, their pro-British foreign policy in an age of French revolutionary fervor, their opposition to the settlement of western territory — such policies played into the hands of Jeffersonian organizers, who exploited the growing disorder and violence of the 1790's to build the world's first mass-based political party. Throughout the decade Jeffersonians were active among rural rebels and riotous city crowds, French sympathizers, and "inflammatory" journalists.[19] Their agitation produced a repressive response by the ruling Federalists — the infamous Alien and Sedition Acts — which, in turn, prompted Jefferson and Madison to promulgate the doctrine of nullification of unconstitutional federal legislation by the states. Had the Federalists insisted on continued repression, continued polarization might well have led to a second American revolution. The wiser conservatives, however, recognized that they had little to fear from Jefferson, whose constituency could be incorporated into the governing coalition without overthrowing the existing social order. They recognized, in fact, that a stable governing coalition in America could not be produced until a working alliance had been forged between the men of small property and the great bourgeoisie. The device which made such an alliance possible — the political party — was an improvisation made *outside* the constitutional "system." First considered un-American, if not treasonable, by the Federalists, it was later sanctified as the sole legitimate method of organizing protest groups to secure political change.[20]

What Jefferson's opponents did not understand (and what many of his admirers still refuse to recognize) is that after 1781 he was not in any sense of the word a "revolutionary." Neither was he a representative of "the people," if one counts black people, red people, and poor whites — easily a majority of the total American population in 1800 — among "the people." Although Jefferson hoped for the development of a Republic of small farmers (and apparently purchased the Louisiana Territory with this in mind), his immediate task was to form a stable, national ruling coalition representing the interests of *all* sections and *all* elements of the great middle class. "We are all republicans," he said in his first inaugural address, "we are all federalists." Jefferson hoped — or, rather, assumed — that his dream of a republic of independent yeomen would be realized naturally, over time. Meanwhile, in order to get on with the task of national reconciliation and effective government, he adopted, in essence, the entire Hamiltonian economic program. Jeffersonians, not Federalists, chartered the first Bank of the United States and enacted the first protective tariff. As the business of America became business, they reversed their earlier agrarian, decentralist principles. With little apology, they interpreted the Constitution loosely, strengthened the presidency, fought aggressive commercial wars, put the government into debt, assisted creditors against debtors, and turned territorial lands over to large speculators. This was a logical consequence of the attempt to make the Democratic-Republican Party coeval with the nation, an unconscious acting out, as it were, of the plan of the conservative framers for perpetuating interclass compromise.

Neither was this plan overthrown by the peaceful Jacksonian "revolution" of the 1830's, which represented a logical development and continuation of the Jeffersonian tradition. Political violence was minimal because the Jeffersonian coalition — an all-bourgeois alliance resting on a mass base of small farmers, skilled workers, and petty bourgeois — remained intact on a class basis while expanding numerically as property qualifications for voting and office-holding were lowered. The Jacksonian reforms, which put the President rather than the congressional caucus at the pinnacle of party power, enhanced the power of this coalition, which governed continuously (with relatively minor interruptions and shifts in emphasis), from 1800 until the 1850's. Jackson correctly judged himself as more rationalist than radical, more restorationist than revolutionary, more a Bonaparte than a Robespierre. Moreover, certain continuities of political praxis, characteristic of the liberal bourgeois alliance, were again present:

(1) *Identification of a small elite as the "enemy of the people."* Under Jackson, the enemy elite was no longer the New England commercial "aristocracy," but the second Bank of the United States and its friends — a group highly unrepresentative even of the big business community, many of whose leaders vigorously opposed the "Biddle clique."

As under Jefferson, the identification of one element of the business elite as the people's enemy (or scapegoat) exculpated all other great-propertied interests and generated substantial support for liberal reform among rising ("new-money") businessmen. While Jackson made war on the Philadelphia bankers, Wall Street applauded, just as later generations of "progressive" business leaders would applaud Woodrow Wilson's attack on the trusts of the 1910's and F.D.R.'s campaign against the holding-company manipulators of the 1930's.

(2) *Adoption of lower-middle-class rhetoric.* Jacksonian political rhetoric reflected the twin lower-middle-class desires for mobility upward and protection against the underclass. It was therefore reformist vis-à-vis the great bourgeoisie and reactionary vis-à-vis the system's "failures" — the debtor, the black, and the Indian. Exhibiting a characteristic political schizophrenia, the Jacksonians established a movement for mass democracy to justify the extension of political power to small-propertied whites, but then resorted to elitist ideology and racist praxis to prevent the extension of power to the nonpropertied underclass. Jackson, the "Great Democrat," saw no inconsistency between his liberal-democratic principles and the illegal deportations of the Indians from South Carolina and Georgia, the revitalization of the southern slave system, or government action on behalf of selected business interests. The Jacksonian rhetorical style was highly puritanical, preaching a return to simplicity, self-restraint, the values of work and saving — the "republican virtues." The continuing function of puritanical political rhetoric is to permit the lower middle class to attack the elite *and* the underclass in precisely the same terms (both classes are lazy, profligate, pleasure-loving, immoral, etc.). Compare the attitudes of modern "white ethnics" towards both the black poor and suburban rich!

(3) *Reversal of decentralist principles.* The exigencies of rule according to the national principle, which require an alliance between the "little men" and those of great wealth and power, reduced the Jeffersonian dream to a pale utopia. Jackson preached laissez-faire but embraced internal improvements, favored free trade but maintained the protective tariff, talked of states' rights but prevented South Carolina from putting nullification into practice, appealed to the small farmer but sustained the large slaveholder, opposed Big Government but became the strongest President the Republic had yet seen, considered government a neutral arbiter but plunged the presidency into politics, venerated law and order but defied the Supreme Court. Decentralist principles were undercut by a nationalism which was used to justify business demands for government aid in opening up the West and farmer demands for "protection against the Indians" — that is, territorial expansion. The nationalism embodied by "Old Hickory" and celebrated by his biographers was — and remains — an effective method of uniting business-capitalist and agrarian-capitalist interests. Unfortunately, it also works to undermine both liberalism and democracy.

(4) *A turn towards militarism* on the part of liberal reformers like Andrew Jackson illustrates this point. Class conflict within the system can be minimized if the total amount of wealth available for distribution is constantly increasing. In earlier days, when the chief source of wealth was land, the liberal dream of class reconciliation based on universal property ownership led directly to a policy of territorial expansion through war. Thus, although Thomas Jefferson was able to purchase the vast Louisiana Territory, his disciples fomented the War of 1812 in an attempt to grab Canada by force. Andrew Jackson was the first "military" President since Washington; *his* disciples, particularly President James K. Polk ("Young Hickory"), en-

couraged American slaveholders and adventurers to seize Texas, invented an excuse for a war of conquest against Mexico, and came close to fighting Great Britain for the Oregon Territory. The absence of serious opposition to these adventures demonstrated the effectiveness of militaristic nationalism in uniting all classes — from eastern workers and businessmen to western dirt farmers and slave-emperors — in a common cause. Even after industrialization shattered the nexus between land and "property," war would prove indispensable to America's economic expansion. With twists and turns to be described a bit later, a "neo-Jacksonian" association of liberalism with militarism led America straight to the jungles of Indochina.

(5) *Elimination of differences between the two major parties.* Once the all-bourgeois alliance has been cemented (often with the aid of wartime nationalism), the governing coalition consolidates its hold on the political system. The consensus which it has called into being requires that the opposition party, if there is one, be reduced to a mirror image of the major party. Thus, between the War of 1812 and the rise of Andrew Jackson, the two-party system literally ceased to exist. Following the Panic of 1837, the Whig party managed to elect William Henry Harrison President, but only after Harrison had out-Jacksoned Jackson in the "log cabin" campaign of 1840. By the mid-1840's it was clear that Whigism could be considered a tendency within the Jacksonian consensus. Both major parties were appealing to roughly the same constituencies, proposing more or less identical programs, and taking orders from the same combination of powerful interests. Creatures of the same coalition, they became progressively more rigid and obtuse as civil war clouds gathered. Since new demands relating to the issues of slavery and secession, free labor and free soil, could not be managed by the old coalition and its parties, protest groups were forced *outside* the

decaying two-party system. A series of group revolts, generating new political formations, shattered the illusory unity of the old coalition. Recapitulating the breakup of the British colonial system in the pre-Revolutionary era, Jacksonianism disintegrated in the violence and disorder of the 1850's.

III

From the point of view of those in power, the principal danger during periods of disorder and change is that men and women of small property will combine with the underclass to form a radical, antibusiness alliance. Relative to the power of big business and its allied professions, the precarious economic situation of the small-propertied farmer, factory worker, or marginal entrepreneur is barely distinguishable from that of the marginally employed or "working poor" underclass. Economically, poor southern whites have always had more in common with blacks than with plantation owners; northern workers have had more in common with ghetto immigrants or blacks than with great industrialists. Even today, the modern blue-collar worker in a city or industrial suburb shares most of the problems and concerns of his black neighbors, and vice versa. During periods of coalitional breakdown and reorganization, then, the chief function of liberal coalition praxis is to block the translation of converging economic interests into an anticapitalist alliance. Liberalism confirms the "little people" in the belief that they belong, actually or potentially, to the middle class, and, conversely, persuades them that an unbridgeable gulf separates them from the underclass.

A good deal has been written about the first half of this equation. We know that reformers from Jackson to Roosevelt helped keep alive the myth of Horatio Alger; many commentators have spoken wonderingly of their success in convincing ambitious workers, petty bourgeois, and even the poor that it is possible to achieve "success" in America *without displacing the upper class.*[21] The immense wealth of the United States contributed to the longevity of the myth: every group, no matter how frustrated or oppressed, could point to a few of its number who had made it "from rags to riches." Nevertheless, the few are not the many. General improvements in living standards do not improve, and may even worsen, the position of small-propertied or poor groups relative to that of the big business elite.[22] Economic reality would therefore have exploded Horatio Alger generations ago were it not for the equation's second half — the willingness of coalition leaders to unleash campaigns of racism and xenophobia in order to drive an unbreakable wedge between the two lower classes. The basic dynamics of the liberal coalition are contained in this equation: (1) rapid increase in available land, goods, and services + (2) continuing hostility between small-propertied class and underclass = (3) the "all-bourgeois" alliance.

In this light, the evolution of the party of Jefferson and Jackson into the party of slavery and secession seems logical, perhaps even inevitable. Slavery, like genocide of Indians and territorial expansionism, was not an embarrassing exception to the principles of liberal-democratic ideology, or a manifestation of "hypocrisy"; it was a necessary consequence of the politics of the all-bourgeois alliance. Jefferson's dream of a Republic of independent farmers required the destruction or removal of Indian tribes and a policy of aggressive continental expansion. Later, the Jacksonian commitment to agrarian democracy *without* a corresponding determination to limit the power of large landholders would lead inevitably to a pro-slavery policy. It is true that many workers, North as well as South, feared that the abolition of slavery might unleash large numbers of low-wage black workers on the economy. But it is also true that the alternative to continuing a tripartite class division in the South was the destruction of the slaveholding "aristocracy" and the redistribution of its wealth and power among all the members of southern society.[23] Between 1800 and 1840, it was a prime function of Jacksonian ideology to convince the mass of whites that no such class conflict was necessary, that being able to vote for Andy Jackson and to call Negroes "boy" made the white man "free" — a citizen, as Calhoun put it, of a Greek democracy. The corruption of Jacksonian democracy was neither an accident nor the result of the machinations of a few evil men. *All* ruling coalitions in America have begun as liberal and ended as conservative, reflecting the ambivalence and manipulability of the small-propertied class which provides their electoral base.

It is customary to describe the Civil War as the great watershed, or dividing line, in American history — the "second American Revolution," the "triumph of capitalism over the slave system," "the beginning of the Industrial Age," and so forth. Certainly, those who lived through the war period had the feeling that America had crossed some sort of definitive historical line; their lives before and after the war seemed separated as by a veil, opaque but impenetrable. Very quickly nostalgic mists surrounded antebellum life in America, while the postbellum world seemed the embodiment of harsh, modern reality. But the terms of our research compel analysis of the *political* changes wrought by the Civil War — and, here, although significant change occurred, it is not at all clear that the war marks a unique dividing line. True, it settled the question of national unity, dispossessed slaveowners of slaves, and unleashed the northern bourgeoisie on a fertile, passive nation. From the point of view of political structure, however, it would seem that the war period's principal effect, in addition to averting secession, was the replacement of a defunct liberal coalition by a viable one.

To be sure, the disintegration of the Jefferson-Jackson coalition and its replacement by the Republican coalition was a momentous political event for a nation which had come to think of the rotation of parties in office as significant political change. (In American terms, coalition changes always seem "revolutionary.") In fact, the Whig party of 1840–1860 bore more or less the same relationship to the Democrats as the Democrats of 1876–1896 bore to the Republicans of those years, or as the Republicans of 1940–1960 bore to the Roosevelt Democrats. That is, their differences were primarily of tone and emphasis; their main sources of electoral and financial support, like their programs, overlapped. Indeed, this "Bobbsey Twins" relationship between the major political parties is an indication and a proof that a ruling coalition based on the national principle of organization is firmly in power. At such times, the opposition party's only hope (if it would "rule") is to *reduce* the ideological differences between itself and the party in power, and then claim the existing "consensus" as its own. With this as the tradition of normal politics in America, the injection of significant (one is tempted to say "real") issues into the political process by new political groups is profoundly destabilizing. By comparison with the static norm, the political struggles which follow appear revolutionary. For the same reason, when one ruling *coalition* replaces another — even if the new coalition's politics are quite similar to its predecessor's — historians are tempted to say that a "revolution" has taken place.

Between 1830 and 1860, the North was undergoing a social and economic transformation created by the development of industry, an enormous increase in population, and the settlement of the free West. Simultaneously, what might in these times be called a cultural revolution occurred; one five-year period saw the publication of Hawthorne's *Scarlet Letter* (1850), Melville's *Moby Dick* (1851), Thoreau's *Walden* (1854), and Whitman's *Leaves of Grass* (1855). During the 1830's and 1840's the New England Transcendentalists (the original cultural revolutionaries) inspired a host of political protest movements, including abolitionism, a women's rights movement, a labor movement, and experiments in anarchism and communal living.[24] Indeed, the parallels between this era and the 1960's are striking. In each period, the threat and promise of profound socio-economic change triggers a movement of cultural and political revolt. The movement is predominantly white and middle class, intensely moralistic, antiracist, pacifist, and utopian; organizationally, it is fragmented, and vulnerable to cooptation by the great bourgeoisie. Political polarization in each period produces a lower-middle-class backlash which confirms the existing political parties in their conservatism, but a more general radicalization of the population continues nonetheless. In both eras, the forces of political change must mobilize outside a decaying two-party system. During the later 1840's and the 1850's, the once-despised abolitionists and free-soilers became the ideological spearhead of a new coalition based electorally on the northern small-propertied class (especially "native American" workingmen and farmers), while all white classes in the South united in defense of the southern system. As the existing political parties demonstrated their inability to deal with the real questions of the day (slavery and the status of new territories), the old coalition, which had governed through both major parties, began to disintegrate. And — again a parallel with the present — the disintegration took place violently, with fistfights in Congress, the lynching of rebel slaves and abolitionists, civil disobedience of the fugitive slave laws, a bloody war-by-proxy in Kansas-Nebraska, John Brown's raid, and the final "irrepressible conflict."

Again, note how marked is the difference between American politics in "normal" times, when the ruling coalition governs through two almost-identical political parties, and seemingly "revolutionary" periods, when the question is not which *party* but which *coalition* shall rule. Indeed, the persistence of this pattern suggests that, under pressure, when the differences between competing political alliances are substantial, the two-party system tends to disintegrate very rapidly. As a consequence, new contenders for power are forced outside the accepted party system. They are compelled to adopt unusual political tactics (William Lloyd Garrison publicly burned copies of the United States Constitution; anti–Vietnam war protestors publicly burned draft cards and United States flags). Violent overreaction by authorities and "patriotic" citizens (abolitionists were mobbed by the 1840s' equivalents of the 1960s' "hard hats") further radicalizes the dissenters. (John Brown's violent attack on Harper's Ferry was approved by men like Ralph Waldo Emerson and Wendell Phillips, who had previously been nonresistants and pacifists.) Attempts at legal repression of dissent by the authorities "politicize" the law and undermine authority's legitimacy (John Brown's trial, the fugitive slave acts, and the Dred Scott decision may be compared in this respect with the political trials of the 1960's and the 1970's.) Finally, the old two-party system collapses and a realignment takes place. The Republican Party swallowed up the Whigs, Free-Soilers, Know-Nothings, and other northern-based parties, while southern delegations walked out of the Democratic Convention of 1860. The critical role in the drama of polarization is played by the mass of small-propertied Americans, whose conservative instincts generally incline at first towards the forces of status quo, but who are progressively radicalized as the status quo itself it undermined by polarization.

Viewing the Republican Party with historical hindsight

as the party of big business and corporate privilege, it is easy to forget that, in its earlier years, the Republican coalition was every bit as "radical" as Jefferson's or Jackson's. In the industrializing East, the Republicans represented not just captains of industry but militant white Protestant workers, New England farmers, intellectuals, reformers, and activists of various stripes.[25] In New York State, for example, Jacksonian "locofocos" and Whig liberals gravitated towards independent political organizations like the Know-Nothing, Liberty, and Free Soil parties, eliminating the chief Jacksonian base in the East and contributing mightily to the breakup of the old party system. At the same time, western farmers were terminating their old alliance with the agrarian South in order to unite with the eastern small-propertied class under the banner of "Free Soil, Free Labor and Free Men." "Progressive" elements of the big business community joined as well, and the Republican coalition came into existence as the political heir to the Jacksonian coalition and the ideological heir to Jeffersonianism. (The Homestead Act of 1863, which offered independent farmers small tracts of western land for next to nothing, was precisely what Jefferson had had in mind!) However, like its predecessor — and like subsequent governing coalitions in the United States — the Republican coalition aspired to national consensus. This it achieved by fighting a war to preserve national unity, joining small-propertied interests with those of the great bourgeoisie and extending its control over both parties. With significant class differences between the political parties virtually eliminated, the desired result could be obtained: no matter which party reigned, the coalition would continue to rule.

Despite its almost continuous string of presidential victories between 1860 and 1912, the Republican Party often failed to gain a majority of the popular vote in the elections, and its hold on the state houses and state legislatures was by no means secure. Nevertheless, the strength of the Republican coalition reduced the Democrats to a pale imitation of the dominant party. By the time Democrat Grover Cleveland was elected President for the second time in 1892, a new generation of dissenters had begun to recognize that policy differences between the parties were insignificant. Each party bid for the votes of a mass of employed workers, farmers, and petty bourgeois. Each was controlled in critical respects by big business interests. (It was President Cleveland's crushing of the Pullman Strike of 1894 and his alliance with New York banking interests that drove men like Eugene V. Debs to socialism.) Each party adopted the liberal rhetoric of the small-propertied class, offering protection against the underclass and promising access to higher socio-economic levels. Each preached laissez-faire while throwing the whole weight of the government behind favored business interests (for example, both parties favored railroad land grants, protective tariffs, a pro-business foreign policy and strikebreaking). Each became progressively more conservative and big business-oriented until the lower classes rebelled again, forcing a third restructuring of the coalition system.

Consider for a moment the "betrayal" of the southern Negro by the postwar Republicans. It is now well known that initial Republican efforts to "reconstruct" the South in the decade following the Civil War were thwarted by a combination of southern insurgency (the guerrilla war fought by the Ku Klux Klan and allied groups) and northern acquiescence.[26] As war fever waned, the handful of "Radical Republicans" who advocated destruction of the southern landowning elite and protracted war against the Klan were repudiated by the majority of Northerners, paving the way for the Compromise of 1877 by which President Hayes withdrew the last northern troops from southern soil.[27] These events are sometimes attributed to a failure of northern will, war-weariness, or corruption in the Republican Party; but in view of what we have discovered thus far, they were as certain as the degeneration of the Jefferson and Jackson coalitions. Big business could not wait for the completion of reconstruction to enjoy the fruits of northern victory, and a war of counterinsurgency against the Klan could not be "good for business." The economic elite therefore asserted its natural strength within the Republican coalition, calling a halt to reform, selling out the blacks, and conservatizing both parties.

What made this possible, again, was the ambiguous position of the small-propertied masses. The "little people" of the North, who had fought to preserve the Union and to end slavery, now sought protection against the underclass and confirmation of their status as bourgeois. They respected property — in particular, landed property — and saw the liberated, potentially mobile Negro as an economic threat. (Immediately after the Civil War, blacks who had migrated into border-state cities like Cincinnati and Louisville were massacred by organized white workers, just as blacks in Washington, D.C., and Chicago were attacked after World War I.) Thus, the Republicans turned the alliance of the whole bourgeoisie to the Right, using the Civil War spirit to keep a conservative nationalism alive ("waving the bloody shirt") and purporting to represent the interests of decent, respectable white folk against the disreputable poor. Those former radicals who did not accept this transformation of their party were forced to choose between joining a pallid upper-class intraparty reform movement (the so-called "Mugwumps" of the 1880's) and participating in the underclass agitation taking place outside the two-party system (populism and labor agitation). Very few chose, as did Wendell Phillips, to exile themselves to this political Siberia.

After a time, however, the effects of the takeover of liberal coalitions by conservative forces become clear. The business elite is firmly in command of the governing coalition; the lower middle class is menaced from above and below; the underclass moves towards open revolt. A period of political disaggregation and disorder then begins, usually initiated by underclass rebellions, but leading rapidly to a revolt of the lower middle class as well. Eventually, after a good deal of violent turmoil has taken place, a political realignment occurs which produces a new configuration of political parties and a new governing coalition. Initially, hopes are high. Reforms benefiting the men of small property are advanced; at the very least, some out-groups acquire new status and recognition. But there has been little or no structural change. The organization of the new coalition on the national principle, the unwillingness of the "little people" to attack the great bourgeoisie, their alignment with "liberal" representatives of the upper class against the underclass, inevitably set in motion a process of decline. Dissatisfaction, at first inchoate, then militant, explodes as the small-propertied masses realize that a fatal separation between politics and economics has occurred — that, while exercising the rights of free men in law, they have become the pawns of rich men in fact. Another period of lawlessness and disorder then begins, but with the same results, for the pattern cannot be broken except by an alliance of lower classes which *eliminates* the business elite as an economic force and returns political power to the people.

The Republican coalition which governed America after the Civil War excluded both the rebel South and the masses of urban immigrants, mostly Irish Catholics, who had entered northern cities between 1830 and 1860. These immigrants, soon to be joined by enormous numbers of Italians, eastern Europeans, Russians, and, in the West, Far

Eastern peoples, occupied a political position in the North roughly analogous to that of the blacks in the South. They were the northern underclass, threatening to underbid employed workers for industrial jobs, speaking strange dialects, practicing a "sinister" international religion, contributing heavily to the crime and pauperism rate, drinking and fighting, "ruining the neighborhood." Threatened by this wave of immigrants, small-propertied Northerners were not inclined to revive the Civil War in order to re-free the southern Negroes, who might choose, as many had immediately after the war, to enter northern cities and join the large surplus labor pool. In fact, from the 1840's on, WASP workers and the petty bourgeois of the North tended to condemn the Irish masses in terms which have since become associated with anti-Negro racism: the Irishman was said to be violent, unintelligent, promiscuous, lazy, dirty, and irresponsible.[28] The coincidence of stereotypes is no coincidence; these are constant terms used by members of the lower middle class to describe underclass groups which threaten their precarious economic, social, and moral security. One cannot help noting that the same set of stereotypical images is often employed by the modern lower middle class to describe rebellious youth and "hippies."

Like Jacksonian ideology, Republican ideology stressed the puritan virtues. The stereotype of the Irishman-Nigger is the precise opposite of the puritan model (diligence, frugality, cleanliness, honesty, self-control). I remarked earlier that ideological puritanism expresses the hostility of the respectable lower middle class to the life styles of the very poor and the very rich, and that some of the very rich are also stereotyped as profligate, lazy, dishonest and promiscuous. Liberal leaders in America from Jackson to Roosevelt have therefore been great puritans, at least in their public pronouncements, since this ideology provides a method of uniting the lower middle with the bulk of the upper middle class. As applied to the great bourgeoisie, use of these moral-political standards enables the critic to distinguish between *most* businessmen, who are felt to be hardworking, honest, self-controlled persons who have *earned* their success, and the minority of frauds, lechers, wastrels, and pseudo-aristocrats who are not entitled to their "ill-gotten gains." The stigma of deliberate evil (for example, fraud) attaches to this minority, the scapegoats of the all-bourgeois alliance. Jackson had affixed these labels to the supporters of the Bank of the United States (clearing, by implication, the vast majority of bankers outside Philadelphia); northern Republicans painted the southern slave-holding caste in these terms before the Civil War, contrasting the honest northern businessman with the degenerate southern nabob.[29] Subsequent liberals, like Wilson and Roosevelt, would use similar standards to attack a small minority of industrial tycoons while vindicating the moral-political character of the majority of "decent businessmen."

Further parallels between the Jefferson-Jackson and Republican coalitions illustrate the persistence of the governing coalition's seemingly irresistible tendency towards conservatism. Both coalitions were created during periods of violent but nonrevolutionary group struggle; both were alliances of small-propertied interest groups with advanced but repressed elements of the big business community. Initially adopting the political rhetoric of the small-propertied class, both were organized on the "national" (consensus) principle, and fought nationalistic wars which enabled them to crush the militant opposition and to coopt the opposition party. In both cases, lower-middle-class groups were pacified by reforms which promised to protect them against the underclass and to improve their mobility upward; nevertheless, political power, following economic power, was increasingly concentrated in the hands of a few tycoons and used for their exclusive benefit. Jackson had fought the Indians and the Bank, promising to secure the position of small-propertied interests, while, in fact, his laissez-faire policies insured the economic supremacy of southern cotton aristocrats and northern industrial barons. Lincoln gave the farmer a homestead, offered the black man his first hope of freedom, and pledged to support the cause of "free labor," while the Republican Party went about the task of mortgaging America to the monopolists and their kept politicians.

Once again, hypocrisy will not explain the inconsistency. What resolves it ideologically is the belief that the interests of upper and lower middle classes, men of small property and business leaders, are identical. Why not give away more western land to the railroads than to all the small homesteaders put together? Why not treat corporations as legally inviolable "persons" under the Fourteenth Amendment? Why not let John D. Rockefeller or James J. Hill "outcompete" small entrepreneurs and put them out of business? Property is property, business is business, individualism is individualism; *the assumption is that size makes no qualitative difference.* It is easy to see why big business should have promoted this assumption, which, accepted by the small-propertied classes, would produce a nice mixture of hope for business success and resignation to the "inevitable" facts of economic life. But why should the men of little property — the constant victims of a brutal industrial process — identify their interests with those of the industrial elite? And why, even during a period of intense class struggle in the United States (roughly 1877–1937) did an oppressed underclass of unskilled workers, blacks, and poor whites tend to identify *their* interests with those of the middle class? Social analysts have frequently attempted to explain these peculiarities by recourse to simplistic psychological and economic theories: for example, the frontier as safety valve theory, the melting pot hypothesis, or mass acceptance of the Horatio Alger myth. But these notions fail to explain why group revolt during the period of class struggle was limited to occasional violent outbursts, when, with less provocation, the victims of industrialization in other lands were making revolutions. We will get closer to the truth, I think, by examining the relationships between American classes and interest groups during this period of struggle.

IV

The hallmark of protest and counterprotest during the last quarter of the nineteenth century was violence — the intense, but sporadic disorder represented by bloody strikes, race riots, dynamitings, lynchings, vigilantism, and excesses of "official violence."[30] The violence was taken very seriously; each crisis generated new talk of revolution, and William Jennings Bryan's defeat in 1896 seemed to conservatives nothing less than the salvation of the Republic. Nevertheless, despite widespread fears of intensified class struggle and revolution, the period of rapid industrialization in the United States produced not communism but the New Freedom, whose prophet, rather than Karl Marx, was the father of "scientific management" of business, Frederick Winslow Taylor.[31]

In order to understand this development, it is necessary to appreciate that, in America, class struggle was, in reality, a three-cornered affair. In labor struggles, for examples, there were almost always three parties involved: management, workers with jobs, and a surplus labor force of underemployed or unemployed "scabs" — very often recently arrived immigrants or blacks.[32] Management resorted to a variety of devices, from the contract-labor system to importation of Negro strikebreakers from the South, to keep skilled and unskilled, organized and unorganized, "native" and "foreign," black and white workers at each others' throats, competing for jobs and living space. Not surprisingly, organized workers resorted to violence more often against underclass strikebreakers (and the private armies employed to protect them) than against management itself. As a result, conservative unions like the AFL were often more violent than left-wing socialist unions which preached unity of the proletariat against management![33] Karl Marx had foreseen intense competition between employed workers and the "reserve army" of the unemployed, but felt that proletarian class-consciousness would grow as production was collectivized and the wage level driven down. The failure of a revolutionary working class to emerge in the United States before World War I was not attributable to error in Marx's economic projections, which were accurate enough, but to the persistence of a *three*-class system in which the predicted political collectivization did not take place. Instead, economic competition between skilled and unskilled workers, intensified by immigration and reinforced by overlapping cultural, religious, and racial conflicts, became a matter of primary importance.

In other words, the underclass in America was not simply the peasantry on the way to becoming a proletariat, or workers driven into the ranks of the unemployed. It was the Irish, seeking to take over the jobs, homes, schools, and churches of "native Americans"; or the Italians, threatening the jobs and life styles of native Americans and assimilated Irishmen; or the blacks, against whom all white working men could unite in defense of job, home, and school. Under the intense pressure of an underclass constantly replenished from the seemingly inexhaustible supply of oppressed foreigners and native blacks, American workers who "made it" into the ranks of the employed were driven to behave like petty bourgeois. Like independent farmers or small businessmen, they felt compelled to stress security and to cut risks to defend their little "property" (their jobs and neighborhoods) against the unemployed and the propertyless. Skilled workers in the United States thus retained attitudes toward work and society which Marx had believed would die out with the advance of capitalism; for example, many were driven to organize along craft rather than industrial lines, to claim prescriptive rights to their jobs, and to protect a precarious respectability against alien immorality. Of course, socialist, communist and anarchist organizations existed among American workers, but radical traditions and organizations would have had to be much stronger than they were to overcome the disparities between small-propertied workers and the huge underclass.[34]

    As a result, from the New York "draft riot" of 1863 through the Detroit "race riot" of 1935, it was generally impossible to distinguish labor violence from racial violence. (Earlier, it had been equally impossible to differentiate between labor rioting and anti-Catholic rioting.) Throughout much of the so-called class warfare period, the objects of worker wrath were more likely to be underclass "scabs" than the bosses themselves — thousands of "scabs" and union men were killed or maimed in these years, but assassination attempts against industrialists were few and well publicized.[35] In other words, for more than a century, the majority of employed white workers in the United States were moved by the apparent threat from the underclass to prefer their "enemies above" to their "enemies below." Upon this rock earlier radicals foundered, because — to oversimplify somewhat — the proletariat which they set out to organize did not yet exist. The army of unemployed behaved more like the *lumpenproletariat* of Marxian analysis; it was extremely vulnerable to manipulation by management and management collaborators. For this reason, unskilled workers just off the boat or the plantation were considered enemies by their more skilled and assimilated fellow workers, while management saw them as natural allies in its battle against labor shortages and high wages. Conversion of the Republican coalition into a big business oligarchy coincided with this shift away from the all-bourgeois alliance and towards a paternalistic alliance of upper class and underclass. In the North, businessmen imported foreign workers, employed immigrants or blacks as strikebreakers, and constructed company towns like Pullman, Illinois, in order to break the unions. In the South they adopted a paternalistic attitude towards poor whites (and even, to some extent, towards blacks) in order to keep "uppity" small-propertied whites in line. Not surprisingly, elements of the hard-pressed small-propertied class were again moved to revolt, this time against the Republican coalition.

Between 1870 and 1900, rapid industrialization without significant political change produced a number of militant small-propertied protest groups. Initially disparate and competing, they began to coalesce early in the present century within the movement now known as Progressivism, and, later, within the New Deal. These groups included staple farmers, who participated in a number of locally successful but nationally impotent agrarian movements (Greenbacker, Granger, Populist); industrial workers attempting to organize labor unions; white Southerners, who remained a rural and colonized people in an industrializing nation; small businessmen driven to the wall by the growth of monopolies; and urban WASPs appalled by the corruption of the big-city immigrant political machines.[36] The critical stage in the development of this new coalition (indeed, the critical stage for all American coalitions to date) was a revolt against the old leadership by advanced elements of the great bourgeoisie — in this case, businessmen beginning to look to international expansion to provide new sources of raw materials, new markets and investment opportunities. Progressive businessmen and lawyers supplied the leadership of the new movement, and shaped it to their ends; it was no accident that Theodore

Roosevelt of the "big stick" and "dollar diplomacy" was the first President who could be called (to some extent) a Progressive.

At the same time, an equally important rebellion was taking place at the level of ideas, again led by upper-class members of the intellectual "establishment" concentrated for the most part in the elite universities. (Morton White has described this movement well as a "revolt against formalism."[37]) In political terms, Progressivism demanded governmental action at the state and federal levels to secure honest government by "professionals," the vote for women, temperance reform, restoration of business competition, protection of the public against impure food and drugs, recognition of conservative labor unions, and (within limits) greater citizen participation in government. The movement achieved gains, which, while significant, were hardly revolutionary: popular election of senators, the vote for women, Prohibition, a Labor Department, more government regulation of business, and (in a few states) cleanups of government, adoption of "direct democracy" devices, and passage of labor-protective legislation. Theodore Roosevelt and a group of maverick senators spoke for the movement within Republican circles; Woodrow Wilson's election in 1912 (through an electoral fluke) brought elements of the new coalition to national power under Democratic Party auspices. The United States' entry into World War I ended its most energetic phase, although some Progressive reforms continued to be enacted during the 1920's.

Three characteristic motions of American politics are illustrated by the rise and decline of Progressivism.

ONE: *The great bourgeoisie, initially allied with the poor against the men of small property, ends by ruling with the small-propertied class against the poor.* When there are very large numbers of unorganized poor people about, or when small-propertied interests are weak and disorganized, the rich-poor alliance can become a reality, as it did during the brief period of Republican rule in the South, and at times of greatest immigrant inflow into the North. The repetition of this pattern in certain modern American cities is attributable to the enormous migration of southern blacks to the cities between 1940 and 1960, and the precarious political situation of a figure like New York's minority mayor, John Lindsay, illustrates the difficulties of this strategy. Eventually, the liberal coalition moves to secure its electoral base by uniting small- and great-propertied interests against those of the poor, as the Progressives did in repudiating the cause of the blacks, the recent immigrants, and the militant labor unions. Even where an alliance of the lower middle and upper middle classes is cemented, however, the threat of a rich-poor combination serves the function of keeping the small-propertied class off balance without forfeiting its loyalty to the ruling coalition. For example, labor leaders like Samuel Gompers counted on "decent" businessmen to stem the tide of low-wage immigration, and in congressional testimony on oriental-exclusion legislation fully embraced the racist WASP position on that question.[38] Progressive businessmen and politicians accepted immigrant exclusion as a method of restoring individualism to American politics and cleaning up the cities, but failed to grant organized labor the legislative recognition which the unions needed to survive and prosper. "Individualism" cut both ways; it could also be used to prevent collective organizations of the small-propertied class from gaining too much power.

TWO: *The small-propertied class, weak and disorganized, flirts with the idea of coalescing with the poor against the great bourgeoisie, but ends by allying itself with big business against the underclass.* The initial flirtation produces excesses of repressive counteraction by the ruling class, since an alliance of the two lower classes against big business would clearly be revolutionary. The possibility of such a union forming drives those in power to use propaganda, public hysteria, legal processes, and even police or military force to avert the dreaded alliance. For example, when radical southern Populists attempted to form a coalition of poor whites, poor blacks, and small-propertied farmers during the 1880's, their efforts were sabotaged by a wave of anti-Negro hysteria whipped up by the southern "aristocracy."[39] Similarly, when northern Socialists scored some notable economic and electoral gains early in this century, they brought down upon their heads all the repressive power of government. The Industrial Workers of the World had demonstrated that it was possible to organize native Americans and foreigners, skilled and unskilled workers, in one militant political organization; it had invaded the eastern textile industry, and had won several major strikes. Eugene Debs, Socialist Party candidate for President, polled almost one million votes in the election of 1912. Socialist politicians held local and state offices, were influencing (and being influenced by) radical agrarian Progressives; and even conservative workers were showing a considerable readiness to engage in violence to protect their unions. But the United States entered World War I because to stay out, risking loss of the European market, would have brought on an economic crisis, perhaps a revolution.[40] Virtually the entire Left of that period was consumed in the holocaust of xenophobic nationalism stirred up by the war.[41]

THREE: *The liberal coalition is established as a nominally united front of the whole bourgeoisie.* Within the coalition, however, power inevitably gravitates into the hands of the great bourgeoisie, and liberalism shades imperceptibly into conservatism. We saw that under Jeffersonian, Jacksonian and Lincolnian liberalism, the "senior partners" of the coalition adopted the political rhetoric of the "junior partners," offering them protection against their enemies of the underclass and selected scapegoats of the upper class; while, for their part, the "junior partners" moderated their demands for radical alteration of the economic and political system. Similarly, the rhetoric of the Progressive coalition — a familiar combination of political egalitarianism, economic individualism, and international moralism — served to placate the farmer, the worker, and the small businessman while big business strengthened its hold over the domestic economy and began a worldwide expansion. As a result, the liberal-democratic line of the Progressives was constantly negated in practice by their racism, distrust of mass-based political organizations, and unwillingness to alienate the "decent" elements of the big business community. Even before the outbreak of the world war, they began systematically to stamp out the radical tendencies within the movement, that is, the tendencies towards allying the men of small property with the poor. Instead, most Progressives chose to link themselves with the "responsible rich." For this reason, it is possible to view the so-called return to normalcy of the 1920's as a continuation rather than a negation of Progressivism. The figure of Herbert Hoover sums up the matter perfectly, for Hoover — social engineer, humanitarian, bourgeois individualist — was enough of a Progressive to have been considered for the Democratic presidential nomination in 1920. And it was not, after all, the famous conservative Hoover but the liberal Wilson who reintroduced racial segregation into government service, yielded to the Ku Klux Klan on matters affecting the South, broke strikes by using federal troops, plunged the nation into a nationalistic holy war, prosecuted pacifists for sedition, sent an expeditionary force to aid the White Russian counterrevolution, and permitted his attorney general to conduct the first (and worst) witch-hunt in American history, the Red Scare.

The outstanding institutional innovation of this era of protest and reform — the government regulatory agency — was a triumph of illusion over reality, another example of the liberal faith that political power alone, without altering the class structure or redistributing economic power, can redirect the social results of enterprise. Forward-looking businessmen recognized readily enough that attempts to "civilize" business (pure food and drug regulation, antitrust and fair trade acts, regulation of public utilities, even wage and hour laws) were not steps towards socialism but towards a business-government partnership which could work to their decided advantage. As early as 1890, the railroads had decided that the Interstate Commerce Act, which helped to cartelize their industry, was a Good Thing, and wiser heads in other industries (particularly large, complex industries depending upon orderly domestic markets and government assistance abroad) recognized that government regulation, within limits, would not restore competition but help to eliminate it. Let older, more inefficient enterprises scream about socialism in Washington. Those who could not tolerate minimal regulation — like that proposed for the stockyards, say — could go to the wall, leaving Armour and Swift (or their equivalents in other industries) in control of meatpacking for the entire country.

With business in control of the liberal coalition, even muckraking exposés like Upton Sinclair's *The Jungle* could be used to advance the cause of oligopoly! The persistent failure of government regulation to accomplish its purpose was *not* attributable to political corruption, human error, or lack of will on the part of the regulators. It was — and is — the result of that wildly utopian faith

which leads those of small property to believe that they can control big business without dispossessing it by allying themselves with "good" monopolists against "bad" monopolists.

The failure of the Progressive foreign policy, the chief ideological innovation of the era, is attributable to much the same cause. After the Spanish-American War, Theodore Roosevelt, Elihu Root, and other Wall Street statesmen had begun the transformation of American attitudes towards the outer world. They initiated a "world leadership" policy which required building up U.S. naval forces to defend American business interests abroad, reviving the Monroe Doctrine towards Latin America, and committing U.S. troops to interventionist actions in weak neighboring countries.[42] Ironically, while the militarist Roosevelt, who had a strong interest in arbitration of international disputes, won the Nobel Peace Prize for his role in settling the Russo-Japanese War, the pacifist Woodrow Wilson led the United States into a futile, murderous war "to make the world safe for democracy." (A comparison of the foreign policies of Presidents Dwight Eisenhower and Lyndon Johnson is suggestive.) In retrospect, it seems clear that T.R.'s hearty imperialism was the reality disguised by Wilson's self-deceiving rhetoric, just as John Foster Dulles's jingoism was the hidden foundation for Johnson's war in Indochina. In both cases, involvement in war represented a betrayal of the small-propertied class, whose main interests were in domestic reform. Nevertheless, when Eugene Debs dared suggest that U.S. participation in the Great War was intended to make the world safe for big business rather than for democracy, he was jailed for sedition. Wilson's Fourteen Points were the foreign policy analogues of the Progressive domestic policy — a set of rules of fair play designed to take international politics out of the "smoke-filled room" and to turn them over to gentlemen and experts. Point XIV of the League Covenant providing for U.S. adherence to the League of Nations was, on paper, the greatest regulatory agency of them all; but the Senate's disapproval of the League Covenant probably had little effect on the subsequent course of world history. What Progressives could not admit (can they admit it now?) was that no regulatory agency can succeed when it is weaker than the powers to be regulated.

The First World War ended the major period of Progressive reform, just as the Second World War ended the New Deal and Vietnam the New Frontier. There is a lesson to be learned here, but the lesson is not that the Democratic Party is a "war party." Liberal democratic coalitions — alliances of the small-propertied and great-propertied classes — begin by reflecting the views of the former. During this period they are intensely domestic-minded, focusing their energies on internal reform and promising to avoid foreign wars and military expenditures. (One recalls Jefferson's early pacifism, Lincoln's profound aversion to war, Wilson's campaign of 1916 — "He kept us out of war" — and Franklin D. Roosevelt's "neutrality" campaign of 1940.) As power gravitates into the hands of the great bourgeoisie, however, coalition policy becomes more internationalist, for the interests of big business are increasingly so. When an international situation dangerous to American business expansion abroad coincides with a failure of liberal reform at home, wide political rifts appear within the coalition, and the all-bourgeois alliance threatens to come apart. At this juncture, using the *Maine* or the *Lusitania*, an invasion of South Korea or an attack in the Tonkin Gulf as *casus belli*, liberal political leaders declare that America's mission lies in fulfilling her reform ideals abroad (this, while admitting privately that they can no longer be fulfilled at home).

War ensues. Military expenditures revive a sagging domestic economy; the unemployed and marginally unemployed are drafted into the armed services, and nationalistic fervor is whipped up to "reunite the country." As the United States goes to battle, domestic reforms are postponed. Sacrifices are called for. While the children of the poor and the near-poor die or are maimed on one battlefield or another, business and government enter into a close "partnership" to win the war. As a result, the economy is stimulated; but the balance of power within the governing coalition shifts even more strongly in favor of big business. The economic elite emerges at war's end stronger than when it began. The masses are bitter but disorganized, and still subject to nationalistic appeals; postwar figures who attempt to revive the reform fervor of the prewar period are written off as Red dupes; if they will not retire quietly, they are retired forcibly by aroused war veterans and other "patriots." Historians now confess that this is, more or less, what happened to Progressivism after World War I. They have been less willing to admit that, notwithstanding the surprise election of Harry S Truman as President in 1948, the same thing happened to the New Deal after World War II.

V

For a time during the mid-1930's, it seemed that the New Deal, recognizing the failures of Progressivism, would move beyond the techniques of liberal coalition government to establish a new political order based on the power of the organized working class. During the first New Deal (1933–1935), the industrial giants, included in a "partnership" with organized labor and government under the Blue Eagle of NRA, dominated the arrangement so completely that many old Progressives and young radicals left Washington in disgust.[43] The shift to a second New Deal, coinciding roughly with Roosevelt's reelection in 1936, was an outcome of a continuing violent polarization reflecting the desperate economic crisis and mass disenchantment with big business's economic leadership. In 1935, the creation of the CIO split the labor movement into radical and conservative wings, with the radicals threatening to vote against Roosevelt in 1936. Rural populists like Huey Long and William Lemke endangered the New Deal's hold on the farm population; the Communist and Socialist parties were steadily gaining strength; and previously apolitical groups like older people (under Francis Townsend) and northern blacks (under William White and W. E. B. DuBois) were organizing for action.[44] Under these circumstances, the coalition made a necessary turn to the Left, but managed with remarkable success to contain emergent social forces within the forms of the liberal coalition. The New Deal offered political recognition and organizational security to certain protest groups without altering the fundamental nature of the economic system, or the preeminent position of the big business community within that system.[45] It utilized a revolutionary method — the creation of a giant federal bureaucracy with new power to regulate the nation's economic life — for conservative ends — the reconstruction of the all-bourgeois alliance. It is worth noting how this was accomplished.

There existed, of course, one consuming public issue — how to end the Depression. New Deal efforts to reverse the cycle of decreasing investment and consumption were crude and largely unsuccessful; on the eve of World War II there remained at least ten million unemployed. (Indeed, it is difficult to say what would happen even now were war and war-related industries, by far the nation's largest employers, to be eliminated.) However, there also existed a related, equally important issue which was not faced publicly by the coalition's leaders: how to end the proletarianization of American labor and the disappearance of the small-propertied class. For without a small-propertied class to form its electoral base, no liberal coalition could survive. The governing coalitions of the past had always rested on realizing the concept of "the bourgeoisie" — the idea that those of small property and those of great property possessed a common bond, a basis on which to unite against the underclass at the bottom and the monopolists at the top. In America, largely owing to the predominance of ethnic over class loyalty among workers, skilled workers could be accorded the status of petty bourgeois, and — so long as competition was not too intense — provincial bourgeois could stand on the same status footing as Wall Street tycoons. The Depression altered this situation (or brought alteration of the situation to mass consciousness) by creating an intolerable tension between the status claims and real power of nonelite groups. In fact, while the "bad monopolist" phantom began to disappear (it was becoming clear that the structure of big business was essentially monopolistic or oligopolistic), all classes below the great bourgeoisie were simultaneously degraded. What if skilled union workers were, by international standards, the best paid in the world? Their bourgeois aspirations were mocked by developments among the petty bourgeois themselves, who now recognized that neither they nor their children would, except by a stroke of fantastic luck, "make it" into the ruling class. The gap was clearly too great to be overcome by hard work, diligence and frugality: this was (and is) the insight which revealed that the old small-propertied class was, in fact, becoming a working class. Similarly, the massive rural, black, and immigrant underclass, aided by relatively radical organizations like the CIO, moved towards conscious membership in the working class, while even professionals, intellectuals, and white-collar workers began to accept their "degradation" to working-class status.[46]

In the American context, this was a truly revolutionary development. Even sober analysts agreed that forms of political organization and demands for change generated by a mass proletariat would almost certainly destroy the old coalition system. Nevertheless, by 1939 the thrust of antiadministration protest had been parried by a political reformation which satisfied key political groups and by a war threat which was beginning to provide both economic recovery and ideological unity. The political techniques employed by the new coalition concentrated on defining selected "interest groups," each one representing a balance of classes, which could then be offered privileges, emoluments, and institutional recognition within a new federal bureaucracy created especially for this purpose. The New Deal's most conspicuous beneficiaries were farmers, for whom the Agricultural Adjustment Administration, the Federal Farm Loan Board, and other agencies were created; "organized labor," which reaped the benefits of the Wagner Act and Fair Labor Standards Act; "small business," which received emergency loans and mortgage relief, a Bankruptcy Act and beefed-up antitrust program; "the South," which gained the TVA along with control of most congressional committees; "the aged," who became entitled to the benefits of Social Security; and "the unemployed," who could now receive unemployment compensation, work for the Works Progress Administration, or join the Civilian Conservation Corps. Other groups were granted special legislation, appointment of their members to important government jobs, or other signs of official recognition. A substantial number of members of each of these groups, of course, was working class; in combination with working-class sectors of other excluded groups they might have produced the first major labor party or socialist party in America. But small-propertied farmers, industrial workers, and white-collar employees were not yet convinced that their position was untenable in the age of monopoly capitalism. The "popular front" policy adopted by the Communist and Socialist parties in 1935 deprived the American working class of an alternative to Roosevelt capitalism. The New Deal was therefore able to appeal to "interest groups" as if they were still composed primarily of small propertyholders and to link large, disaffected groups with the executive branch of government, furthering an identification with the President which did much to overcome their previous sense of isolation and political alienation.

What was not recognized, however, was the price such groups paid (and continue to pay) for the status of "special client of the State." For the least conspicuous but best-served client of the New Deal was the big business sector dominating each multiclass interest group. The farmers, pacified by agricultural programs established to maintain prices and control production, were helpless to prevent large-scale operators, speculators, and "agribusiness" corporations from using the same legislation to increase their competitive advantage over the small fry. The result: continued concentration of power in large corporations, three decades of farm depopulation, and the creation of rural slums within every major American city. Small businessmen were sold on the New Deal's policies of punishing selected "evil" tycoons (such as the holding company magnates) while aiding business through government loans, tax relief, antitrust prosecutions, Federal Trade Commission actions, stock exchange regulation, bankruptcy protection, public works and defense contracts, and so forth. But, again, aid to business benefited businessmen, generally speaking, *in proportion to their existing economic power*. Even antitrust regulations proved a blessing in disguise for corporations strong enough to manipulate them to their own advantage. Adding up the results of the small business programs, the best one can say is that if they had not existed, the trend towards business concentration and elimination of the petty bourgeoisie might have proceeded more rapidly and ruthlessly than it did. On the other hand, if the New Deal had not helped to legitimate the "honest" tycoon, might not the whole structure have toppled by 1940? The question must have also occurred to women, the elderly, the unemployed and marginally employed, blacks, the rural poor, and others who voted happily for F.D.R. because the New Deal made them, to some extent, the wards of government welfare agencies. Early in the 1960's, reformers would be compelled to "rediscover" poverty, noting that the distribution pattern of income in America had not changed materially since World War I. Under the impact of riots and movements of human liberation, they would also rediscover racism and sexism — which the New Deal had not considered to be problems at all.

The test case of the New Deal, however, must be the labor movement, whose recognition and empowerment was the Roosevelt coalition's greatest claimed achievement. During the economic disturbances of the 1920's and 1930's, the workers' militancy had compelled most of the world's industrial nations to move strongly in the direction of socialism or fascism, either of which would ultimately undermine the power of the business elite. (At the very least, the basic "public" industries in the fields of transportation, power, communications and credit were nationalized, as in most western Europe and Scandinavian countries.) The New Deal, however, aimed at solving the problem of labor-management relations without significantly altering the nation's economic structure. This it seemed to do (after a brief experiment with the organization of industrial interest groups under the NRA) by creating an "interest group" composed of organized industrial workers in national industries and dealing with this collection as if it were a privileged small-propertied interest. The New Deal's labor legislation was an economic version of "law and order" — an attempt to use government as an economic policeman rather than as an agent for class realignment. The Wagner Act's federalization of labor-management relations was intended to bring economic "order" out of "chaos." In place of intense, often violent struggles at the local level between workers trying to organize unions and bosses trying to destroy them, the new legislation substituted collective bargaining, governed by federal rules, between legally recognized unions and legally protected managements. Bosses in interstate industries gave up their struggle against unionism, and were forced to accept federal minimum wage, hour, and overtime standards. Workers in those same industries gave up their dreams of worker control over industry and government, and agreed to bargain only over wages and working conditions, leaving "management decisions" to management and government to the "experts." In effect, labor agreed to operate in relationship to government as one recognized interest group among many.

Did this represent a triumph for American workers? A fair compromise between competing interests? Or a successful short-term pacification of the working class by an increasingly powerful business elite? Viewed against the experience of other industrial nations, and in light of subsequent economic development in the United States, the latter seems the correct view. Federal labor laws guaranteed the existence of both unions and management, labor and capital, thus continuing the tradition of preservation of all classes in the coalitional structure. Moreover, they left the *substance* of any bargain reached to a trial of strength (threatened or actual) in a strike-lockout situation. The "civilizing" of labor-management struggles has been compared to the removal of a street fight from the sidewalk to the boxing ring — but, in this case, one combatant was permitted to keep a club. Since the New Deal legislation did *not* weaken the economic power of the great bourgeois or loosen their hold upon the state machinery, a continuing dependence of labor upon capital was inevitable. In fact, the New Deal's labor legislation accomplished for private business what business could never have accomplished itself: it institutionalized the subordination of wage worker to capitalist at a time when revolutionary changes in that relationship were threatened. As subsequent events proved, the growing "partnership" between big business and big unions worked to the disadvantage of small businessmen unable to handle increased labor costs, unorganized or unemployed workers excluded from the game, and consumers, who bore the brunt of simultaneous

wage and profit increases in the form of higher prices. Industrial workers gained that "junior partner" status within
the Roosevelt coalition which economically dependent
groups often take for power. They lost the opportunity to
lead a mass working class towards worker government
and tied their fortunes fatally to those of the monopoly
corporations.

The point, of course, is not to deny that the New Deal
brought about changes in American politics which affected
millions of Americans — obviously, it did. Still, the New
Deal can be best understood as the last of a series of liberal
coalitions which solved the problem of militant dissent by
granting small-propertied groups institutional recognition
— membership cards in the alliance of the whole bourgeoisie — while continuing to maintain the great-propertied class in its accustomed position of preeminent power.
Often, the efforts of New Dealers to preserve the great
corporations' dominant position were painfully obvious:
for example, both Roosevelt and Truman obtained the
support of leading companies in new industries (air transportation, armaments, motion pictures, radio and television, petrochemicals, electronics, etc.) simply by turning
over to them huge defense contracts and vast amounts of
the public domain.[47] At other times, the service was
performed more subtly; for example, while the graduated
income tax was graduated even further (amidst cries of
"soak the rich!"), loopholes were quietly opened up for oil
producers, corporations doing business abroad, the holders
of stocks and bonds, the owners of real estate, etc., with
the result that the income tax became a method of soaking
the small-propertied class and protecting favored forms
of investment.[48] Generally, however, at least in domestic
affairs, the governing coalition served the interests of big
business best by nonaction. So long as government avoided
removing from corporate hands the power to set prices,

allocate production, multiply brands, advertise at will, re-
locate plants, make foreign investments, alter capital structure and the like, while at the same time requiring the
public to pay for the industrial infrastructure (roads, har-
bors, schools, defense, and basic research), the ruling class
would remain as powerful as ever. The continuing passivity of government towards business (and business's allies
in the professions, the universities, and the military services) usually goes unnoticed by members of the small-
propertied class, who make specific demands on the
business community only when their own group interests
are directly threatened. It was not until the postwar period, however, that big business domination of the Roosevelt coalition became apparent.

One effect of World War II on the New Deal — the
termination of its "progressive" phase domestically — was
announced by Roosevelt himself.[49] Nevertheless, it has
been said, the basic drive and direction of the New Deal
were maintained during the war, when workers and farmers realized the benefits of war spending and increased demand for almost all commodities, and afterward, when the
Truman administration assured a continuation and extension of Rooseveltian politics (including high levels of defense spending) under the Fair Deal label. The thesis was
consistent with the idea that the New Deal was not just
another shallow movement of liberal reform but something more profound and proletarian. The memory of the
collapse of Wilsonian liberalism following World War I
was very much alive to the "old New Dealers" of the
1940's. Their proudest claim was that the post–World
War II years produced no depression, no civil strife, and
no Red Scare. The ratification of the United Nations
Charter and continued military preparedness averted a
Third World War while the continuation of New Dealers
(including liberal Republicans) in office after 1948 ex-

tended the benefits of "positive government" to additional millions of Americans, including racial minorities. In short, the ideology of the New Deal remained alive and its political structure intact. This time the return to normalcy, such as it was, was essentially benign.

For a time, the New Dealers' claims seemed accurate, although during the early 1950's, the United States did experience a second Red Scare, fomented by right-wingers led by Senator Joseph McCarthy. The electorate which defeated Adlai Stevenson in the "Communism, Controls and Corruption" campaign of 1952 was clearly in a conservative mood. But it was the administration of Dwight Eisenhower which signaled most clearly that the essential ideological commitments and political institutions of the New Deal would remain unchanged. The extreme Left had already been disposed of by McCarthy, Nixon, and Red-hunters within the Democratic Party and the labor unions. Eisenhower outlasted Senator McCarthy, appointed the liberal Earl Warren to be chief justice of the U.S. Supreme Court and the urbane John Foster Dulles to be secretary of state, and, repudiating the Taft wing of his own party, left the Roosevelt legacy pretty much intact. The ghost of reaction, which would appear again briefly in 1964 in the person of candidate Barry Goldwater, was exorcised. Nevertheless, as early as 1951 the political analyst Samuel Lubell was announcing the imminent breakup of the Roosevelt coalition,[50] and by 1968, when President Lyndon Johnson resigned rather than face certain defeat at the polls, almost everything that could go wrong had. During the 1960's, with Roosevelt's heirs in power, rebellious blacks burned dozens of urban ghettos, U.S. military forces became hopelessly bogged down in Indochina, the postwar economic boom was ended by inflation and unemployment, students and antiwar demonstrators disrupted normal campus life at hundreds of universities, politics became polarized between a new radicalism and a new conservatism, and a direct clash between militant police and militant students made a shambles of the Democratic Convention of 1968. What had happened to the promise of the New Deal? What had happened to Roosevelt's unbeatable coalition?

A search for answers to these questions must lead back to the thirties, for the New Deal was not a single political philosophy or set of institutions; it was a changing balance of forces with limited parameters, whose public stance at any point represented the product of intracoalitional competition. Therefore, when one avers that "the New Deal" continued during and after World War II, the question is whose New Deal? The years 1935 to 1940, for example, saw an enormous increase in labor union militancy and radicalism. For the first time, workers in industries like automobiles and steel were organized along industrial lines. Fiery CIO leaders, taking the Wagner Act as their opening gun rather than as a final victory, led their troops into bloody confrontations with management, won a series of unprecedented sitdown strikes, intensified organizational activity among the poor, and began to welcome Negroes and other previously thought "unorganizable" into their unions. Students and teachers sympathetic to labor and to socialism participated in a multitude of Left organizations, as did black writers and intellectuals of the "Harlem Renaissance." For the first time since the destruction of the IWW after World War I, there was a movement in America (factionalized though it was) dedicated to forming an alliance between the underclass and the working class. Much of this movement entered into coalition with Rooseveltian liberal-democrats during the "popular front" period from 1935 to 1945. But the radical workers who supported Roosevelt in 1940 believed that the New Deal which would emerge after Hitler's defeat would be *their* New Deal, an intensified struggle by "the people" against the big business community. In 1948, following a wave of strikes, Roosevelt's former vice president, Henry A. Wallace, led the remnants of *this* New Deal into the Progressive Party.

The business community, on the other hand, was coming to see the New Deal as a new version of the alliance of the whole bourgeoisie, in which elements of organized labor might be included — if they behaved. Although some great bourgeois remained right-wing and isolationist down to Pearl Harbor, preferring to let Hitler and Stalin destroy each other, most "progressive" industrialists welcomed the revival of defense spending under Lend-Lease, the prospect of economic recovery through further spending, and the burst of nationalism which influenced even Communist Party propaganda. Advocates of preparedness perceived that the war economy would promote both economic growth and political stability at home. It would cement the alliance between big business, which would direct the economy in "partnership" with the federal government, and organized labor, which would gain jobs, higher wages, exemption of defense workers from the draft, and a chance to consolidate union power in exchange for agreements not to strike or to stir up the underclass. Increased demand for consumer goods would pacify small business; farm prices would inevitably soar; conscription and the war industries would eliminate unemployment; and an ideology of national unity raised to a fever pitch would make class conflict (or, indeed, any serious group conflict) seem absolutely treasonous. (In fact, the Roosevelt administration's wartime measures against dissenters were tougher than those of the Wilson administration.)

Thus, although Americans had vigorously criticized Germany for solving her economic and social problems through military rearmament, war, national unification and the *führerprinzep*, the fact was that no capitalist nation found a better solution. While decrying fascist excesses, the United States entered upon a stage of economic and political development which, in some respects, resembled fascism: the executive department of the State centralized political power in its hands, while permitting the giants of private industry to centralize economic power in theirs. The "war emergency" which justified these measures was continued, thanks to the Cold War, into and beyond the 1950's, with the result that the United States remained a warfare-welfare state. Although many tend to think of the "conservative" 1950's as the era of the corporate state, it was the wartime New Deal which initiated the hegemony of the giant corporations, development of a military-industrial empire, creation of the intelligence establishment, the termination of labor militancy, and the repression of dissent. All of these trends were initially New Deal responses to the fascist threat, authoritarian reactions which big business hoped would become permanent features of a new centrist order.

The question at war's end, then, was not whether *the* New Deal would continue, but *which* New Deal would continue: the quasi-social-democratic government of the late 1930's, moving steadily to the Left under pressure of a lower-class alliance, or the nationalist government of the 1940's, consolidating an all-bourgeois alliance against Right and Left "extremists." After a brief period of struggle (1946–1948) the advent of Harry S Truman and the Cold War settled that question. By 1952, *before* the "conservative" Eisenhower assumed office, the great corporations had reasserted their economic supremacy. Military spending had surpassed World War II levels, and the congressional powers to declare war and to control defense appropriations were effectively abrogated. Labor unions and liberal political organizations had purged themselves of radicals, governmental "loyalty" programs had been instituted (and judged insufficient by Senator Joseph McCarthy), and radical reform was a dead letter.[51] Once again, without waiting for a conservative "reaction" (which never materialized), the liberal reformists buried reform themselves. By contrast, the conservatives who succeeded them would appear relatively liberal, for although they served the same masters, they did so more candidly.

Viewed from the perspective of the turbulent sixties and seventies, Franklin Roosevelt's New Deal seems more a technique of conflict-management than a movement for radical change. But it is easy to make jejune criticisms of movements like the New Deal ("Look at the opportunity you missed!") and easier still for aging liberals to defend their youthful achievements with pride ("But look at what we *did* accomplish!"). It is more important to understand the true position of those former out-groups whose association with the New Deal gave Roosevelt's government its ultraprogressive image: the industrial workers, the urban ethnics (particularly Jews, Irish, and Italians), the independent farmers, poor whites, the blacks, the aged, and the unemployed. With regard to these groups, our analysis suggests that the New Deal did not obliterate but rather strengthened the distinction between underclass and small-propertied class: only the latter achieved representation. Moreover, especially after 1940, small-propertied groups within the coalition were increasingly subordinated to the interests of big business and its allies. They obtained the right to compete for power, property, and prestige in the boxing ring rather than on the street corner, but surrendered the right to win. As a result, the New Deal gave ground steadily to the overwhelming economic power of the great bourgeoisie. Tragically like its predecessors, it proved incapable of conquering racism, poverty, militarism, or the domination of politics by private power.

VI

World War II and a new burst of technological innovation in the postwar period profoundly altered the situation of the American ruling class. The corporate elite and its allies in the political, military, and professional establishments were now committed to methods of production which raised both expectations of abundance and fears of overproduction. Moreover, the interests of this class were becoming more and more international — so much so that the "multinational corporation," an exception before the war, was becoming the dominant force in both the world and domestic economies. Thanks to the war, the elite found itself heir to colonial interests abandoned by Britain, France, the Netherlands, and other old colonial powers. Thanks to the reconstruction of Europe and Japan by American taxpayers, it gained important new markets in the more advanced industrial nations as well. Between 1950 and 1970, direct private foreign investment by United States companies climbed from 11.8 billion dollars to more than 77 billion dollars.[52] *Business Week* explained the development as follows:

In industry after industry, U.S. companies found that their overseas earnings were soaring, and that their return on investment abroad was frequently much higher than in the U.S. As earnings abroad began to rise, profit margins from domestic operations started to shrink. . . . This is the combination that forced development of the multinational company.[53]

Multinational companies could not operate, of course, without the close "cooperation" of United States government agencies concerned with international trade, foreign policy, economic and military aid, monetary policy, and the like. Indeed, the postwar experience confirmed what "forward-looking" businessmen had been saying since the First World War: a very close working partnership with the federal government was essential to the new economic order.

Enormous government expenditures were required to protect foreign investments, markets, and sources of raw materials, and to keep domestic demand high enough to prevent a new Depression. Planned obsolescence, the use of mass-media advertising, and the expansion of consumer credit within the private consumer market were insufficient, over the long run, to support massive technological overproduction. It was necessary to maintain government consumption at wartime levels or higher — and what better way to do this than by creating a separate "defense" economy based on automatic obsolescence, endless "consumer" credit, and guaranteed profit for the corporate giants?[54] The cost item increasing most dramatically on most corporation ledgers was research and development. In this respect, World War II military spending had set a precedent which was to be followed in every "crisis": the taxpaying worker would foot the cost of R & D, and private industry would reap the profits.[55] Old-line corporate opposition to Big Government and "foreign entanglements" was clearly counterproductive, as was opposition to foreign aid, the welfare system, and other programs designed to put money into the hands of potential consumers. Similarly, despite ritualistic handwringing about excessive labor costs, advanced corporations were not inclined to fight expensive strikes at home, since under conditions of monopoly capitalism, wage increases could be passed on to workers in the form of price increases. If necessary, labor costs could be lowered somewhat by replacing workers with machines, using antiracial discrimination legislation to increase the labor supply and put pressure on the unions, or instituting wage controls; but so long as inflation did not go entirely out of control, why take the risk of creating a proletarian spirit among wage earners? Why bother, when the international proletariat created by European colonizers was ripe for plucking by their neocolonialist heirs?

This new situation split the corporate community politically, driving its modern, more international wing to embrace the "postwar New Deal" with passion. While Old Guard Republicans, businessmen with purely domestic interests, and the petty bourgeoisie might grumble about unbalanced budgets, high taxes, and wage increases, the international corporations recognized a bonanza when they saw it. Senator Taft and the Republican Right had fought their greatest battle in opposition to the Marshall Plan for the reconstruction of Europe and the Truman Doctrine of intervention to support "Free World" allies — but it was precisely this sort of intervention, financed by tax dollars, which created the richest markets, the most lucrative sources for capital export, and the largest government contracts for the American monopolies. The lesson was clear. The federal grab-bag was chock full of goodies labeled Foreign Aid, Defense Spending, Food for Peace, Highway Construction, Urban Renewal, Mass Transportation, and the like. Industry tasted of the tax dollar, and found that it was good. Old-style conservatism had become a sentimental luxury which the Henry Fords, Thomas Watsons and Nelson Rockefellers of the new era could not afford. The Goldwater presidential campaign of 1964 was therefore the last gasp of the old Republicanism while the election of Richard Nixon in 1968 represented the triumph of a Republicanized New Deal. Big business and the federal bureaucracy were now "partners."

This development has been widely noted,[56] but its political effects are not as well understood. For if the corporate elite stands on an equal footing with government or exercises governmental functions itself, its relationship to other classes has changed and must be redefined. In theoretical terms, this development further erodes the distinction between Society — the arena in which social classes, ethnic groups, and other interests slug it out — and the State. In liberal theory, the State stands above Society, representing *all* its members, arbitrating class conflict, and supporting the public interest against various private interests. At present, however, to use lawyer's language, *private interests vest in the State*, often in institutional form. Class conflict in the old, extragovernmental sense vanishes as the "system" becomes all-embracing.[57] Grasping a part of this truth, social scientists of the 1950's began to write about the disappearance of classes, the end of ideology, and the politics of a mass society. But this vision of harmonious consensus can be — and was during the 1960's — turned on its head. Marxists had long predicted that the centralization of power in advanced capitalist societies would *decrease* their political stability, since conflicts formerly fought out "behind the back" of the State, would now, of necessity, become struggles for State power.[58] The system which had seemed so stable during the 1950's began to fall apart in the following decade precisely because it *was* so all-embracing — because the great bourgeoisie and its allies, now confirmed in power and clothed in law, demanded total allegiance to their authority.

We often forget that current movements of rebellion against authority, decried as lacking in "respect for law and order," were preceded and largely generated by unprecedented demands on the part of the *authorities* that the public respect their law and standards of order, demonstrate loyalty to their State, and conform to their social code. The conformity of the 1950's, with its consumerism and loyalty oaths, its pious politics and politic religiosity, was not a spontaneous growth, it was the cultural correlative of this advanced (monopoly) capitalist order. Mass docility was a necessity for the ruling class, which wished to govern a highly centralized, technologically integrated society without effecting a fundamental redistribution of income, goods, or power. In a sense, then, the powerful became their own gravediggers exactly as Marx and Engels had prophesied. The consensus produced its opposite, which was not the traditional rebellion of the disenfranchised but a sweeping antiauthoritarianism, expressed initially by urban blacks and alienated students, but now moving contagiously through the ranks of the working class.

The Cold War, a critical consensus-producing myth of the 1950's and early 1960's, collapsed dramatically as a result of the Chinese-Soviet split and the American experience in Indochina. This illustrates, again, the effects of overreaching by the ruling class, which had attempted to convert an occasional strategem — whipping up patriotic hysteria to "unify" the country — into a permanent feature of American life. Herein lies the enormous significance of Vietnam: popular revulsion against the war, producing anti-State activities of various kinds, signified a widespread refusal to accept a permanent state of war and permanent emotional unity as normal for the United States. As a result, the ideological glue which bound the American nation together came unstuck before one's eyes. The war produced a Left calling for immediate withdrawal from Indochina and a Right calling for immediate victory. The Flag, once a symbol (and, by reflex action a creator) of national unity, became the badge of one political faction. The Dove of Peace, formerly incorporated in the military myth of "peace through preparedness," became the symbol of another. Centrists hoped, of course, that the removal of American ground troops from Southeast Asia would eliminate the war as a divisive issue, and cut down mass support for left- and right-wing movements — but they were wrong. In the first place, Nixon centrists found it impossible to "wind down" the war without conceding South Vietnam to the National Liberation Front. They therefore mechanized it, replacing ground troops with air power and men with machines.[59] Equally important, war or no war, the Center's position continued steadily to weaken. Both the ideologies and the spirit of protest awakened by the war persisted, the disaffection spreading to new groups concerned with new issues. If forms of protest were now less dramatic their content was now even more corrosive. The war, it seems, was merely a trigger for disaggregating forces already present in American society. Its end would not restore the lost consensus or eliminate the long-term potential for massive domestic revolt.

Analyzed correctly, the dissensus of the period after 1963 seems a logical and inevitable sequel to the prior period of consensus. During the late 1940's and the 1950's, big business embraced the wartime New Deal and took charge of the Roosevelt coalition, capturing the federal agencies established to service the New Deal's client groups and striving for a consensus which would express mass consent to business leadership. We have already seen that at such periods in the life of any American coalition, consensus (or its appearance) is temporarily established by silencing Right and Left "extremists," reducing differences between the two major parties to variations in style, and assuming that the coalition is omnirepresentative. We have seen also that the appearance of such a consensus is as much a sign of coalitional decay and coming disorder as of perpetual peace. Nevertheless, American social scientists declared that the 1950's ushered in a new age and a new society — an "affluent society" (J. K. Galbraith) whose political genius, Daniel Boorstin said, was for institution-building and compromise.[60] Noting that the prewar Left and Right had been eliminated as significant factors in American politics, and that postwar "liberals" and "conservatives" were brothers under the skin, analysts like Seymour Martin Lipset and Daniel Bell assumed an "end of ideology" — the creation of an unshakable national consensus based on institutionalized affluence, middle-class mores, and centrist politics.[61]

The scholars believed that the scarcity of goods and services which had always provided the framework for political conflict between haves and have-nots was, at least in America, giving way to abundance. Technology had not only increased industrial productivity enormously, but was also providing new solutions to the old problems of overproduction and business cycles (e.g., mass-media advertising, technological obsolescence, installment buying, and the creation of a world market). The new abundance had already mitigated labor-management conflict; it had created a leisure "problem," millions of new jobs in service occupations, and a new white-collar "class"; it had made poverty unnecessary and would soon make it obsolete. Moreover, although the new age might be expected to raise individual and group expectations, technology could also deal with the problem of temporary instability by using a wide range of devices of social control, from television programs and "management" of the news media to new techniques for policing unruly communities.[62] Against this background, class conflict in America — and the ideological conflicts which it generated — seemed an anachronism. Whether or not postwar America was characterized as a "mass society," a "pluralistic society," or a society ruled by the "power elite" was irrelevant in light of the visible *fact* of consensus.

These were the assumptions of postwar regimes in America which attempted to govern on what might be called a technocratic basis. The technocratic approach to government administration came into its own under Presidents Kennedy and Johnson. Former Secretary of Defense Robert McNamara and his "whiz kid" systems analysts put the new technology to work helping to make business decisions more "rational." Of course, this was a procedural, not a substantive "rationality": while systems analysts developed ingenious new methods to make corporate outlays more cost-effective, the corporate goals — profit maximization and political power — remained unquestioned. Applied to government, the technocratic method proved disastrous. It sent hundreds of bright young men to work in the Bureau of the Budget, the Pentagon, and other key federal agencies developing sophisticated scientific methods to implement goals which remained unexamined, and which were themselves "irrational" — either impossible of fulfillment, self-contradictory, or evil.[63] To intervene militarily in Southeast Asia without seeking a military solution, to seek a military solution without destroying the same people whose "independence" was allegedly in question, to make war on poverty without redistributing income, to liberate black people without redistributing power — these were some of the goals of Franklin Roosevelt's successors. The downfall of Lyndon Johnson, for example, which has been attributed to his autocratic style, his isolation in office, or his inability to duplicate the Kennedy charm and charisma, really had less to do with style than with the combination of technocratic methods and inherited goals which, then and now, characterize government administration in America. For it was in Johnson's administration that the most intolerable of all contradictions made itself felt. The great corporations demanded an orderly society of passive consumers at home and an open field for capitalist expansion abroad. But, abroad, the tide of revolution was rising, while domestic tranquillity was shattered by a chorus of demands for an end to poverty, inflation, high taxes, military spending, sexism, racism, and injustice. The notion that a Kennedy, or even a Roosevelt, could have steered a clear course through these waters is unconvincing. No reformer holding office at the pleasure of the great corporations could satisfy their interests while serving the people, although another President might not have veered as wildly and erratically as Lyndon Johnson did between pacific rhetoric and all-out bombing, civil rights enactments and police repression, poverty programs and machine politics.

The problem lay not in the Johnson style, but in the implications of that consensus which had so intrigued the scholars and upon which Johnson had premised the Great Society and his Senate majority leader technique of politics. Apparently it did not exist! What attracted most attention during the late 1960's and early 1970's, of course, were the dramatic rebellions of the old underclass — principally urban blacks and other nonwhite minorities — and the new underclass — radicalized students, hippies, antiwar demonstrators, and women. A widely accepted view has it that the first of these groupings was excluded from the postwar consensus by racism,[64] while the second excluded itself "counterculturally," originally because of opposition to the Indochina war, later out of disgust with American hypocrisy and materialism.[65] Note that this view *accepts* the main lines of the consensus analysis described above, assuming that postwar America has solved the fundamental "quantitative" problem of politics (the conflict between the haves and have-nots), and implying that both rebellions may be "dealt with" by a combination of force and gradual amelioration of conditions. Blacks want a larger share of the pie — and they shall have it, because the quantitative problem has been solved. Students, women, and others want social equality and liberated life styles — and they shall have them, because America now has the capacity to solve even these "qualitative" problems.

The analysis, however, is incorrect on both counts. The distinction between quantitative and qualitative problems or demands is meaningless. Moreover, "quantitative" questions, however defined (for example, the problem of wages and working conditions for industrial labor), have not been solved and cannot be solved by technological means, since they are political questions. Technology defines social potential, not political reality; it does not, for example, enable us to solve the basic problem of *politically manufactured* scarcity.[66] Shortages of jobs, goods, services, power and status are not necessary to a technologically advanced and educated society, but they exist. Why? Because such shortages serve the interests of the ruling class. Among other things, they serve to divide small-propertied workers from unpropertied workers, to delay political consolidation of a mass working class, and to keep alive the bourgeois consciousness on which the old system of coalition government depends. Thus, black frustration and anger are generated not merely by white prejudices, but by competition with lower-income whites for scarce jobs, living space, public resources, and social status. Most "working poor" and lower-middle-class whites have been excluded from the benefits of the so-called affluent society: the gap which separates them from the ruling class is increasing rather than decreasing, and they know it.[67] White labor unions do not exclude blacks out of prejudice alone, but because unemployment has become endemic and *real* wages in the United States have been stagnant or declining since 1967. As survival values — the preservation of the little they have — become paramount among hard-pressed whites, a downward pressure is exerted on blacks and other poor groups seeking entry into the work force. Trapped beneath this crushing weight, they are imprisoned in urban ghettos — but the whites who guard these prison walls are no less trapped. Like all prisoners, the black poor occasionally vent their rage on their own cages. Like all guards, the white near-poor occasionally vent theirs on the prisoners.

Clearly, with regard to blacks and other poor minorities, "quantitative" problems still exist. Is it not true, nevertheless, that rebellions among students, women, and other predominantly white middle-class groups are the result of the attractions of a hedonistic "counterculture"? On the contrary, these groups have all been blocked and frustrated by the rise to power of the great corporations. Like black demands, their demands are neither "quantitative" nor "qualitative," but a mixture of both, since the opportunities offered by the existing society for useful work are so limited. In fact, the youth rebellion, like that of women, seems in part a protest against being *declassed*, in part an acceptance of the new status of *worker*. For the sons and daughters of the bourgeoisie understand that their fate, once on the job market, is to become menials of the corporate state, so long as there is a corporate state, and partners in its crimes. (Conscription into the armed forces but dramatizes this more general destiny.) In a weird reversal of Hegelian principles, quality becomes quantity for the vanishing middle class. Students begin by worrying about the Vietnamese peasantry and end by worrying about finding jobs — but those who are being radicalized see that the two questions are related: the corporate state makes serfs of all. Therefore, symbolic acts of self-declassification, from joblessness to identification with the exploited peasantry of the Third World, expresses a gut recognition that a real declassification has taken place, that the white-collar employee is merely a worker who lacks the protection of labor organization bargaining, a "house nigger" to the great corporations and their captive State. And, of course, as workers themselves, little by little, become technologically obsolete, the young perceive that even a suburban executive may be little more than a machine-tender, although he pays a tremendous price in human terms for the privilege.

Thus does Janus-faced consensus turn its head and reveal dissensus seething among those who had been ranked among the privileged members of the governing coalition. If the consensus scholars' analysis were correct, ending the revolts of the 1960s' out-groups would have restored the consensus supposedly existing throughout the "new industrial state," but we see that something very different has happened. While out-group discontent smoulders, revolt spreads through other segments of society, *including* those very groups whose problems were thought to be forever solved by New Deal politics and new industrial economics.

For example, consider the development of a spirit of civil disobedience among normally law-abiding segments of the population. Civil disobedience is the term ordinarily used to describe conscientious acts of nonviolent lawbreaking by protestors — acts like the burning of draft records at Catonsville, Maryland, by Fathers Daniel and Philip Berrigan and the Catonsville Nine.[68] But this very clear and well-articulated type of civil disobedience proves to be the tip of an iceberg, the self-conscious manifestation of a tendency towards *mass* resistance to laws considered oppressive and unjust. Strikes against the government, for example, which are illegal in most jurisdictions, have become regular practice for the millions who now work for state, local and federal government agencies. How could it be otherwise? Labor-management conflict, which had been limited to "Society" prior to the New Deal (with the State intervening from time to time), became subject to federal rules and regulations during the 1930's and 1940's. However, this institutionalization still assumed the existence of a State separated from Society — an impartial arbiter operating, in the case of industrial labor, through federal agencies like the Bureau of Labor Standards and the National Labor Relations Board. When the State itself became an employer — in fact the largest employer and the largest industry in the nation — government employees discovered that preservation of their rights to organize and bargain collectively required regular acts of civil disobedience.

The risks of such disobedience are real; major strikes of policemen, transit workers, schoolteachers, postal employees, and office workers against governments frequently entail injunctions, fines and jail sentences for union leaders, and the risk of firing for strikers. Nevertheless even among workers who might consider antiwar protestors like the Berrigans "kooks," the spirit of civil disobedience spreads.[69] For these workers, the Marxian prediction has become a reality. Every strike involves the "public interest"; every conflict over wage and working conditions is, in a small way, a struggle for State power. The same thing is true, moreover, for workers in other centralized, interstate industries: their wage demands affect the "public interest" in inflation, and their strikes so affect the "public convenience and necessity" as to call forth constant government intervention. Wage and strike control represent the domestic equivalent of a "state of war" mentality which workers will ultimately end by rejecting as militantly as students reject the draft. Or, conversely, those in power may attempt to avert further conflict by failing to

enforce laws against labor organizations, just as they now
refuse to enforce price control and other laws against industry. Either way, the law is broken and falls into disre-
pute. Driven by the imperatives of class rule, the nation's
rulers seem bound to continue this process which renders
reformist demands revolutionary.

The tendency of private conflicts to become public, with
intense destabilizing effects, is further illustrated by the
steady expansion of the area of federal criminal law, and
the consequent growth of the United States Justice Department and its multifarious agencies, including the FBI.
Hannah Arendt has pointed out that governments losing
authority generally resort to *force* in a vain attempt to
stop what we might call a leakage of legitimacy; but in so
doing, they open the leak even wider.[70] Behind the current concern for law and order lies the "gravedigging"
dynamic described above. Impelled to set impossible
standards of civil order, the State compels its citizens to
violate them, and ends by becoming the prime violator
itself. Conscription of young men for the unpopular (and
very likely unconstitutional) Indochinese war produces a
movement of draft resistance, also illegal, which produces,
in turn, unconstitutional use of the Selective Service System to punish resisters. The assassination of Dr. Martin
Luther King, Jr., triggers a riot in Chicago in which poor
blacks perform illegal acts of looting; the mayor of Chicago then advises his police to violate state law and their
own regulations by shooting the looters. With unemployment, income disparities, and low-class aspirations all
rising, the crime rate rises as well. The world's richest
society effectively compels men without hope to engage in
criminal activity, and then, in order to contain this activity, sanctions unconstitutional searches and seizures, pre-
ventive detention, aggressive patrol, wiretapping, and

other affronts to constitutional "law and order." In other words, as politics becomes more criminal — as authority violates its own standards and resorts more openly to naked force — crimes become more political. And political crimes — assassinations of policemen, bombings and the like — accelerate the tendency towards federalization of crime, growth of the secret police, use of infiltrators, spies and technological surveillance against suspect groups. The entire process is best summed up, perhaps, by the events of the Democratic Convention of 1968. There in Chicago, while demonstrators protesting an illegal war (some acting illegally) were illegally beaten by policemen, U.S. Army intelligence agents illegally tapped the telephone of a candidate for the presidency (Senator Eugene McCarthy) because, an agent later admitted, he was in telephonic contact with some of the demonstrators.

The movement from consensus to dissensus, as we have seen, is well precedented. In America, when governing coalitions begin to loose legitimacy, revolts by underclass groups are usually succeeded by revolts of small-propertied groups. But the dissensus of the present time provides evidence of an entirely new development (which suggests that, in a strange way, the consensus scholars' perception of novelty was correct). It appears that our traditional three-class system itself is moribund, and that society is finally dividing into two great classes composed of workers and the great bourgeoisie. We shall have to postpone concrete analysis of this development until Part III. Let me just suggest here that the period of post–World War II consensus in America was produced, not by abolition of class conflict or class consciousness, but by tendencies undermining the preexisting *three-class* structure, and the consciousness which accompanied it. What happened to the pre–World War II class structure, in short, was this:

(1) The *great bourgeoisie* assumed control of the governing coalition in partnership (but *primus inter pares*) with political, military, labor, and educational elites controlling key federal institutions. In so doing, however, it ceased to be a bourgeoisie in the old sense, and became coincident with the State. The struggle within the Republican party between "conservatives" and "liberals" expressed the conflict between the old, extragovernmental bourgeoisie and the new elite — the international corporations which have already assumed many of the planning functions of a centralized State. The triumph of the latter, isolating the old Right as a political force, was a key to construction of the postwar consensus.

(2) The *small-propertied class* was silenced initially by a combination of reward ("cooperation" of government with unions, the benefits of defense business, etc.) and punishment (the "Red purges" of the late 1940's and early 1950's). However, as the great corporations extended their hegemony, the security of small property was further undermined. Threatened by underclass aspirations, hemmed in by concentrated monopoly power, it could no longer function as a springboard to great wealth — or, for that matter, as a guarantee of one's children's education and a comfortable old age. A new consciousness therefore began to develop among blue-collar and lower echelon white-collar workers, a consciousness not based on personal property and status, but on social function and class. The small-propertied class, slowly and painfully, was becoming a working class.

(3) The *underclass*, for the first time in American history, rejected its alloted role, developing within the forms of racial solidarity the closest thing to proletarian consciousness since the demise of the Industrial Workers of the World. Ironically, the new wave of labor union militancy was fed by the influx of blacks into the unions, just

as white militancy in urban neighborhoods profited from the black example. Equally important, a new segment of the working class composed of students, women, intellectuals, and others appeared, or rather was *created* by the insatiable demands of the technocracy for replaceable human parts. The consciousness of these groups was initially countercultural and hedonistic but, as the 1970's dawned, this, too, began to change. A new class consciousness was emerging.

Sooner or later, these mass forces would discover each other humanely and meet on common ground, the ground of defense against a common oppression. For the time being, the ruling class could be counted upon to sow disunion and discord between the new proletarians, alternating between liberal promises to bring business under control and conservative attempts to fan the fires of racism, "law and order" hysteria, and militaristic nationalism. One could nevertheless wonder, without being a Pollyanna, whether either strategy would again serve its historical function of dividing to conquer the working class. Did not the success of these devices depend upon an immature capitalism which permitted a small-propertied class to exist? In the early 1970's, at any rate, it seems clear that militaristic nationalism undermines rather than strengthens the reactionary "consensus" — in fact, that the armed services serve as a training ground in cooperation among the oppressed. The race issue is similarly losing its sting as blacks and whites come to realize that they want and need the same things, and that the same forces stand in opposition to their aspirations. Even the promises of liberal politicians to create a new liberal coalition — a "new New Deal" — meet with unprecedented (and deserved) disbelief; we have been down that road before. One who believes, as I do, in the enormous capacity of the ruling class for self-preservative evil will not underestimate its willingness to cajole, lie, create domestic discord, or resort to force in order to maintain its privileged position. Perhaps this time, however, Americans will recognize that they must take control of their nation away from the business elite or lose it, possibly forever: they must choose, and soon, between socialist democracy and fascist oligarchy.

PART 2

THE DYNAMICS OF COALITION GOVERNMENT

. . . the alliance of the petty bourgeoisie and the big bourgeoisie is not indissoluble. Since the petty bourgeoisie is incapable of an *independent* policy . . . no other choice is left for it than that between the bourgeoisie and the proletariat.

— LEON TROTSKY,
"The Only Road for Germany," 1932

I

Political philosophers, like other kinds of philosophers, premise their work on a distinction between outer form and inner reality. For American political philosophers, it is a truism that the forms of constitutional democracy often obscure the realities of power politics. Most would agree with James Q. Wilson that, "if the study of urban politics has taught us anything, it is that, except on referenda, and perhaps not even then, 'the people' do not govern — organizations, parties, factions, politicians, and groups govern. The people choose among competing leaders and thereby constrain them."[1] The modern analyst views American politics as an extremely complex system in which elections play a less important role than had formerly been assumed. In order to answer the question, "Who governs?" he must therefore write a lengthy book (or two or three!) describing the roles of "organizations, parties, factions, politicians, and groups." Which of these factors is most important? Why, "groups," of course. For to say that elections serve a limited function in a modern democratic state is to imply that the function of political parties (which is to win elections) is also limited. Downgrading the independent significance of parties, one upgrades the importance of those interest groups which so obviously influence the behavior of both parties and politicians.

Piercing the forms of democratic government, forms which relate masses of individuals to officeholders through electoral processes, political scientists thus discover the reality of groups. "The people" is abandoned as a relevant political concept; democracy is redefined, in Robert A. Dahl's language, as "a political system in which all the active and legitimate groups in the population can make themselves heard at some crucial stage in the process of decision."[2] Occasionally, some dissenter will be heard to object that James Wilson's list of governing entities and Robert Dahl's definition of democracy omit the most important factor of all — economic *classes*. For is it not true that the United States, like other nations, possesses a ruling class and subordinate classes, that even in America the rich rule and the poor serve? Not really. In the eyes of the pluralistic political scene, interest groups are perceived as *superseding* classes. Why talk about a "working class," for example, when the relevant groupings are unionized industrial workers, nonunionized agricultural workers, white-collar workers, black workers, and so forth? Why speak of a "ruling class" if the coalition in power includes, say, labor unions, civil rights organizations, and groups representing the unemployed?

Karl Marx distinguished a class inchoately "in itself" — definable only in economic terms, without political consciousness, hence, without immediate relevance — from a class "for itself," conscious of its political role and historical destiny.[3] It may seem obvious that politics in America has *not* been dominated by classes, at least in the latter sense, or plagued by European-style class conflict. But this is to confuse form with content. It is not necessary to choose between pluralist description and Marxist understanding, for interest groups in America, far from superseding or dissolving classes, provide the mechanism which makes class rule possible in a bourgeois democracy. Many commentators have remarked upon the narrowness of the effective political spectrum in the United States. The tendency of the vast centrist majority to reject extremes of radicalism and reaction has been attributed by some to the American character or the ideology of natural rights, by others to interest-group pluralism or the two-party system, and by still others to the superabundance of natural resources on the American subcontinent and the success of the capitalist system. I maintain, however, that this centrism is characteristic of politics in a *three-class society*.

To most of us, the idea of class suggests polarity, for example, the "haves" and "have-nots." Political philosophy correctly relates revolutionary change to the existence of *two* classes: in the Marxian dialectic, for example, socialist revolution depends upon the reduction of all classes to two — proletariat and bourgeoisie.[4] Conversely, if there is no polarity, we tend to think that there is no class struggle, or even that there are no classes, only "interest groups." But the United States Constitution is the product of a philosophy of "balanced government" reaching back to Aristotle, which assumes that "in all states there are *three* elements; one class very rich, another very poor, and a third in a mean." Where two classes predominate, the stronger will sooner or later attempt to destroy the weaker, thus producing either democracy (rule by the numerous poor) or oligarchy (rule by the few rich). But where the majority of citizens are neither poor nor rich, conflict gives way to compromise, and a "constitutional" form of government may be realized.[5] For the Founding Fathers, as well as for Aristotle, a three-class system pivoting on a large small-propertied class provided the best defense against class warfare and radical change.

The ruling class in the United States, as in other advanced capitalist nations, is the great bourgeoisie — that small minority of business and financial decision-makers which controls the vast bulk of the nation's invested wealth.[6] Its mode of rule, however — the exercise of power through domination of interest groups within a governing coalition

— is uniquely American. Coalition government of this sort is possible only if the ruling class is confronted not by a united proletariat but by two mutually hostile lower classes which bid against each other for the favor of the elite. America's enormous natural wealth provided the material basis, first of all, for a *small-propertied class*. In the present period, we would be more inclined to speak of the lower middle class, but, in any age, this class comprises individuals a generation or two removed from poverty, whose economic position and social status are based on small-property holdings in the form of land, small capital, personal possessions, or jobs secured through contract or bureaucratic regulation. Historically, this grouping in America has included the petty bourgeoisie, middle-level farmers, skilled craft and industrial workers, and lower-level white-collar workers. All share a petty-bourgeois consciousness characterized by fundamental insecurity of economic position, conservatism in moral matters, yearning for social and economic advancement, and a profound fear of being done in by those without land, capital, jobs, or possessions.

According to Marx, of course, the petty bourgeoisie is a declining class which sinks into the proletariat as monopolists take control of the capitalist economy.[7] And over the long run (as I attempt to show in Part III) this observation has proved accurate; the small-propertied class *is* being annihilated under modern conditions of capitalist production. But what will explain the unusual scope, strength, and persistence of this class in America? Why, rather than shrinking, has it seemed at times to expand to encompass the whole mass of employed workers, farmers, and white-collar employees, as well as entrepreneurs of all sorts? One explanation, widely accepted, has it that the great wealth of the United States has been the prime inhibitor of class conflict and preservator of small property.[8]

We know that our skilled industrial workers, for example, are generally more prosperous than their counterparts in other countries, and able to acquire those small holdings in land, goods, or even investments which convey membership in the extended petty bourgeoisie. Nevertheless, social scientists have emphasized that the *absolute* level of prosperity of a class has little to do with its propensity for class struggle or rebellion. It is its deprivation *relative* to class expectations and the position of other classes which makes the difference.[9] Relative to the position of big business, small property has for a long time been at a serious disadvantage; the consistent trend of the past century has been towards industrial concentration and the undermining of the petty bourgeoisie. Furthermore, we know that, notwithstanding its privileged position measured by international standards, the small-propertied class in America has had a strong propensity for violence and rebellion.[10] Why then does this class not revolt on a massive scale when economic crisis strikes, as during the 1930's? Why is it not revolutionary?

The answer, I think, is that a small-propertied class is preserved, and the development of a united working class postponed, by maintenance of a permanent *underclass*. Existence of the underclass divides American workers into more or less congruent categories of employed and marginally employed, skilled and unskilled, organized and unorganized, "foreign" and "American," "racially superior," and "racially inferior." It creates intense competition for control of "scarce" resources between those who possess a little and those who possess nothing. It drives the men and women of small property into the arms of the great bourgeoisie, impels them to trade political power for social status, and offers the ruling class an irresistible opportunity to achieve stability by recourse to the tactics of "divide and conquer."

In Karl Marx's two-class analysis, there is no underclass. There is a *lumpenproletariat*, which Marx refers to caustically as "scum, offal, refuse of all classes," and whose role he and Engels describe as follows: "The 'dangerous class,' the social scum, that passively rotting mass thrown off by the lowest layers of the old society, may, here and there, be swept into the movement by a proletarian revolution; its conditions of life, however, prepare it far more for the part of a bribed tool of reactionary intrigue."[11] But Marx was thinking about "the whole indefinite, disintegrated mass, thrown hither and thither, which the French term la boheme"[12] — the bohemians of Paris — rather than a massive class, rural as well as urban, embracing unskilled workers as well as the unemployed, composed of groups whose collective identity and social status are based on race or ethnicity. The American underclass has not always been black, although most black people have been of the underclass; at various times it has included American Indians, Scotch-Irish, Chinese, Japanese, Mexicans, Puerto Ricans, Germans, Irish, Italians, Poles, Jewish and Slavic immigrants. At present, working women, whose median income is lower than that of black males, form an increasingly large and important segment of the underclass. Two factors present in America, but not in the nations of old Europe, originally combined to produce this third class here: the existence of castes of aboriginal Indians and black slaves, and the "open door" immigration policies which prevailed until the middle 1920's. Several great waves of migration — the forced migration of slaves, the European inpouring, and the internal migration of rural blacks and whites into urban areas — assured a steady supply of cheaper labor to the high-labor-cost economy of the United States. Therefore, instead of rapidly "decaying" as a class, which was the fate predicted by Marx for the *lumpenproletariat*, the underclass became a powerful factor in American politics, its economic, social and political functions remaining constant while its personnel changed.

The sine qua non of American-style coalition government is the displacement of class conflict; instead of the poor and near-poor struggling together against the rich, here they have alternated in uniting with the rich against each other. Nevertheless, this struggle is not generally recognized as a form of class conflict, since liberal ideology insists upon dissolving classes into "interest groups." For example, from 1863, when Irish workingmen in New York City unleashed a pogrom against that city's blacks, until 1968, when Mayor Daley ordered the Chicago police to "shoot to kill" black rioters, there has been constant conflict between small-propertied whites and poor blacks based on competition for jobs, living space, public facilities, political power, and control of neighborhood cultures. Although such a long and bitter conflict points logically towards a social contradiction — a conflict between social classes — no such contradiction is admissible in liberal ideology, which insists that the interests of "the people" (expressed, of course, through diverse "interest groups") are to be upheld against the selfish demands of a "privileged few." But so long as shortages of jobs, income, living space, social services, and political power exist there is no coherent "people" to represent. If people with property are compelled to fight people without property for scarce resources, even liberal politicians must *choose* between competing classes. In 1863 the mayor of New York and in 1968 the mayor of Chicago did choose; they both opted to represent the white small-propertied class against the black underclass (the usual choice of our ruling class leadership). Later, since their political principles would not tolerate admission of a fundamental cleavage among "the people," they were compelled to resort to explanation, qualification, and denial. Mayor Daley a racist? Of course not: he merely "overreacted" in a difficult situation. The rioters were not "representative" of the black community, etc.

An alternative method of fusing principles and practice is not hard to imagine. Forge an alliance between the two lower classes against the big business community and its allies in order to redistribute available wealth and power and end the shortages which divide "the people" into classes. However obvious this strategy may seem to the innocent, it is anathema to liberal capitalist thought. The undifferentiated concept of "the people," utilized to gloss over class conflict between those of small property and the poor, also serves to deny the existence of the more profound conflict between small-propertied and big business classes. We are all "the people" — ghetto-dwellers and surbur-banites, union men and coupon-clippers, stock boys and stockbrokers — and the liberal coalition theoretically represents us all (with the exception of a few, specially selected "malefactors of great wealth"). This eighteenth-century ideology, which has long misrepresented the facts of economic and political life in America, now takes the form of "interest group" analysis. What this analysis ignores, however, is that interest groups and governing coalitions have not replaced social classes; on the contrary, in a three-class society, the governing coalition represents all classes *in proportion to their existing economic power.*

The "active and legitimate" groups of which Robert Dahl speaks are not free-floating atoms. They exercise power through a process of coalition-formation and bargaining, a process in which the political party, with its highly de-centralized structure, serves a crucial function. The party is the matrix upon which the coalition is constructed, the forum in which intergroup conflicts are settled informally, the engine which mobilizes mass support for the coali-tion's candidates and programs. But the party is not the coalition. History as well as logic leads us to a conclusion which pluralists have been loath to recognize: it is not the party which governs, but the coalition. Most major political movements in American history, from Jeffersonian democracy to the New Deal, have exercised power as coalitions; that is, in each case, major decisions have emerged out of the interplay between members of an alliance of interest groups. As Dahl's definition of democracy implies, coalitions firmly in power attempt to represent virtually every "active and legitimate" political group in the nation — industrial (including labor), occupational, geographic, ethnic, racial, and ideological. In other words, coalition government both assumes and generates a national consensus. Insofar as democracy implies justice and equality, however, the continued existence of subordinate and dominant classes mocks the democratic ideal.

Within any governing coalition, there are some "interest groups" which have the power to move the administration or to obtain the passage of legislation, some which can veto objectionable activities by the government, some which have only the right to be consulted, and some which possess no power at all — their membership in the coalition is merely "token." (Whether, as Dahl says, such groups can "make themselves heard" is beside the point.) Why is this? Why is it that there are groups which lack even token membership, either because they have been excluded deliberately (they are not "legitimate") or because they lack political consciousness, or have developed it too late for inclusion (they are not "active")? I suggest that imbalances of power among interest groups, or among subgroups within complex interest groups, generally reflect the more profound imbalances characteristic of a three-class society. To take just one recent example: in 1972, the nation's largest agribusiness corporations — a great-bourgeois interest group — demanded and received advance information from the Department of Agriculture about the impending sale of grain to the Soviet Union (in fact, key members of this group helped negotiate the deal), while small-propertied farm interests represented by national farmers' organizations did not. In turn, although small-propertied farmers stood to gain something from increased exports of grain and were at least strong enough to protest the "insider" status of the large corporations, underclass farm laborers — an unrecognized interest — could not have taken advantage of the information even if they had possessed it. In fact, since governing coalitions usually embody an "all-bourgeois" alliance of small- and great-propertied interests, underclass interests *do not exist* from the point of view of the governing coalition. They must be "discovered" by dissidents, as William Lloyd Garrison discovered the oppressed slave, Lincoln Steffens "the shame of the cities," and Michael Harrington "the other America." After such discoveries take place, the coalition may attempt to extend the consensus by gaining the support of "responsible elements" among the disenfranchised. Quite often, it attempts to isolate such groups and to keep them passive, or, failing this, to destroy them.

The realities of class structure account for the tendency of the American political system to fluctuate over time between periods of stifling consensus and wild disorder. In a formally democratic system (even granting the influence of money in politics), it is relatively easy to vote any politician in or out of office. But it is another matter altogether to displace a governing coalition, since the all-bourgeois alliance, once constituted, usually controls both major political parties. Therefore, while coalitional rule is based almost by definition on consensus among groups, members of lower-class groups overtly or covertly excluded from coalition membership experience increasing frustration and rage as "normal democratic procedures" fail to produce a breakthrough to power. The mistake is to assume that political parties, rather than coalitions, govern; for if party and coalition were coterminous, excluded groups could obtain coalition membership merely by associating with the opposition party and working to make it the majority party. On the contrary, until the New Deal, industrial workers were effectively excluded from both parties by the coalition which controlled them both, while black people at present can bring neither party to support their demands. In effect, our system says to the powerless and disenfranchised, "Get out of the underclass, and *then* we will give your interests limited recognition. Join the small-propertied class, and *then* you may acquire membership in a governing coalition." Similarly, notwithstanding the myth of lower-middle-class power, our system predicates the power to innovate (as opposed to the power to be consulted or "heard") on membership in the *great* bourgeoisie. The responsiveness of political institutions to interest groups in proportion to their preexisting economic strength gives the lie to the reformist notion that, without abolishing classes, large, relatively powerless groups may secure their advancement through conventional politics. (In fact, as William Shannon has pointed out with regard to the Irish, overconcentration on politics at the expense of attempting to "get ahead" in the economic jungle may actually hold a group back.[13]) With this in mind, we can take a fresh look at the coalitional process in the United States in order to determine how governing coalitions take power and how they are reorganized or replaced.

II

Unlike politicians, coalitions in power are astonishingly difficult to displace. Consider that, with only minor interruptions in each case, Jeffersonians and Jacksonians controlled both the White House and Congress from 1801–1841, Republicans from 1861–1913, and New Deal Democrats from 1932–1969! Moreover, even where the parties play revolving chairs in the White House or Congress, a strong coalition may remain firmly in power, as Jackson's did between his retirement and the breakup of both parties during the 1850's, or as Roosevelt's did through the eight years of Eisenhower government. (This is particularly obvious when the same party which controlled Congress under a strong President continues to control it under a series of weak ones.) To some, this may appear old hat, but its unrecognized implications are startling. If coalitions do govern America, the United States has had numerous regimes, but no more than five or six *governments*: Federalist, Jeffersonian, Jacksonian, Republican, Progressive, and New Deal. None of these came to power without using novel methods of protest and organization decried as illegal or un-American by its opponents. And none was evicted from power without an interregnum involving intense and violent civil disorder, verging at times on civil war and potential revolution.[14]

This tendency to plunge from seemingly unshakable consensus to a condition apparently bordering on anarchy is a characteristic of coalition government; when a coali-

tion loses its grip, the pieces fly apart. Richard Hofstadter
and other historians have remarked on the sudden and
unexpected appearance of civil disorder during eras like
the 1790's, 1850's, 1890's and 1930's.[15] I believe that
these turbulent times mark periods of coalitional breakdown, periods during which the stakes of conflict are
raised too high for the "politics of civility." Why should
this happen? Because at such times *real* power, and not
just the illusion of power, is up for grabs. In "normal"
times the existence of an effective governing coalition has
a dampening effect on political activity and interest, since
voters, interest groups, and organizations sense that a
change in representation will not make a great deal of difference; redistributing offices is not the same thing as
redistributing power. Conversely, the breakdown of governing coalitions raises the amount and intensity of
political interest. Polarization and politicization take place
when there is something to be genuinely gained or lost by
political activity, during those rare periods in American
history when *governments*, and not just *regimes*, are
changing.

Participants in governing coalitions therefore recognize,
from the moment of taking power, the nexus between
effective coalition government and consensus: in America, you either govern as a "national" (consensus) government, or you may not govern at all. As a result, however
uproarious the circumstances of its birth, however radical
and divisive its earlier ideological commitments, the coalition in power always claims to represent the *whole* people
and not just one class, section, or set of interest groups
against another. Normally, we do not worry about mass
refusal to accept a new government; the prospect is so
unlikely as to be impossible, practically speaking. But
"normally," coalitions are not changing. When they are,
following decades of disorder like the 1790's, 1850's, or

1930's, it is not so clear that the "loyal opposition" will remain loyal. The passions aroused during periods of riotous politics do not subside once a new coalition has gained national office, and the defeated coalition often comes close to withdrawing from the social contract — as some Federalists did, for example, at the Hartford Convention of 1815, and as most Southerners did after Lincoln's election in 1860.[18] (Compare the role of the Republican Supreme Court in striking down New Deal legislation between 1933 and 1938, a tactic which provoked Roosevelt's famous "court-packing" scheme.) Frequently, the enemies of the new coalition picture its leader as the Antichrist and wrecker of the Republic, a stereotypical villain (even down to allegations of physical and mental malformation) to whom allegiance may not be due. And sometimes, when political parties are disorganized and elections hotly contested, there *is* genuine doubt as to their legitimacy. Again, with power, and not just office, at stake, electoral processes are strained to the breaking point; in this respect America is no different from Vietnam or Chile. Jefferson's first election was achieved only because a number of Federalist electors preferred him to Aaron Burr; Lincoln was a minority President in 1860, and might not have been reelected without the absence of the South and the dubious "soldier's vote" of 1864; Wilson owed his first election (by less than 40 percent of the electorate) to a Republican split in 1912. Of all the great liberals, only Franklin Roosevelt had a clear electoral mandate in his first term, although it was the kind of mandate a drowning man gives a lifeguard.

Even where the situation is not so dramatic, it takes time for the new coalition to achieve both organizational coherence and the consent necessary to effective rule. Under these circumstances, it is not surprising that its leadership moves as quickly as possible to become "national." In his first inaugural address, Jefferson, prince of party organizers and political infighter par excellence, immediately announced the subordination of party politics to the cause of national unity: "We are all federalists; we are all republicans." Denied the consensus necessary to coalition government, Lincoln fought a civil war on grounds of union alone ("if I could save the Union without freeing one single slave I would do it"), and was prepared at war's end to sacrifice Reconstruction for a rapid restoration of national unity. Woodrow Wilson made it equally clear that the rhetoric of reform would not lead him to attack or alienate any major interest group: "I am for big business, and I am against the trusts."[16] And Franklin D. Roosevelt, as Frances Perkins said, "took the status quo in our economic system as much for granted as his family. . . . He was not even a vigorous antimonopolist."[17] His "first New Deal," featuring the business-government-labor partnership of the NRA, was preeminently a government of national unity.

Responding to the imperative of consensus, the new coalition's leadership moves to conciliate the opposition by appointing its leaders to high position and by adopting its political attitudes on critical issues of foreign and domestic policy. The leader himself undergoes a reverse Jekyll-and-Hyde transformation — from politician to statesman, advocate to compromiser, publicist, as it were, to diarist. The result is often hard for the coalition's more militant members to swallow, since the new leadership seems to (and often does) reverse both principles and practice in order to achieve the desired mandate. In a sense, liberalism begins its decline into conservatism from the moment of the liberal President's first inaugural address, pledging to govern on behalf of "all the people." In practice, this means that *no class will be destroyed* — not even the monopolist elite. But if all classes are guaranteed survival under the new coalition, it is only a matter of time until their political power becomes proportioned to their economic power and is then used to secure even greater economic advantages for the more powerful. Omnirepresentation assures not only the survival of all recognized interest groups, but the domination of the strongest. Only a step separates Jefferson's "we are all federalists" from his adoption of Hamiltonian economics; Wilson could *not* be "for big business" without also embracing the trusts; and F.D.R., playing father to the nation, could do little more than chastise the naughty "economic royalists." (To go farther would have risked patricide!)

Basing the new coalition's legitimacy on a claimed national consensus not only enhances the position of already-powerful interest groups, it also undermines the position of the weakest. Keep in mind that the claim of any government to represent all the people is a lie except in times of gravest national emergency — and usually it is false even then. Some underclass or small-propertied groups have been excluded from coalition membership *ab initio*; some develop political consciousness later on and are shut out as "illegitimate"; and some, initially included in the coalition, become dissatisfied with their lot and drop out. But once the claim to all-national representation or consensus has been put forward, it may not be withdrawn without impairing the legitimacy of the coalition. Therefore, groups opposing the government are frequently denied recognition and the right to bargain, for if the coalition claims to be all-representative, it must deny the very reality of groups outside its pale.

Thus Federalists watched in horror as groups without political "standing" rose in revolt against their excise taxes and their foreign policy, and had no hesitation in jailing Jeffersonian publicists under the Sedition Act. Jeffersonians returned the favor by driving some Federalists into violent opposition to their foreign policy and then declaring them traitors. Old Jacksonians could not comprehend the rise of abolitionist and secessionist groupings, nor would Republicans (and Republicanized Democrats) recognize the right of labor organizations to exist. New Dealers felt a similar bafflement and anger when confronted by rebellions of militant blacks and students; candidate Hubert Humphrey's silence in the face of the actions of Chicago policemen during the Democratic Convention of 1968 spoke louder than words. Agitation by rebellious groups outside the coalition is almost always condemned as illegal or un-American when it is merely outside the universe of political activity recognized as legitimate by those in power.

Note especially that the illiberalism of the governing coalition is not the result of evil men assuming positions of authority; it is implicit in the coalitional dynamic itself. The necessity for consensus drives the coalition to identify itself with "the nation," with the result that its opponents are excluded therefrom. If their opposition is passive, they remain unrecognized; if active, they become "enemies of the state." Although democratic principles and procedures may govern the relationship between interest groups, political organizations, and parties operating within the framework established by a governing coalition, they are easily abandoned when it comes to dealing with groups outside the coalitional consensus. Each wave of repression, from the Alien and Sedition Acts to the Red Scare of the 1920's and the McCarthyism of the 1950's, seems an undemocratic anomaly to those who come after; but even while the liberals of today condemn the repression of yesteryear, they move inexorably towards identifying *their* coalition with the nation, and dissent with "foreign agitation" or treason.

The principle of omnirepresentation therefore drives

the governing coalition towards illiberalism even in its early, reformist phase. A second self-contradiction producing similar results is implicit in the role of coalition leader. One of the more significant ironies of American history is the tendency of movements of reform and reconstruction, dedicated to expanding the mass constituency and democratizing the techniques of government, to accelerate the tendency towards authoritarian leadership. Each new coalition comes to power behind a leader who is attacked as dictator by his enemies and acclaimed as messiah by his supporters. The "strong President" is a father figure to the nation, and coalition leaders like Washington, Jefferson, Jackson, Lincoln, and Roosevelt played that role to the hilt. To an extent, the strong executive was foreseen by those who framed the Constitution, but it was thought that the President, like a European monarch, would represent the forces of tradition and property against the decentralist, antiauthoritarian tendencies of the popular assembly. The constitutional "balance of power" was intended to favor the former by aligning the conservative executive with a conservative Senate and judiciary, all possessing some form of veto power over the acts of the House of Representatives. What the framers did not anticipate was the emergence of the *authoritarian liberal*, typified by Napoleon Bonaparte, whose power would be based on a new kind of mass mandate, a Rousseauian legislator who would interpret and execute the "general will" of the community against all partial wills. But a further irony lay in store — a contradiction analyzed best, perhaps, by the sociologist Max Weber. Weber pointed out that while charismatic leaders might take power in the name of any number of ideals (including the ideal of "democracy"), society's irresistible tendency was towards centralization and routinization of authority.[18] Every Jesus must sooner or later have his St. Paul, and every

Tom Paine his Alexander Hamilton. Coalition leaders in America, however, generally undergo an even more rapid transformation. Before election they are all Tom Paines; after assuming the "responsibilities of power," they are all Hamiltons.

It is not hard to understand why new coalitions, no matter how democratic their principles, have risen to power in the United States under the banner of the strong central leader. Prior to the formation of a new coalition, dissident groups representing a wide assortment of class, geographical, occupational, ethnic, and ideological interests survive by securing *local* power bases. Indeed, it has often been remarked that this is one of the chief virtues of a federal system: interests which do not succeed in securing their objectives at the national level may live to fight another day by "digging in" at the level of state, city, or county government. However, the relationship of local power to group survival is complex: local power is necessary, but not sufficient, to enable an interest group to maintain its position in American society. It follows that the process of alliance-formation and coalition among interest groups is not usually motivated by an aggressive will to power or an abstract desire to make society over so much as the desire of group members to survive. It is in the process of alliance-formation that the role of the Leader is defined.

Local power is necessary. Groups outside the governing coalition fight desperately, and often violently, to gain and maintain a hold on some physical or economic "territory." Unless the group controls some source of power — land, votes, jobs, businesses, or politicians — it will have nothing to bargain with, nothing to bring to an alliance, and will be unable to either join the existing coalition or to participate in forming a new one. More important, without local power, the group is subject to destruction at any time by those wielding national power. (Destruction means elimination as an independent political entity; it may also mean physical extermination, as in the case of the American Indians.) A single thread links the politics of Sam Adams and Tom Paine with those of later dissident leaders from Aaron Burr and John C. Calhoun to Malcolm X and Tom Hayden: give us local autonomy, control over our own communities, for without local power we are subject to political extinction (through integration or repression). Let us govern ourselves at the local level, for democracy means participation in self-government, not delegation of power to distant representatives. Permit us to develop our own culture on our own territory, for constitutionalism means that minority cultures will not be destroyed by the majority. Thus dissidents in America often begin as decentralists, if not separatists. How else does one find breathing space within a centralizing society dominated by a "national" coalition?

But local power is not sufficient. Once obtained, the breathing space threatens constantly to disappear as local political power is suffocated by inexorable tendencies towards economic and political centralization. Southern nationalists obtained political control over their territory, bolstered by legal power at the national level (Fugitive Slave legislation, the Dred Scott decision, etc.) — but to no avail, since they could not control the progressive economic (and hence, political) subordination of their section to the North. Western staple farmers put Populists in control of state legislatures from Ohio to California — but state legislatures were unable to control international commodity prices or to alter the national coalition's commitment to industrialization. More recently, urban blacks began to elect mayors of large, northern cities and to form political organizations independent of the major parties. Excellent — but neither Cleveland's Mayor Carl Stokes nor Gary's Mayor Richard Hatcher, neither traditional street gangs nor militant peoples' organizations, proved able to arrest the decline of the ghetto or to obtain a reversal of national priorities. Without local power the group is nothing. But, having gained local power, its relative position in the society continues to slip unless it becomes part of a new coalition with a share of central power. Therefore, groups which possess local power, but which remain outside the ruling coalition, tend eventually to surrender their separatist militancy for the sake of militant alliance. (The dark *doppelgängers* are groups within the ruling coalition which possess apparent but not real power, and which may surrender their integrationist conservatism for the sake of a reactionary alliance.)

But once the necessity for alliance is recognized, how will it be formed? How will former separatists become cooperative partners? What will link these diverse, far-flung dissident groups, which represent a multiplicity of interests and *types* of interest? Lacking "horizontal" links (for example, a common class position), they search for "vertical" links — principles of organization which will make alliance possible notwithstanding this diversity. One vertical link is the leader, the "father" who is capable of providing a home for all his "children" within a new national coalition. In theory, of course, there is an organizational principle which should serve to ally dissident groups regardless of their differences. In theory, the minority party should collect these dissidents until it becomes a majority party, the nucleus of a new coalition. In fact, since coalitions are no respecters of parties, but rather (if they are strong) easily control the major parties, the problem of new groups is generally solved extrasystemically, through innovations which seem illegitimate or illegal at the time (although history is later rewritten to restore their legitimacy). The Jeffersonian party was pure invention; the Federalists were surely correct in labeling it extra-constitutional and would have destroyed it "legally" if they had had the power to do so. Similarly, the parties of union and secession were less political parties than the governments of competing sectional nations; the Republican right to rule could be proved only by force. And although the Roosevelt coalition utilized the Democratic Party to unite the "outs" of 1932, what made the Democrats a winner in 1932 was not the smooth workings of the two-party system but the most catastrophic depression in world history — a depression which made almost every interest group in America an out-group.

Emergent groups do *not* generally come to power merely by rallying behind the minority party and waiting for the tide to turn. They may join the minority party, which is happy to have their votes; but unless these votes are absolutely essential to its success, and unless a threat to withhold votes is credible (a rare situation), the party will subordinate their interests to its own interest in sharing power with the existing coalition. Thus Southerners interested in preserving slavery were thrust aside by nationally oriented Democrats interested in getting a piece of the industrial-railroad action, while northern abolitionists were excluded from the Whig Party by "moderates" who did not wish to see the national scramble for wealth derailed by a fight over principle. Similarly, despite the long years of Republican rule, the Democrats managed for decades to avoid becoming the party of labor and the immigrant. Into such gaps between two-party principles and single-coalition practice steps the leader. The new coalition may come to power by using the political party as an organizational device, but only after the existing party structure has been torn apart by some economic or social catastrophe. It is here — in putting the pieces back together in a new way — that the leader's role becomes critical, for it is he that mediates between past and present, the old coalition and the new, the ruling class and the lower classes.

Every important liberal-democratic leader in the United States has been called a "traitor to his class" — Jefferson, the Virginia aristocrat; Jackson, the plantation owner and army general; Lincoln, the ex-Whig; Wilson, the genteel southern professor; and, of course, the two Roosevelts, Hudson Valley patricians both. This is not an accident, for these are men whose background or ambition places them in the upper or upper middle class, but who are capable of leading a coalition whose mass membership is lower middle class or poor. Damned as demagogues by influential folk, they often seem saviors to those dissident groups which, prior to the upheaval, had been excluded from positions of influence in both major parties. As the old coalition begins to lose its hold on its mass constituency, dissident groups compete intensely and often physically among themselves, helping through their own factional struggles to keep the old alliance in power. Even during eras of disorder like the pre-Revolutionary and pre–Civil War periods, the "era of class struggle" (1877–1914) and the present, out-groups fight bitterly among themselves for crumbs from the governing coalition's table. Left to their own devices, these groups might, out of sheer desperation, develop an alliance capable of challenging the old coalition's right to rule. They might even organize a lower-class party to oppose the two parties controlled by the upper class. But before this can happen, elements of the old coalition representing powerful but discontented great-bourgeois interests break off to join (and to control) the dissident alliance. A basis for coalitional agreement appears in the person of the leader, whom all can agree to support since he embodies both the dream of order and the dream of change. Initially, his leadership is highly personalistic. His own background and prior career insure that he will *not* have formulated a comprehensive program prior to taking power. The legendary "pragmatism" of the great liberals is thus a response to the situation which produces them — the necessity of leading a coalition which exists at first for electoral purposes only. The emergent coalition combines out-groups of various stripes, functionaries and factotums of the old minority party, dropouts from the old coalition — and a host of formerly apolitical groupings which have "crawled out of the woodwork" during the period of civil strife. The leader is called upon to forge out of this raw material both a majority party and a ruling coalition. In performing the first task he realizes the dream of order. In accomplishing the second, he betrays the dream of change.

As organizer of an emergent coalition, the leader adopts the rhetoric of democratic antiauthoritarianism, attacking centralized government, calling for sweeping reform of the old system, and justifying out-group rebellion. Occasionally, he utters vague threats of revolution, adopting the tone and reflecting the demands of the outcast groups which are, initially, the most active in opposing the old regime. Nevertheless, the problem which confronts the new leadership is supremely practical: how to forge a coalition whose mass electoral base will assure victory at the polls without actually creating a *mass organization* which could overthrow the great bourgeoisie and utterly revolutionize the political system. The first imperative requires an appeal to mass discontent, the second a diversion of mass anger away from the ruling *class* and towards selected *groups* within the old coalition, who thus serve the time-honored functions of the scapegoat. The solution is to adopt the political style of the middle classes, especially the petty bourgeoisie, which singles out for attack a few "economic royalists" or "malefactors of great wealth" within the old coalition, while identifying its vital interests with those of the larger business community rather than the oppressed underclass.

This means that the liberal leader seeks to unite his

diverse followers on the basis of a conservative appeal: he will restore the values of a vanished America. By attacking a few monopolists (the Federalist "aristocracy," the Bank of the United States, the "slavocracy," the trusts, etc.) and restoring competition, he will return control over an irresponsible government bureaucracy to the people. (That means the "people" who possess a little property, a little education, and a little hope — not the masses of oppressed and disenfranchised blacks, immigrants, or poor people.) The leader is certainly *not* a revolutionary, but so catastrophic, in the American context, are changes of governing coalitions that he is often seen as one. As a result, when he attains high office, he must speak as an embodiment of the nation, appealing to the entire body politic which has "elected" him (including his enemies) to consent to the results of his election. Empowering the new coalition must await this second verdict of the people — a verdict taken for granted in democratic theory, but as we have seen, not always affirmative in practice. As a result, the leader's first term in office is often in the nature of an interregnum; the new coalition does not assume power or final form until his second term. By that time, however, continuity has been reestablished and the upper-class leadership is firmly in control of the coalition. Again, the leader's role in this process is critical since, with the coalition and its program yet unformed, he is able to identify the nation's abstract loyalty to the constitutional system with personal loyalty (fealty, really) to him. "Many of us have fought hard against the new President, but now that he is elected, we must all get behind him."

The revolutionary potentials of a refusal to make this identification lurk just below the surface of consciousness, yet it is probably this awareness, conscious or not, which explains the astonishing submissiveness of candidates defeated in disputed national elections — the unwillingness of the victims of manifest vote-stealing to jeopardize the system's stability by shouting "fraud" and throwing electoral results into doubt. In a system in which vote-stealing has become a fine art, every close election is, in effect, won by fraud. For Americans to demand "Free, honest" elections of themselves (as they do of other nations) would potentially invalidate the results of a great many critical elections, including the presidential contests of 1800, 1824, 1864, 1876, 1884, 1896, 1916, 1948, 1960 and 1968. The last elections mentioned provide a classic example of turnabout being fair play — fair, at least, to the monopolists of power. In 1960, after John F. Kennedy's narrow victory had been insured by vote fraud in Chicago, Richard Nixon refused to heed the pleas of his enraged supporters to challenge the election results — a wager on stability which paid off handsomely in 1968, when Hubert Humphrey refused to challenge the vote-stealing in rural areas without which Nixon might not have won.

In the first phase of a new coalition's rule, then, loyalty to the leader has many of the characteristics of feudal fealty or recognition of familial authority. The leader is the "father" who promises to protect and do justice to all his individual "children," provided only that they acknowledge the authority of his office. Such efforts to dissolve the crisis of authority immediately build into the emerging coalition a set of complex contradictions. The leader has made himself "father of peoples" — but groups in rebellion against the old coalition have declared their unwillingness to play the child; their style is often violently anti-paternal. The leader has distinguished the Constitution, which he now represents, from "mere politics" — but dissidents ordinarily fight bitterly to abolish this distinction. The leader now sees his "children" as individual wards, each of whom is entitled to his paternal care, whereas new coalition members insist on their political existence and rights as groups. The leader promises the nation equal and impartial enforcement of the laws, when what his lower-class supporters desire and need is partiality *towards* them as a corrective to years of partiality *against* them. Weaker groups within the coalition will soon claim that the leader has "sold them out"; stronger groups will perceive the same phenomenon as the leader "rising above politics." What this usually means is that the leader has turned his back on the interests which intended to use him to redistribute economic and political power. By founding his authority *ab initio* on "the people," he attempts to blur the popular divisions which produced his election. The next phase of the coalition's rule inevitably brings this father figure into conflict with the rambunctious children of his own house, for in becoming the instrument of the mystical "nation," the leader inevitably becomes the tool of a national elite.

To summarize: active political interest groups are the atomic units of traditional American politics, and they govern by forming coalitions. Governing coalitions in America are formed, with great difficulty and amidst serious civil disorder, on the matrix of the political party. Once in power, they are extremely hard to remove, for they quickly coopt middle-class dissenters and move savagely to prevent opposition on the part of unrecognized or "illegitimate" groups. The fundamental principle of organization of the governing coalition, necessitated by the nature of its multiclass interest-group membership, is the "national" principle, or the principle of omnirepresentation. Although an aspiration, omnirepresentation is believed for ideological purposes to be a fact. This contributes to the tendency of the American system to swing between poles of apparent uniformity or consensus and seeming anarchy. A fundamental organizational device is the leader, who mediates between change and order, the volatile mass and the existing elite. Although branded a "class traitor" by his enemies, he customarily disappoints less powerful members and nonmembers of the coalition by adherence to the principle of omnirepresentation. What weaker groups frequently fail to understand, however, is that omnirepresentation and paternalistic leadership are of the essence of bourgeois coalition government, since they protect the supremacy of the ruling class even while they veil its existence. It is not this leader or that, this group or that, this party or that which frustrates their expectations, but the coalition system itself.

III

It is not entirely fanciful to imagine a similarity between governing coalitions in America and those ancient empires that rose and fell so regularly as to give rise to cyclical theories of history. In fact, witnessing the birth, growth, maturity, and decline of successive coalitions, one senses the same rhythm described by the ancient historians — ceaseless, regular flux without fundamental change. "The sun also rises, the sun also sets. There is nothing new under the sun."

Flux, in our system, is guaranteed by the inability of governing coalitions to be truly omnirepresentative. First, groups outside the coalition, persecuted and outlawed, move into violent opposition to the status quo. Later, they are joined by disenchanted groups within the coalition who often desert behind their leaders' backs (as the membership of the labor movement appears to be doing at present). Next, as disunity and repression increase in tandem, "illegitimate" and apostate groups begin to form alliances; there is talk of new political parties, new coalitions. Polarization deepens; violence and disorientation become endemic. Eventually, amidst scenes of disorder not contemplated by the Founding Fathers, a new order does come to power, flying the flags of mass democracy. Fundamental political change does not take place, however, since the new coalition, like the old, claims to represent a national consensus, cutting across class lines. No matter how loudly great private interests may protest while the old coalition is under attack, the capitalist vanguard always manages to make the leap from the old order to the new, thus insuring the celebrated continuity of American politics. In large part, this continuity reflects the continuous domination of successive coalitions by interest groups representing the most powerful elements of big business and its satellites. The logical consequence of this domination is the necessity for new out-group revolts, new in-group desertions, and finally, a new coalition. The cycle begins again. *Plus ça change, plus c'est la même chose.*

With variations, this pattern is repeated during the life of each subsequent coalition. At first dynamic and seemingly radical, the coalition comes to power by joining previously excluded and alienated groups representing small property and the republican virtues with powerful groups representing great property and the "iron laws" of economics. Frequently, the new government is financed by new money; it attracts wealthy businessmen and professionals who have not achieved sufficient influence or prestige under the old regime. The coalition's initial "radicalism," representing the desire of small-propertied groups for power, property, and status, produces a democratic ideology and generates some reform. It is undercut, however, by the principle of multiclass organization and by great-bourgeois domination of the coalition. The lower middle class requires protection from the underclass below. This protection is offered by men of wealth and power in exchange for self-protection — that is, the little people are not to make radical alterations in the operations of the economy or to challenge the "partnership" of government and big business. Stability is achieved by creating an all-bourgeois consensus which requires the elimination of significant differences between the major political parties. Then problems begin. The underclass is excluded *ab initio*, and the goals of the small-propertied class are impossible to realize. Economic and social change generate new protest groups whose demands threaten the old coalition's hegemony. Under the pressures of business concentration, economic and sectional competition, and the demands of new political groupings for recognition, consensus becomes dissensus. Disorder bursts forth anew (it always comes as a surprise) and the old coalition finds itself again in a struggle for power.

In the American context, this process seems revolutionary, although, as a method of preserving the hegemony of an advanced business elite, it is antirevolutionary in effect. In America — to push the analogy further — the *ancien régime* is the old governing coalition, dominated by a small, upper-class elite whose economic position is undermined by industrial-technological change while its political authority is challenged by dissident small-propertied and underclass groups. Up to the present time, the American equivalent of revolution has been the process through which a new coalition, claiming to represent a new alliance of enlightened businessmen and dissidents, overthrows the old. In order to take power and hold it, the new coalition is compelled to employ improvised and extra-constitutional devices like the political party, the labor union, and the regulatory agency and unusual political techniques, like the mass demonstration and the strike. It works in part "outside the system" because the inherited "system" provides only for adjustments *between* interests represented in the governing coalition; it does not provide for the overthrow of the coalition itself. Following an initial consolidation-conciliation period, the coalition, under pressure from lower-class groups, enters a "Jacobin" stage. In this period (which I discuss shortly), selected small-propertied interests receive institutional recognition and protection, and selected monopolistic villains are vigorously attacked. The reform impulse spreads, sometimes until the very structure of monopoly capitalism is threatened. At this point, the period of reaction — the American "Thermidor" — takes place. Big business elements within the all-bourgeois alliance assert their true strength. Frequently a war breaks out or is fomented; class conflict is subordinated to national unity; and the coalition turns away from reforms promised the small-propertied class. "Normalcy" returns. Gradually, the coalition becomes a new *ancien régime*, excluding the underclass, alienating small-propertied groups, and driving into opposition even the more "progressive" (that is, technologically advanced) elements of the business community.

Pluralist theory, the former orthodoxy of political science, cannot penetrate these processes since it fails to provide a "depth analysis" of American society which would explain the recurrence of discontent. According to pluralists, no class analysis or other form of "depth" reasoning is needed, since interest groups which succeed in joining a governing coalition naturally tend to become a new "establishment," and to resist challenges by newer, upstart groups. Each coalition includes groups representing those formerly oppressed and discontented, which are admitted to power when they become well organized or prosperous enough to control votes. Therefore, according to pluralist thinking, the existence of "new" dissident groups like the urban blacks and antiwar students of the 1960's does not imply that the pluralist system has in any way broken down. On the contrary, these new malcontents are protesting against an "establishment" which *includes* pre–New Deal malcontents like the labor unions and the farmers. What their protests really amount to is a request for early admission to the club; their threats to bring down the walls are merely the results of impatience. Pluralists therefore look forward to a new surge of reform — the "new New Deal," so to speak — which will transform out-groups into in-groups and end the present period of discontent.

Critics of this perspective have pointed out that our system requires groups to become middle class, in effect, before they can be admitted to power, and therefore discriminates against the poor; that advancement into the middle class is not automatic; that even middle-class groups can be denied entry into the governing coalition, for example, because of racism; that pluralism can run amok when influential groups intervene *after* the public interest has been discovered (e.g., by influencing a government agency not to enforce an enacted law); and that some protests and demands which are qualitative cannot be satisfied by offering the protestors a "piece of the action."[19] Our purpose, however, is not to add to what seems to be a rather sterile debate, but to suggest a basis for the depth analysis which pluralism lacks. To do this, it is worthwhile to examine the "Jacobin" phase of coalition government, when the dissidents who gave life to the new coalition succeed in placing their impress upon it. For if the recurrence of discontent in American society is caused solely by the emergence of *new* out-groups outside the governing coalition, then the criticisms of pluralism noted above lose much of their point. We will assume, for purposes of discussion only, that with patient organization and hard work, the most oppressed group can eventually gain coalition membership.[20] What *is* such a group's true position and role within the coalition?

In the second phase of coalition government, after powerful national groups have been conciliated and the new coalition's legitimacy established, member groups representing the small-propertied masses begin to clamor for attention, reminding the leadership of its promises of reform and political reconstruction. Agitation for change, temporarily dampened by the need to reestablish consensus, begins again with a vengeance; impatient coalition members threaten to break with the leadership if their demands are not met. (The clearest example of this, perhaps, is the CIO's split from the AFL in 1935, and its threat to oppose Roosevelt in 1936 if the New Deal failed to meet labor's demands.) Rising pressure from the mass-based groups within the coalition demonstrates the need to consolidate the electoral base. The leadership therefore turns soberly towards implementation of reforms which dissidents have demanded in the intoxicating period of coalition-formation. This is the period of active domestic reform, when the coalition will make the record entitling it to be called "liberal" — the period in which Jackson challenged the financial monopolists, Lincoln emancipated the slaves and opened up the West to homesteaders, Wilson pushed through antitrust legislation and other reforms, and Franklin Roosevelt became the hero of organized labor.

The problem faced by coalition leaders is how to keep mass support without expropriating the great bourgeoisie. It is solved, typically, by admitting small-propertied groups to coalition membership on what might be called a *recognition-of-interest basis*. That is, the big unions, or farm organizations, or civil rights organizations are "recognized" politically, and some of their basic interests (including their right to exist as political entities) are given institutional protection. In a sense, they become wards of the government, with recognized claims against tax revenues and other government resources. This is more than nothing — but it is a good deal less than the power to rule. Accepting the status of small-propertied "interest group," the group cuts itself off from other members of its class, surrendering any claim the class may have to direct the affairs of society. It admits, in effect, that innovation is the function either of impersonal social forces or of more powerful groups. It accepts the legitimacy of intracoalition bargaining and redefines its goals so as to assure continuity of bargaining relationships. Equally important, the new "in-group" acquiesces in self-redefinition; its members are henceforth those recognized by the coalition, and its leaders those entitled to speak for it in coalition councils. The classic example of this process is the labor movement under the New Deal, but it is equally descriptive of antislavery forces within the Republican coalition, women in the Progressive coalition, or blacks at the present time.

Put another way, what the coalition grants its "junior partners" is protection against their enemies below and a few, specially selected monopolists above. The price which it extracts for this service is a reconciliation of small-propertied dissidents with the big business community (which means, for small property, a form of gradual economic suicide). In the coalition's liberal phase, farmers are given homesteads and protected against Indians, but reconciled to the existence of privately owned credit institutions, railroad monopolies, and the uncontrollable fluctuations of commodity prices. Workers are protected against scabs and contract labor, but reconciled to management ownership and "management rights." Small businessmen are protected against certain kinds of price-cutting and price-fixing, but reconciled to the "laws of economics" which favor large, efficient, integrated corporations. Suburbanites are protected against public housing and school busing, but reconciled to the spread of industry into their areas and the urbanization of the suburb. Thus do the coalition's "senior partners" focus the attention of small-propertied groups on threats which are concrete and immediate — these are usually the threats from below — while softening and confusing the more serious threat from above. If necessary, however, they will punish one of their own in order to personalize the threat from above and to defuse radical dissent: therefore, the special attention meted out to a few railroads by Republicans, a few "trusts" by the Progressives, a few holding companies by the Roosevelt Democrats, and a few defense contractors by modern liberals. These big business villains are always painted as deliberate scoundrels or frauds; the element of malice aforethought serves to distinguish them from their "decent" brethren.

It is incorrect, therefore, to say that small-propertied groups "come to power" under new coalitions. What such groups seem to gain by adhesion to the coalition is the right to *compete* for power, as groups, within a political universe in which power has already been distributed. The unwritten rule is that they are not permitted to question this prior distribution or to seek to alter it *ab initio*. Notions of compensation for past injustice suffered are ruled out.[21] Like new members of a private club, new coalition members join a going concern; they will not be permitted, at the first or even the hundredth meeting, to move the abolition of the club or the expulsion of senior members. What this means, in effect, is that the coalition's junior partners surrender even their claim to *group* advancement into the ruling class for the chance that some of their members may gain *individual* access to the executive boardrooms and government offices where the fates of men and nations are decided. The vast majority, of course, will not be able to enter the anteroom, much less the inner sanctum of power, but many are pacified by this combination of group recognition and individual gambler's hope. Temporarily pacified, that is, for when hope runs out and recognition proves a sham, it is time for the "forgotten men" to rise again.

Now we can dispose of the pluralist contention that, in each age, "new" interest groups arise to challenge "older," more successful groups for power. This, we are told, represents progress when, in fact, capitalism's "progress" produces legions of victims of industrial concentration and automation who become, in each age, the "little men" of liberal ideology — reincarnations of Jefferson's yeomen farmers and Jackson's artisans. While a handful of individuals succeed in escaping from the small-propertied class into the great bourgeoisie, the farmer, the skilled worker, the government employee, and the small businessman remain powerless in the face of concentrated wealth and terrified by the prospect of further proletarianization. Big government and political collectivism are pressed far enough to save these clients from immediate economic destruction, but the movement always stops far short of the goal. Gradually, small property is undermined by great property, and (as Marx predicted) the lower middle class sinks into the working class. Underclass groups do advance in the direction of petty-bourgeois respectability, but the ship they so eagerly board is sinking. (Indeed, how can a group achieve "security" without control over the market? Under capitalism, the goal is illusory to begin with.) Thus, 25 years after Franklin Roosevelt's death and 150 years after Jefferson, the lower middle class is again restive — even militant — making its traditional dual demands for upward mobility and protection against the poor. And, once again, the political analysts cannot decide whether this class is "radical" or "reactionary." In fact, as small property becomes more and more irrelevant to life in a monopoly capitalist system, the initial reaction of declining small-propertied Americans is to resist proletarianization; that is, to become reactionary, or to embrace some variety of right-wing "populism." Over time, however, membership in the mass working class is accepted and these same Americans become a force for radical, even revolutionary change.

IV

Liberal reform, I am contending, is the traditional method by which interest groups representing the small-propertied class are attached to the governing coalition, usually through the medium of a major political party. Once this electoral base has been secured, those holding innovative power (and who finance the party) are free to move on to the "Thermidor" of the coalitional cycle: the establishment of big business supremacy. This is an exceedingly complex process, however, whose true nature is disguised rather than described by the ordinary terms of American political discourse like "liberal" and "conservative." In the first place, although it displays a much stronger class consciousness than any other American class, the great bourgeoisie is not exempt from division into interest groups. This means that big business rarely moves as a united class. More typically, advanced, "progressive" groups within the large corporate community — those most closely linked to the latest advances in technology and business organization — will have acquiesced or even led the fight for reform during the coalition's "democratic" heyday. Now, their supremacy guaranteed by destruction of the old coalition and pacification of the lower classes, they move with new energy to collect their reward. The political behavior of business during this period is not easily described as "reactionary" or "conservative," since it appears forward-looking and benevolent. The identification of aggressive, innovative business groups with the cause of liberal reform makes it difficult to recognize the gradual process through which this elite imposes its will on the coalition. Some years later, when intellectuals have awakened to the reality of business domination, they characterize the development as "reactionary," ignoring the fact that the elite's right to rule in the name of the people — its expertise, creativity, and social consciousness — had been conceded by liberals early in the coalition's reign.

Who are the progressives of the great bourgeoisie, and what leads them to throw in with liberal coalitions? They are the vanguard of the expanding economy, those businessmen able and willing to participate in the process which Marx described as the continual revolutionizing of the means and relations of production under capitalism. During the Revolutionary period, this group was dominated by New England shippers and merchants chafing under the restrictions of British mercantilism. Under Jefferson, it was forced to yield supremacy to a more dynamic combination of large-scale producers of agricultural export goods, suppliers of agricultural credit, and those with interests in western land. (A nascent class of domestic manufacturers also began to flourish behind the walls of Jefferson's embargo.) Jacksonian democracy subordinated the interests of coastal producers and credit suppliers to those of interior producers of staples (now including cotton), new local banking and manufacturing interests, and the rising transportation industry. Under Lincoln and his Republican successors, domestic manufacturing and transportation gained complete ascendancy over agriculture, with credit control gradually reconcentrated in the East. Progressivism began, and the New Deal continued, a process by which supremacy passed to those financial and industrial corporations whose interests were international in scope. Since 1945, the corporate vanguard has been identified by its capability to manage and exploit technological innovations — hence, the rise of the military-industrial complex, the electronics and communications industries, and the multinational corporations.[22]

A combination of factors initially attaches the advance guard of capitalism to the liberal coalition. Under the rule of the old coalition, their march to supremacy was impeded by older business interests vulnerable to charges of monopolizing economic opportunities and relying on government to accomplish narrow, self-interested purposes. Initially, therefore, the new money interests are antimonopolistic. The desire of small-propertied interests to break up monopolies and to reestablish government as an impartial arbiter therefore coincides neatly with the requirements of rising economic power. For while small-propertied groups believe that such reforms will restore a lost world of competitive equality and make it possible for them to rise into the established bourgeoisie, the industrial vanguard (whose economic leadership is already established) uses reform to remove the last obstacle to its political supremacy. For rising business power — for example, heavy industrial manufacturing before the Civil War, or electronics before World War II — the initial step is to join in attacks on "vested interests" whose competitive position is artificially maintained through governmental ties or institutionalization. Northern industrialists used radical Republicanism to break the nexus between government and slave agriculture; electronics manufacturers used New Deal reforms to break the nexus between government and older industrial interests like the utility holding companies. Historians have often quarreled about the role of "rising" and "declining" groups in supporting liberal figures like Andrew Jackson and Woodrow Wilson. The fact seems to be that *both* types of groups participate in liberal coalitions, including many whose economic status is ambiguous — e.g., "declining" groups participating in a "rising" industry, like petty land speculators under Jackson or craft workers in defense industries under Roosevelt and Truman.[23] (Such groups rise relative to other sections of the small-propertied class; relative to the position of steadily concentrating capital, however, their fall is continuous.)

I do not mean to imply, however, that big business liberalism is merely a cynical tactic. On the contrary, the economic vanguard's willingness to tolerate social change reflects the linkage between revolutions in production and revolutions in social relations. Those in the forefront of economic development can envision and plan for the coming of a new society. They have both an ideological and an economic stake in "liberating" the poor and small-propertied classes from bondage to the old economic elite, so that new, "more equitable" relationships can be established with *them*. The businessmen who supported Jefferson's attack on New England shipping interests, Jackson's assaults on the Bank and other chartered monopolies, and Lincoln's war against the slave power believed — with some justification — that they represented the forces of progress and enlightenment. So, with less justification, do the computer technocrats and international corporation men of the present era. Business "progressives" therefore participate actively in the second phase of coalition government, which involves the disestablishment of certain entrenched business interests. Phase three, their own establishment as "leaders of the business community" (which is to say, monopolists relying on government favor), is the inevitable sequel.

How does this happen? How and why do militant small-propertied groups, the electoral base of the coalition, acquiesce in a return to big business domination? In the next section, I discuss in greater detail the role played by the State apparatus in bringing about this result. For now, it suffices to note that war is often the midwife for reorganization of the governing coalition. In earlier days, when small-propertied farmers looked westward to the undeveloped lands controlled by American Indians, Mexico, and the European powers, strong expansionist impulses emanated from this class, and a continued cultural expansionism (characterized, for example, by the desire to Christianize China) was evident even after the continent was conquered.[24] But there is little doubt that, at least since the coming of the Industrial Revolution, the principal force in America promoting massive military engagements has been the rising big business elite.[25] The lower classes, whose interests are generally insular and whose sons are potential cannon-fodder for foreign wars, have extracted from every coalition leader a pledge of peace. Professions of pacifism and isolationism are standard fare in the early phases of coalition rule. Nevertheless, a turn towards militarism and foreign intervention, supported by the business vanguard, is equally predictable following the period of reform. For example, the Civil War was initially opposed by most northern abolitionists and workers; in mounting the war against the South, Lincoln counted upon and received the powerful support of the large industrialists, including leading "conservatives" of the period. Similarly, Wilson campaigned for reelection in 1916 on a platform of peace and neutrality, but committed the nation to world war one year later with the strong support of international business interests. (Secretary of State William Jennings Bryan, representing the old Populist streak within the movement, thereupon resigned.) F.D.R. also pledged peace in a reelection campaign (1940), although France had fallen to the Nazis and England was preparing for a German invasion. Rearmament and war came as a godsend to the Depression-ridden big business community, which extracted a no-strike pledge from the labor unions while industrial demand soared. More recently, in 1964, Lyndon B. Johnson campaigned for reelection as the "peace candidate," accusing his Republican opponent of favoring escalation of the war in Vietnam. In fact, Johnson himself planned to escalate the war, and did so in 1965 with the backing of big business, particularly the technologically oriented "military-industrial complex."[26]

In each case, war accelerates tendencies towards industrial concentration, centralization of political power, reliance of government on technologically advanced business interests, and creation of a new big business–big government "partnership" to win the war. "Divisive" demands of small-propertied interests are set aside in the interests of national unity and military efficiency. Dissenters who refuse to accept subordination are damned as traitors and jailed or otherwise silenced. Domestic reforms are shelved, with reformist energies directed away from oppressive institutions of the home country and towards the international aggressor: the war for democracy at home becomes the war "to make the world safe for democracy"; the struggle for freedom in America is subordinated to the struggle to free the Cubans, Koreans, or South Vietnamese from communism. Like Napoleon's France, the American coalition attempts to project its former idealism onto the world stage, but even its ideology soon becomes defensive and conservative: we are fighting to protect *what we have* against foreign enemies who would destroy our institutions. (As President Johnson stated in an address to United States troops stationed in South Vietnam, "They want what you've got."[27]) The ideological shift reflects a shift in the balance of power within the coalition, for the predominant role of big business is now unquestioned. The new business elite emerges from the war clothed in patriotic glory and determined to continue the productive "partnership" with government which permitted it to expand during wartime. For example, the large, technologically advanced companies which acquired the habit of having Uncle Sam bear their wartime research and development costs did not give up the habit after 1945. Indeed, since R & D had become even more expensive while military research generated huge civilian payoffs, the corporations found themselves "hooked" on government subsidies — dependent, that is, on a permanent state of war.[28]

But is this sort of "partnership" not just another name for government-supported monopoly? Was not the coalition determined to break the stranglehold of monopolies on the economy and to sever their marriage with government bureaucracies? Perhaps — but the turnaround is now complete. The dissenter who evokes the old radicalism of the coalition in order to question the new business-government arrangements becomes the target of late-wartime ideology: he is in league with a foreign enemy which intends to undermine our fundamental institutions. It is no use for him to claim, as Henry A. Wallace did in 1948, that he speaks for a coalition which came to power promising to destroy monopoly influence; if he attacks the institutions America has fought a war to defend, he must be an agent, or at least a dupe, of some foreign power. Thus, the coalition's small-propertied idealism, which was projected onto wartime ideology and thereby corrupted, is now introjected back into domestic life in the form of the witch-hunt. The business elite consolidates its hold on the postwar coalition by sanctioning a campaign of government-sponsored terror against such "extremists," for example, the Red Scare of 1919–1924, the "loyalty-security" hysteria and McCarthyism of 1949–1954, and the political trials of black militants and antiwar radicals, 1969–present. What follows is a decade or more of uninterrupted big business rule, which sooner or later gives rise to new dissension, new revolts, and the formation of a new coalition.

This sheds a rather lurid light, perhaps, on the claim that more recent liberal coalitions represent a qualitative break with the past. Progressive and New Deal historians have maintained that the liberalism of Wilson, and, even more, of Franklin D. Roosevelt, marked a qualitative turn toward "positive government" — not just neutral, umpire-style governmental activities, but active intervention *against* business on behalf of previously neglected constituencies. The contrast between "positive" and "negative" liberalism, it seems to me, is just as misleading as the contrast between "liberalism" and "conservatism" mentioned earlier, for it totally misconceives the relationship between business and government in the United States. Viz., *every* new governing coalition sets out to roast a few monopolists and to sever the links binding the old business elite to government. *Every* governing coalition ends by serving the interests of a new business elite which is both monopolistic and interwoven institutionally with government. Jefferson and Jackson conducted active campaigns against certain established monopolies, then limited government interference with the activities of expanding enterprises, and finally became "partners" with business when new elites demanded tariffs and subsidies, land grants and wars in aid of continued expansion. The Republican leadership intervened actively against the slave-holding South, then limited interference with northern industry, and finally intervened again against labor unions, radical state legislatures, cheap foreign imports, and other dangers to the elite. The steady growth of business influence on government meant that Wilson and Roosevelt would have to intervene even more "positively" both to reduce the power of the old elite *and* to protect their new "partners" against foreign competition and domestic danger. Indeed, the vigor of their attacks on older entrenched interests was nothing compared with the ferocity of their defense of new entrenched interests. At present, a new crop of "populists" is again calling for action against certain "vested interests" — for example, oil producers who reap the benefits of special tax provisions and companies which pollute the environment. The interests attacked are, as a rule, fat and vulnerable, and attacks against them are financed by a new crop of "progressive" industrialists who hope to replace the old elite (or, at least to join it) in the wake of liberal reform.[29]

The expanding role of government under modern coalitions has not been intended to thwart the development of large-scale private enterprise but to aid it. Recognizing this, representatives of the most far-sighted sections of the great bourgeoisie — particularly international finance, international corporate enterprise, and technologically advanced domestic corporations — took key positions within both the Progressive and New Deal coalitions. From Elihu Root to Robert S. McNamara, a long list of sophisticated financial and corporate leaders flocked to Washington to help "activist" politicians govern. What did this vanguard have to gain by shedding its "robber baron" image and attacking unreconstructed robber barons, embracing the positive State and engaging in liberal politics? The answer is — a world! Capitalists with vision recognized that the United States was becoming a mature, developed economy, and that the windfall profits of the era of continental development could not be expected to continue indefinitely. They saw that economic slowdowns or depressions at home posed an increasing danger of genuine class war, which could be followed by some anticapitalist form of "statism." At the same time, they recognized that the twentieth-century analogue to continental development was international development. If political stability, steady profits, and a moderately healthy economy could be achieved at home, a base could be secured for foreign adventures that would make Commodore Vanderbilt look like the village grocer! The business vanguard's twofold aim, therefore, was, first, to rationalize the home market, securing permanent monopolistic or oligopolistic positions while keeping the level of domestic demand high and the risk of class warfare low. Second, to obtain a free hand, uninhibited by welfare state restrictions and aided by the diplomatic and military might of the United States, to exploit economic opportunities abroad. To achieve both these purposes, a new relationship with government was necessary.

It is entirely misleading, however, to characterize this relationship as entailing "more active government intervention in the economy." Such a characterization assumes the existence of a neutral government independent of private economic power, when, in fact, the chief aim of the business vanguard has been to *interpenetrate* government — to identify its interests more, not less intimately with those of the State. And, clearly, this aim has been realized beyond the wildest expectations of Elihu Root or Bernard Baruch. On the domestic front, it is now widely accepted that antitrust laws and agencies have become devices for stabilizing oligopoly; that regulatory agencies are administered for the benefit of their most powerful regulatees; that taxation, interest rates, and monetary policies systematically favor the upper class and the largest enterprises; that the executive departments (Defense, Agriculture, HUD, Transportation, etc.) regularly practice socialism for the rich and "free enterprise" for the poor; and that labor and other social welfare legislation has served to pacify the lower classes without freeing them from economic insecurity.[30] Similarly, with regard to foreign affairs, it is admitted that State Department politics and diplomacy have served primarily the interests of the corporate elite; that military force has been employed both directly and indirectly in their service; that foreign aid (both economic and military) is a thinly disguised form of aid to domestic corporations; and that the Department of Defense has created a separate "economy within the economy" whose main benefits accrue to the technological giants, while the taxpayer foots the bill.[31] Notwithstanding a growing agreement on these facts, the theory persists that these developments are somehow "accidental." It is said to be "ironic" that the rich receive more "welfare" payments than the poor, that regulators have become the creatures of regulatees, that each "war to end all wars" intensifies the struggle for world power. The true irony, however, is the acceptance of "accidental" theories of history by the victims of historical logic.

Recall that the building blocks of governing coalitions in the United States are not classes or even subclasses, but interest groups. Recall, too, that governing coalitions in America have been founded upon a union of small-propertied and great-propertied classes — what I have called the "alliance of the whole bourgeoisie." Since interest groups are combinable (like molecules), each one frequently acts as a member of a larger interest group: the large group of farmers, for example, includes within its membership both the tenant farmers of Mississippi and the General Foods conglomerate. It is this sort of combined interest group which provides the framework for unification of small- and great-propertied classes. For example, let us say that the government decides to aid "farmers," as the New Deal and Fair Deal did in the 1930's and 1940's by providing farm mortgage relief, easy credit, technical aid, price-support payments, and extension programs. Enacted amid great hand-wringing over the plight of the small or "family" farmer, these measures benefited the large, efficient farmer in proportion to the size of his holding and his efficiency in managing it. They helped smaller farmers survive long enough to be eaten up gradually by the farm corporations, for there was no attempt to repeal the "economic laws" which reward efficiencies of scale. Simple logic dictates that if government bounties are paid, say, for nonproduction of agricultural commodities, they will benefit the man who does not produce a lot more than the man who does not produce a little. But the same logic applies (although the symmetry is more complex in other cases) each time the government intervenes on behalf of a multiclass interest group or combination of interest groups.

The principle may be formulated as a law: government aid to any combined interest group will end by benefiting its component subgroups in proportion to their preexisting economic power. For example, the Defense Department provides massive aid to "defense industries." Defense contractors are assured of recovering their costs, plus profits, and are thus able to pay relatively high wages to their workers. The workers, in turn, may consider themselves members of a privileged interest group and develop a strong concern for the welfare of "their" industry. As soon as defense cutbacks begin, however, the differential treatment of *classes* within the same combined "interest group" become painfully obvious. While the workers were acquiring jobs, homes, automobiles and appliances — usually purchased "on time" or otherwise subject to reacquisition by business corporations — the defense corporation was acquiring capital, market position, and influence, hedging against cutbacks, diversifying its interests, and preparing for the inevitable. The nice thing about being a great bourgeois is that one gets to be a member of so *many* "interest groups"!

Henry D. Thoreau put the matter well: ". . . though a crowd rushes to the depot, and the conductor shouts 'All aboard!' when the smoke is blown away and the vapor condensed, it will be perceived that a few are riding but the rest are run over — and it will be called, and will be, 'A melancholy accident.' "[32] Melancholy, yes; an accident, no. This result follows from the business vanguard's capacity to monopolize not just wealth and the opportunity to multiply it, but *the economic planning functions of industrial society*. While the poor and small-propertied classes stumble along through economic storms like primitives attempting to propitiate the lightning, the great bourgeoisie, combining science with power, harnesses the lightning to its own use. The great corporations are not all-powerful — they are not yet gods — but their powers of foresight and adaptation are so far advanced, compared to those of the lower classes, that they are able to function somewhat like the Connecticut Yankee in King Arthur's Court, their computers the modern analogues to Sir Boss's cigarette lighter and pistol. The nonelite majority know this, and even joke about it, but fail to pursue its political implications. Thus, few workers fighting for a guaranteed annual wage tied to cost of living recognize the sad resignation underlying this supposedly "radical" demand. Labor at its most militant still says to management, "We understand that *you* will create the future. All we ask is to be permitted to survive in it." Ironically, many American scholars have distinguished between "developed" and "less-developed" peoples precisely on this basis: "underdeveloped" peoples, like the peasantry of Third World nations, are chiefly concerned with survival, while "developed" peoples inhabit the new world of economic surpluses and the self-created future.[33] By the same criterion, the only "developed" class within the American economy is the monopoly bourgeoisie; all others, factory workers as well as the poor, small retailers as well as government employees, are chiefly concerned with surviving in a world created by others. The political implications of this imbalance in creative planning power are left unexplored because they leave much of democratic theory in a shambles.

In a sense, I am paraphrasing Marx, who described the European bourgeoisie as the creative, aggressive, modernizing class while condemning as reactionary those classes whose hostility to big business masked an opposition to industrialization itself (for example, the petty bourgeoisie and the peasantry). Conventional liberal history, on the contrary, is designed to convince the poor and small-propertied classes that *they* are winning. It portrays a steady series of victories by farmers, workers, immigrants, blacks and poor people over the forces of greed and corruption, when in fact, the American bourgeoisie has been the innovative, aggressive class — the consistent "winner" no matter what the political complexion of the governing coalition. This would be better understood if students of American society paid more attention to the political implications of corporate innovation. What John C. Calhoun wanted for the South — a veto over attempts to alter the status quo in favor of the modernizing North — is essentially what all small-propertied opponents of the industrial vanguard have demanded. The labor movement's great improvisations — for example, the industrial union, the collective bargaining agreement, the minimum wage, and the guaranteed pension — were all designed to secure a minimum of stability for the workingman in a world of uncontrollable change. In other words, *they were intended to maintain the worker's position within the small-propertied class*, and to keep him from being thrown into the marginal world of the underclass. Compare these defense-oriented devices with the innovations of private corporations in search of new worlds to conquer: central banking; integrated and conglomerate corporations; the stock, bond, commodities, and currency markets; the modern tax structure; the tax-free foundation; the quasi-public corporation; the automated factory; mass-media advertising; the multinational trade agreement, and so forth. Up to the present time it has been these innovations, rather than the adaptations of small-propertied interests, which have constantly revolutionized the American economic and political systems. And it has been the bearers of innovation — the members of the corporate vanguard — who have thus far dominated every liberal coalition.

V

Subliminally, if not consciously, Americans recognize that the business elite's monopoly of planning power makes a mockery of political democracy. Any movement of liberal reform will, sooner or later, therefore begin to talk about "bringing business under control" or "making business live up to its social responsibilities." (Indeed, Henry Demarest Lloyd's *Wealth against Commonwealth*, the liberal bible of the 1890's, could easily be issued today by supporters of George McGovern or John Lindsay.) The trouble with all of this, as I have tried to indicate above, is that the power of the big business community resides not just in its privileged social or political position or in its access to police and military force, but in its economic power, which carries with it the actual task of ruling America. The experience of ruling produces, in turn, a high degree of confidence and creativity — a willingness and ability to rule — which is the principal psychological advantage of the great bourgeoisie. The goal of "bringing business under control" really concedes this point; it assumes that there is no other class capable of making the fundamental economic and political decisions which big business has made for more than a century, and decrees that business should continue to rule — but with one eye on its social obligations. This praxis is clear if one keeps in mind that the false distinction between "public" and "private" decision-making permits private business to make such significant *public* decisions as what to produce, how to produce it, when, where, and at what price.

Ironically, for all its emphasis on government regulation and social responsibility, modern liberal doctrine annihilates the very basis of democratic theory. The notion of benevolent dictatorship, we learn, is a contradiction in terms, since any minority entrusted with full power will ultimately wield it in its own interest. It does not take a Marx or a Lenin to see that corporations which are stronger than their regulators will come to control them, that businesses which "elect" political candidates by footing their campaign bills will dominate elected officials, or that communications monopolies owned by business will present to the public a generally favorable view of their owners and advertisers. The traditional responses, however, are also predictable: let's have "stronger" government regulation; let's "do something" about campaign financing; let's "break up the monopolies" in this industry or that. In short, let's make the dictatorship more benevolent again! Clearly, this will not do. As I hope to show in Part III, the business elite does not require regulation, but replacement. However, since many readers will quarrel with words like "rule" and "dictatorship" to describe the functions of the great bourgeoisie, let me illustrate briefly how business rules in a nominally (and potentially) democratic state.

There are many excellent works now available which describe the composition and function of the American ruling class. These leave little doubt that there is a definable group of men (and a few women) which, in G. William Domhoff's words, "owns a disproportionate amount of the country's wealth, receives a disproportionate share of the country's yearly income, contributes a disproportionate number of its members to governmental bodies and decision-making groups, and dominates the policy-forming process through a variety of means."[34] I have no intention of duplicating or paraphrasing the work of Domhoff, Mills, Lundberg, or other analysts of the ruling class[35]; my concern is to illustrate how this class functions in the context of coalition government, and in so doing, to raise some theoretical questions which others may have overlooked. For example, Domhoff's use of the word "disproportionate" might bring us back to the liberal dilemma described above: if big business has "disproportionate" power over this or that, is it possible to reduce that power to a "proportionate" level (say, by stronger government regulation)? Is "disproportionate" power (or "more" power, or "too much" power) what characterizes a ruling class, or must there be something more? Domhoff himself answers this question affirmatively by referring to the elite's "domination" of the political process: "Legally, the government is all of us, but members of the upper class have the predominant, all-pervasive influence. In short, they dominate it."[36] It may be difficult to formulate this concept scientifically, but when one says that the upper class "rules" or "dominates," one means not just that it has *more* power than other classes or groups in the society but that it has *critical* power, the power to define available choices, and to decide among them when the chips are down.

The analysis seemed somewhat simpler, perhaps in the days of Marx and Engels, who could state without quibbling that ownership of the means of production conferred upon the owners power to dominate the State. To this fundamental concept of scientific socialism two related objections have been made by some analysts of modern industrial society. First, they say, it is not clear what "ownership of the means of production" signifies. Those who "own" General Motors (several million stockholders) do not collectively control its stock or its Board of Directors; those who do control its stock do not manage the company on a day-to-day basis; those who manage the company are subject to multiple influences from labor unions, the government, the public, the competition, etc. The day of the tycoon who owned, controlled and managed his company like a primitive tyrant-king is long past. Second, it is not true, as Marx and Engels said, that "the executive of the modern State is but a committee for managing the affairs of the whole bourgeoisie."[37] The State is independently powerful, and responsive to conflicting demands from various segments of the business community, other social classes and groups within those classes, and political interests of different kinds — including intragovernmental interest groups. It by no means carries out the orders of the ruling class (whatever that is) as, say, the United States Congress once carried out the orders of the railroad tycoons. In fact, business has become dependent upon government, not vice versa.

But if this is so, why does the nation awaken every generation or so to the fact that business again dominates the political process and must be "brought under control"? One key to the problem, it seems to me, is the coalitional process which we have been describing, which vindicates the Marxian insight that business rules, while accounting for changes which have taken place in advanced industrial nations like the United States. True, big business does not control the State precisely as a board of directors controls its executive committee. But neither has it become fragmented into interest groups which, with other equally powerful interest groups, make conflicting demands upon an independent State. The bourgeois State is the governing coalition in action; "big government" means that, as coalition members give their interests institutional form, *the coalition becomes coterminous with the State*. The coalition is dominated, however, by what I have called the capitalist vanguard — the most creative and advanced elements of the great bourgeoisie operating as a uniquely potent interest group in combination with weak, defensive groups of the lower classes. As a result, the predominant political power of big business is not overthrown by developments in advanced industrial society; it merely finds a new (in many ways more effective) means of expression. In Marx's day, for example, railroads and canal companies bribed government officials to secure favors, and fought off attempts at regulation. Today, railroads and airlines express their interests through government agencies like the ICC, FAA, and CAB, whose officials are generally appointed with industry consent and are guaranteed postgovernment jobs in the offices of grateful corporations. The capitalist vanguard does not stand apart from the State, attempting to manipulate it on behalf of a united monopoly bourgeoisie. It now operates *within* the governmental apparatus, speaking the language of the bureaucrat-expert, easily dominating the "other" interest groups within the governing coalition without the necessity for hostile confrontation. It has discovered that interest group pluralism, far from dissolving classes, permits a business elite to dominate all other classes without even seeming to try.

The development of American foreign policy in this century offers a clear illustration of this relationship. Those who seek to establish the existence of a simplistic nineteenth-century imperialism, for example, in order to explain the origins of the Indochina war, will not be able to do so even if oil is discovered on the sea bottom off the coast of Vietnam. On the other hand, foreign policy "experts" who dismiss imperialism as a cause of the war because they have not discovered a vulgar economic motive for intervention in Indochina are worse fools.[38] Their talk of blunders into war and a military caste making foreign policy obscures the fact that the foreign policy bureaucracy *is* the bourgeoisie making foreign policy — that the task of this bureaucracy is to identify the "national interest" with that of the great bourgeois vanguard and to make the identification stick. Failing to see this, liberal analysts also fail to ask the pertinent questions about U.S. involvement in Indochina: for example, what is the interest of the corporate vanguard in Southeast Asia (including Thailand, the Philippines, Malaysia, and Indochina)? What is its interest in sustaining an 80-billion-dollar annual defense budget? How important is it to the American corporate community to secure areas of potential economic expansion like the Southeast Asian preserve? What role does competition between Japanese and American business elites play in stimulating American intervention in this area? Is there an incipient or actual crisis of capitalism which drives the great bourgeois bureaucracy towards war? The questions are not asked, I believe, because their answers would illustrate *too* clearly the extent to which "domination is transfigured into administration" (Herbert Marcuse).

We know that since the 1890's, the international business community has supplied most of the high-level officials responsible for the making of foreign policy, and a good many low-level officials as well. William Jennings Bryan, who resigned in 1917, was the last antibusiness secretary of state. All subsequent secretaries, and most undersecretaries, deputy secretaries, ambassadors, legal advisers, CIA directors, presidential advisers, etc., have been closely connected with international companies, law firms or private foundations representing such companies, elite organizations like the Council on Foreign Relations, university institutes financed by the corporations and their foundations, or a State Department hierarchy which serves as a recruiting ground for these same companies, law firms, foundations, institutes and organizations.[39] In recent years, the steady erosion of congressional power to decide important issues of foreign affairs has enormously increased the power of executive agencies to determine available choices in the area of foreign policy, and among these agencies, the State Department has recently lost ground to the Defense Department and the White House. Precisely at the moment that the Pentagon came into its own as a foreign policy–maker, however, civilian control over the armed services was established in the person of Robert McNamara, a leader of the business vanguard, present director of the World Bank, and one of the chief architects of the Indochina war. Under Richard Nixon, the mantle of chief foreign policy–maker passed to presidential assistant Henry Kissinger, a Harvard professor who has long functioned as an intellectual mouthpiece for the liberal industrial vanguard. Do such men's policies express a class interest, a bureaucratic interest, or both? Again, Herbert Marcuse's words are suggestive:

The capitalist bosses and owners are losing their identity as responsible agents; they are assuming the functions of bureaucrats in a corporate machine. Within the vast hierarchy of executive and managerial boards extending far beyond the industrial establishment into the scientific laboratory and research institute, the national government and national purpose, the tangible source of exploitation disappears behind the façade of objective rationality.[40]

In key government positions, these private-public men ordinarily reflect a sophisticated outlook, sincerely believed, in which the interests of the most advanced and rapidly expanding companies merge with the "national interest." Potential conflicts between foreign policy decisions in the interest of advanced business and those in the interest of other coalition members are ordinarily ignored or defined out of existence: "the tangible source of exploitation disappears behind the façade of objective rationality." Or, when conflict appears irrepressible, the administration's primary access to the rhetoric and symbols of patriotism is employed to whip dissenters into line. To take one rather obvious example, the "national interest" did not dictate the isolation and attempted overthrow of Fidel Castro's government in Cuba until 1960–1961, when the Cuban government expropriated the properties of American companies which owned her sugar industry, her telephone and telegraph system, her hotels, and virtually everything else worth owning in Cuba. Why, suddenly, was opposition to Cuba vital to the United States? Because, the nation was told, the Cuban expropriations proved that Fidel was a Communist who intended to make Cuba a Red "bridgehead" in the western hemisphere. Several critics pointed out that, assuming this were true, the United States was getting along very nicely with several communist nations at the time — that one could trade and have friendly relations with Cuba as easily as, say, Yugoslavia. They were informed that only "communist dupes" or traitors could ignore the paramount interest of the United States in preserving a free, noncommunist Latin America. At the time there was precious little evidence that Fidel was planning to "export revolution" to the Latin American continent, and, in any event, revolutions are not exported like Volkswagens. What, then, did the American foreign policy establishment fear? Certainly not the "destruction of democracy" on a continent largely controlled by U.S.-supported military dictatorships! The answer is simple: They feared (and still fear) indigenous revolutions, violent *or* peaceful, which would continue the pattern of expropriation of American monopolies, or which would impose new restrictions on United States private investment in Latin America.[41]

American "national interest" is involved in such cases only if the national interest is coincident with and defined by the interests of large American banks and companies. This notion may seem ridiculous on its face, but it has long been accepted in practice by those responsible for United

States foreign policy. For example, in the 1940's and 1950's, when American companies were extending their control over Middle Eastern oil resources controlled by Arab monarchs or reactionary politicians, the "national interest" dictated the overthrow of left-wing nationalists like Iran's Mohammed Mossadegh, and a policy of "neutrality" (which, in fact, favored the Arabs) vis-à-vis the Arab states and Israel. Vainly did American Zionists contend that the Jewish "bastion of democracy" in a sea of dictatorship and reaction deserved massive military support from the United States. In the 1960's, however, with neutralist or socialist governments rising throughout the Arab world, oil in short supply, and profits in jeopardy, the "national interest" was redefined. It now dictated support, not only for the monarchies of Iran, Saudi Arabia, Jordan, and the Persian Gulf, but for the "bastion of democracy," Israel, which, like the monarchies, was locked in conflict with Palestinian and other Arab leftists.[42] Following the Six-Day War of 1967, which brought the Soviet Union to the aid of Egypt, the Soviet presence in the Middle East was added as a reason for making new commitments to Israel — but this was ex post facto. In fact, should the oil kingdoms be overthrown, there is little doubt that the U.S.-Israel alliance would cool considerably. The "national interest" would again be redefined, as it is now in the case of solidly communist nations like those of eastern Europe and China, whose permanence is accepted by advanced big business for the sake of regional stability and potential trading opportunity. What a strange coincidence! The "national interest," like the corporate interest, dictates opposing revolutionary movements all over the world — except when there is money to be made by recognizing stable communist governments and trading with them.

Again, I am not suggesting that a business community

outside the government acts in a Machiavellian way to adjust the "national interest" to its immediate needs. On the contrary, even where there is little visible economic interest, as in Indochina, business-in-government may commit the United States to intervention or war in support of long-term corporate needs, which are easily equated with the national interest. For example, the "domino theory" predicting the fall of Southeast Asia to communist revolutionaries conjures up a triple nightmare, whose images merge the concepts of national and corporate welfare. First, the Indochinese nations, Thailand, Malaysia, the Philippines, and Indonesia, may become "unfree" or "captive" nations. Second, these nations may be lost as markets, sources of raw materials, and outlets for U.S. investment. Third, some other power — probably the Soviet Union or China — may come to dominate the area, in which case it may proceed to dominate other areas, and finally the world. In the light of day, of course, reason to some extent dissolves the nightmare. "Free" nations like South Vietnam are, in fact, venal and dictatorial puppet regimes. The independence of such nations from United States domination would obviously not prevent America from trading peacefully with them for needed goods and commodities (we have been told often enough that attempts to monopolize markets and sources of raw materials are uneconomic and a principal cause of revolution and war). And the facts of twentieth-century history militate solidly against the notion that the socialist camp is a monolith bent on some sort of Hitlerian world conquest. But one can easily see that each element of the domino theory is a nightmare *for the great corporations,* since socialist or neutralist nations independent of *them* may deny private companies the right to monopolize their natural resources, take over their business enterprises, manipulate their currencies, flood their markets, and exploit their labor forces. With the international corporations facing a declining rate of profit in the advanced industrial countries, loss of monopoly power in Third World nations may indeed seem threatening over the long run, so much so that the business elite in government identifies its own demise with "the end of the world." This solipsism is understandable — "when I die, the world dies" — although its effects are incalculably vicious. Less understandable is acceptance of the equation by the Americans whose sons it regularly murders.

Clearly, the interests of the vast majority of the American people are not the same as those of the elite which plunged the nation into the Indochina war. Nevertheless, a major question remains: why *should* an identity of corporate and national interests be assumed not just by the McNamaras and Kissingers, but by salesmen, workers, housewives, farmers — even the poor? Why should those who do the fighting and dying in foreign lands accept the leadership of business-in-government in matters of foreign affairs? There is an easy answer which must be rejected: the people are ignorant of the extent of corporate influence within the foreign policy establishment; they have been lied to, fooled, misled; they believe that America is defending freedom around the world when she is only defending the freedom of a few giant corporations to monopolize the world market. These contentions miss an important point: even if their truth were accepted by most Americans, the corporations would most likely remain in power. The "corporation conspiracy" theory overestimates the deceptive power of government and underestimates popular intelligence by implying that the people, ignorant of the true extent of private corporate power, routinely accept the "national interest" rationalizations offered by government officials and act on the basis of this false ideology. Surely, this is nonsense! If the problem were merely one of ignorance and deceit, existent criticism of the corporate State would have already provoked a revolution in the United States. The publication of the *Pentagon Papers*, dealing with the origin of the Indochinese war, generated some outrage when it was discovered that the American public had been deliberately misled by the Johnson administration. But if Lyndon Johnson had been candid about his war aims in 1964, can anyone doubt that he would still have defeated Barry Goldwater?

Although they are often misled, Americans understand better than many radicals realize that ruling power — especially in the field of foreign affairs — is in the hands of a few powerful men closely related to big business. By actions, if not in words, they have in the past *consented* to this exercise of power, believing that, in the long run at least, the interests of elite and masses would coincide. As suggested earlier, this faith is based on the persistence of a small-propertied class consciousness which dictates that although big business and its experts are alone fit to rule, *all* bourgeois (or potential bourgeois) are brothers. Fidel's attack on the sugar monopoly or the ITT in Cuba is therefore sensed as an attack on all men of property. The small farmer in Topeka or the homeowner in Brooklyn perceives Cuba as a greater threat to his security than the local banker, even though the banker, and not Fidel, holds his mortgage. And, in a sense, this fear is not entirely unrealistic. Since the great corporations do dominate the domestic economy, events which weaken their international position can cause economic dislocation on the home front, and the small-propertied class is extremely vulnerable to minor dislocations. Viewed with more detachment, however, it seems clear that this sort of dependence on a few giant corporations is as unhealthy for Americans as the one-crop economy is for Cuban or Thai farmers; it is capital concentration, not anticapitalist agitation, which directly and indirectly injures the small-propertied class. It is hard to convince a Third World farmer to abandon his one-crop economy, and it is difficult to show American working people that they have more to lose by maintaining the private monopoly economy than by destroying it. In both cases, however, history proves a hard but effective teacher. As an American working class emerges, small-propertied consciousness disappears, and with it the assumption that corporate and national interests coincide.

Were it not for the coalitional system of government in America, the growing disparity between ideology and reality would (as in many other nations) long ago have destroyed the sense of bourgeois brotherhood. Although dominated openly by big business, the governing coalition still promises Americans that, properly organized into interest groups, multiinterest groups, and political parties, they may retain the status of bourgeois and gain the protection of the elite against attacks from the underclass. In foreign policy terms, this means, first, that some interest groups included within the coalition may use their membership to gain marginal economic advantages. For example, small farmers who are members of national farmers' organizations benefit to some extent from exports of foodstuffs and other foreign trade or aid programs, just as workers in "defense industries" gain short-term advantages as a result of cold war policies. (In both cases, of course, the big gainers are the big companies, whose increased strength undermines the position of small property over the longer run.) Second, and more generally, the threat from the poor and nonwhite underclass at home translates easily into fear of the international underclass, which is also poor and nonwhite. Those who look to the local police for protection against expanding black or brown neighborhoods look to the armed forces for protection against yellow, black and brown insurgencies abroad. Since all threats from below seem to merge, they may be convinced, for example, that the "fall" of South Vietnam or Laos will be followed by the fall of southern California. (This accounts, in part, for the peculiarly intense hostility of the lower middle class towards hippies and radicals, who seem to combine aspects of both negritude and "disloyalty.") Moreover, those who, at home, are willing to trade off upward mobility for protection of their precarious status as bourgeois are even more willing to yield control over foreign affairs to the "experts." To the corporate or government official, international politics is a contest in which one seeks national (that is, corporate) advantage; aggression, in one form or other, is the name of the game. The masses which delegate power to them, however, speak the language of national *defense*, since their own posture as a class is fundamentally defensive. Colonialist racism is merely domestic racism writ large; in either case, the lower middle class accepts the word of upper-class rulers that its only protection against the colored hordes lies in submissiveness to established authority. But again, these values tend to erode as the small-propertied class is undermined by economic and political change. The growth of antiwar protest in connection with the Indochina conflict is both a symptom and a cause of new developments in American politics which we will explore further in Part III.

Traditions die hard, especially traditions which attempt to institutionalize popular incapacities. In analyzing the relationship between the great bourgeois leaders and lower-class followers, one is struck by the persistent lack of confidence of the lower classes in their own capacity to rule. Those dominated by the necessity to defend a precarious economic position or social status can hardly contemplate much less undertake the activity of *ruling*, which requires, or seems to require, qualities of confidence, expertise, aggressiveness, innovative ability, and long-range foresight — the ability to calculate risks and the willingness to take them. President John F. Kennedy is accounted a hero, not because of his sympathy for the downtrodden, but because he "faced down" the Soviets during the Cuban missile crisis of 1962. The combination of bourgeois risk calculation and old-fashioned *machismo* fascinates Americans even while it endangers them, perhaps because our political culture so closely links economic success and political power with sexual potency. (The best exploration of this theme I know is Norman Mailer's novel, *Why Are We in Vietnam?*) The economic insecurity and political impotence of our people tend to generate unrealizable fantasies of power which are lived vicariously through the exploits of a successful and belligerent elite. Thus, few objected that President Kennedy's *macho* performance in 1962 created risks all out of proportion to those it was intended to allay. Similarly, few think to question the domination of American legislative bodies by lawyers and businessmen, or to object that, in the entire United States Congress, there is not one "failure" whose occupation and income level are consistent with membership in the working class.

Although changing, the prevailing attitude remains one of deference to the authority of "the experts." Political theorists from Aristotle to Madison have identified democracy with active participation in government. Nevertheless, American practice limits mass participation to voting in elections through the medium of the political party, and expressing opinions between elections through the medium of the interest group. In effect, lower-class Americans are granted a choice of oligarchs and the right to address them while they rule (which, to be sure, is a good deal more than many rulers grant their subjects). But any disposition to question the oligarchy's superior right to rule or its alleged monopoly of ruling talents is systematically suppressed. In this regard, as analysis of public education shows, it is not hard to teach humans to doubt their own capacities, to condition them to fail, or at least to follow.

But if the great bourgeoisie appears to have a monopoly of ruling talents, this is, at least in part, because Americans have accepted a business executive's definition of "ruling talent." In foreign affairs, for example, it is assumed that the good diplomat is a tough-minded hard bargainer who will enter into international negotiations in the same spirit in which a Wall Street lawyer conducts business negotiations. As pointed out earlier, however, "national advantage," in the eyes of such negotiators, merges into "corporate advantage." The competitive world-view extrapolated from the business world to the international community dictates, for example, that the United States avoid such "unbusinesslike" moves as aiding the socialist government of Salvatore Allende in Chile, or recognizing Castro's Cuba, or withdrawing military forces unilaterally from Southeast Asia. In business or in bourgeois government, one does not give "something" for "nothing," even if, as in the examples just cited, the "nothing" means saving human lives and reorienting American foreign policy towards peace. We continue to assume that businessmen or their lawyers make the best negotiators, then, because we accept not just their leadership but their world-view. Life (including international life) is seen as a Darwinian struggle to survive; "get them before they get you." I would suggest, on the contrary, that Social Darwinism has now become a prescription for species suicide. The peculiar training, perspectives, and abilities of the business elite actually *unfit* it to usher in the era of peace and social justice which all people desire.

The disposition to identify ruling capability with bourgeois talents has severely limited the antibourgeois agitation of the past decade. Protest, whether by the nonwhite minorities of the underclass, militant elements of the small-propertied class, or students and intellectual drop-outs from the upper bourgeoisie, has been generally limited to pointing out the failures of the ruling class. Taking over — substituting another class or classes for the present ruling elite — has not been on the agenda of protest except for a small number of revolutionary Marxist political organizations. Slogans like "Power to the People," whose implications in the concept of local power struggles are clear enough, conceal an inability to answer the critical question: *at the national level, who has the capability to rule?* Even where protest and its repression have produced violence in urban ghettos or on college campuses, the violence has usually been localized, infused with notions of territoriality and local autonomy, aimed at "liberating" specified areas from unwelcome intrusion by central authority. Or else out-groups have engaged in strikes, demonstrations, boycotts, sit-ins and other activities which are sometimes useful in securing attention or minor concessions, but which do not threaten to displace the elite. The great problem for American radicals, omnipresent although seldom confronted directly, is not lack of mass support for radical change, for this will develop over time, but a crippling assumption (shared by much of the New Left) that *no* class or group is fit to rule. Hence the necessity for "participatory democracy" and experiments in anarchism.[43]

Of all American protest groups of the 1960's, those of the underclass best understood (through bitter experience) that an all-bourgeois alliance still existed in the United States, that it worked politically to incapacitate and emasculate all but a wealthy, aggressive elite, and that the elite would not be overthrown until the alliance itself were shattered. Unfortunately, the underclass remained too weak and isolated to put this knowledge to use. In the present period, there are signs that the all-bourgeois alliance is collapsing, and with it, the assumption that the business elite has a monopoly of ruling talents. Before analyzing this development, however, we must first describe the important role played by the underclass in the coalition system.

VI

Economically, the underclass serves the function of that section of the proletariat Marx called the "reserve army" of the unemployed. Whether jobless, working as "scabs," or laboring at the hardest, least remunerative jobs, members of this class intensify wage and job competition among industrial workers, keeping organized labor off balance and focusing attention on the twin issues of wage levels and job security. Socially, the underclass has traditionally served the functions both of threat and scapegoat. In the context of a three-class system, the heterogeneity of American society fostered a social and cultural distinction between acculturated, "civilized," small-propertied Americans and the uneducated, "savage" underclass. The class division within the working community, which operated to the advantage of the great bourgeoisie, perpetuated and was perpetuated by racism; the underclass was therefore considered not merely a class but a *caste*. (In the case of women, class, caste and sex overlapped to produce particularly brutal forms of isolation and exploitation.) As a result, economic competition between underclass and small-propertied class members almost invariably took on aspects of communal or race war (this was true even where the combatants were white, as during the period of so-called nativist agitation.)[44] Equally important, the presence of an out-caste provided the most marginal members of the small-propertied class with superior social status; it furnished a group which could be looked down upon culturally and morally, as well as economically.[45]

Two contemporary versions of this traditional American theme are worth noting, since they illustrate a powerful systemic impulse to *preserve* the underclass rather than eliminate it:

(1) The "war on crime" recently declared by local, state and federal governments focuses feelings of self-righteous superiority and anger upon a "criminal class" composed of nonwhite and poor white members of the underclass. Indeed, as overt racist stereotyping becomes socially unacceptable in modern America, the impulse to preserve the caste identity of the underclass takes just such subtle and devious tracks. "Criminality," although rationally acknowledged to be the product of poverty and social degradation,[46] is irrationally considered to be a racial or caste characteristic. Enormous resources are committed to combating "crime" — that is, violations of the law by the poor — while the crimes of the rich, from conducting an undeclared war in Indochina to wholesale evasion of price control regulations, go unpunished. Why this passionate concentration on lower-class crime? Because the same imperatives of class rule which produced and sustained the underclass in times past produce and sustain it now. The "threat from below" helps to preserve the puritan consciousness of the small-propertied class, which might otherwise come to view itself as part of a working class mass whose interests are opposed to those of the elite. For this reason, the bourgeois elite *requires* the existence of an underclass which is also an out-caste; and if old-fashioned racism is now out of fashion, a substitute — fear and hatred of the "criminal class" — is invented and exploited.

(2) The underclass is periodically replenished through incorporation of large "backward" groups into the work force as a source of relatively cheap, manipulable labor. By "backward" groups, I mean groups originally not urbanized or integrated into the regular industrial economy,

lacking formal education and political consciousness, and dominated in paternalistic fashion by more advanced and powerful groups — for example, slaves, first-generation urban immigrants, and rural black immigrants to northern cities. The latest replenishment of this surplus labor pool involves the mass movement of American women into the work force. The majority of American women now work for pay, occupying the most marginal, insecure and lowest-paying jobs on the job market.[47] Like other underclass groups, women emerging from a background of precapitalist exploitation are extremely vulnerable to a paternalistic style of capitalist exploitation. Desperate for work, hard to organize, and "easy-to-manage," they give better-established workers an illusory sense of superiority; at the same time, however, they are used to keep wage levels down and labor organizations off balance. There is good reason for the emergence of a women's movement in the United States paralleling the development of black liberation movements in the urban ghettos. Although there are important differences between the two movements and the two groups, certain parallels are striking: both movements are "nationalistic" responses to the particularly brutal forms of economic-cultural exploitation which are reserved for the underclass — racism and sexism. Both affirm a group identity against the tendencies of the system to pulverize and fragment underclass groups. Both echo an alienation experienced only by those excluded from the alliance of the whole bourgeoisie.

The political role of underclass groups is not easy to describe, since, in some respects at least, this class responds to Marx's bitter description of the *lumpenproletariat* as "the bribed tool of reactionary intrigue." That urban blacks, women, Chicanos, Puerto Ricans, the rural poor, and other oppressed groups are often vulnerable to individualized manipulation is undeniable: one thinks of

Chicago, for example, where Mayor Richard J. Daley's Democratic machine regularly turns out large majorities of black voters by resort to bribery, intimidation, and old-fashioned ward heeling, or of the passivity of most wage-earning women in the face of the most outrageous sexist exploitation. Nevertheless, since the American underclass is not merely a *lumpenproletariat*, the description, as applied to them, is inaccurate. The same Chicago ghettos which provide the Daley organization with regular votes produced the West Side riots of April 1968 and the largest Black Panther chapter in the United States, Reverend Jesse Jackson's Operation PUSH and the Honorable Elijah Muhammad's Nation of Islam, Angela Davis and Fred Hampton.* The same Mexican-American community which provides bracero serfs to the California farm industry produced Cesar Chavez, the United Farm Workers Union, and an independent political party —the Raza Unida Party. Sociologists worrying about such contradictions seek to explain them in terms of group subclassifications, but to no avail: studies of black urbanites, for example, reveal that the same man who votes for Richard Daley may despise the police and admire the Black Panthers, that the same nonrioter who "disapproves" of riots often believes they are justified and serve a useful function.[48] Psychologists rush to the rescue, armed with theories of lower-class "schizophrenia" and "paranoia," "frustration" and "rage": the black man is pictured as a psychological child who loves-hates the white parent, etc. But the matter may be explained with less mystification.

We have seen that apparent inconsistencies in the political attitudes of the small-propertied class can be

---

* While this book was in preparation, Chicago blacks broke with the Daley organization to defeat State's Attorney Hanrahan, who had ordered the raid in which Panthers Hampton and Mark Clark were killed.

comprehended as rational responses to the strategic alternatives available to the middle grouping within the three-class system. Looking "up" at the corporate elite, the small-propertied class seems radical; looking "down" at the underclass, it seems conservative. The convergence of these forces produces an alliance of the whole bourgeoisie, periodically disrupted by spasms of revolt and abortive moves toward a lower-class alliance. Analysis of the underclass in such a system reveals a different concatenation of forces and a different result. The underclass is the one class *excluded* from the traditional alliance of the whole bourgeoisie. It is therefore uniquely outside the system, rejected by the ranks of bourgeoisified labor, unwelcome in the inner circles of either major political party, a stranger to both the "conservative liberalism" of the small-propertied class and the "liberal conservatism" of the progressive bourgeoisie. This estrangement generates two responses which are not so much contradictory as two sides of the same coin.

First, the underclass plays a shadow version of the "divide and conquer" game of the ruling class, except that it is a strategy of "divide and survive." In order to survive, members of out-caste groups often permit themselves to be used, sometimes by the ruling class against the small-propertied class, sometimes by the latter against big business. Desperate for jobs, they frequently cooperate with businessmen attacking the "monopolistic" labor unions; urgently in need of government aid, they have usually joined the labor unions in demanding greater government "paternalism." When threatened by danger from the lower middle class, they appeal over the heads of workers and farmers to business liberals and those in positions of great power (thus, the alliance between militant blacks, Ford Foundation executives and affluent liberals against the Teachers' Union during the New York City public school controversy of 1968–1969). Conversely, when the danger emanates from the top — for example, when the Nixon administration eliminates social welfare programs, or abandons the struggle for desegregation in order to pursue a "southern strategy" — underclass members seek alliances with those middle strata also opposed to business conservativism.

At the level of sophisticated, interest-group politics, the game of divide and survive requires political skill of a very high order. At the mass level, however, the game combines desperate seriousness with deep cynicism; the street version of "playing both ends against the middle" is to accept bribes from both candidates and to vote for the highest bidder. The much-noted "political apathy" of blacks, women, or the rural poor is not the result of indifference, but of despair — or, as Charles V. Hamilton has said, "pulverization" of the underclass community. Middleclass Americans may have difficulty recognizing the politics of survival as politics at all, since most share the essentially aristocratic Aristotelian notion that political communities exist to bring about the good life, not merely to guarantee survival. But the same despair which produces a politics of survival is the earth which nurtures an extraordinary political sensibility — a combination of passion and detachment, clarity of vision and emotional depth, which often makes the "radicalism" of more privileged groups seem anemic by comparison.

"Conservatism" in America's politics means "Let's keep the niggers in their place." And "liberalism" means "Let's keep the knee-grows in their place — but tell them we'll treat them a little better; let's fool them more, with more promises." With these choices, I felt that the American black man only needed to choose which one to be eaten by, the "liberal" fox or the "conservative" wolf — because both of them would eat him.[49]

These are the words of a former con man, dope pusher, hustler, pimp, and jailbird named Malcolm Little, who took the name Malcolm X after his prison conversion to Islam. Malcolm, like certain other black leaders, was a living refutation of the conventional wisdom which declares that leadership of the lower class by lower-class members is an impossibility. The lower class, we are often told, is incapable of leading itself, and must therefore await direction by disenchanted members of the middle class or alienated intellectuals. This observation contains a good deal of truth for American groups which have not yet discovered their underclass identity — or for any society in which a common feeling of "nationhood" pervades all classes, and in which the class struggle is overtly and principally economic. (A continuing source of amazement, to an American, is the extent to which peasants and workers in other societies permit themselves to be led by intellectuals; imagine Leon Trotsky leading the Red army during the Russian civil war!) By contrast, since American underclass groups are excluded not only from the bourgeoisie but from the bourgeois "nation," they have produced their own indigenous "national" leaders and thinkers — slaves and former slaves, unlettered immigrants, dirt farmers, and children of the city streets — all sharing with Malcolm X a profound sense of "us" and "them," a tragic sense of the alienation and isolation of their people from the nation, a hard and unsentimental perspective on the "other" America.

At the risk of overstatement, let me deepen this contrast. In most other countries of the world, the concept of the "nation" denotes not only geographical boundaries and historical continuity but a mass of people who are mostly workers and farmers. Although it is correct, in such a context, to speak of industrial workers being alienated from the product of their labor, it makes no sense to describe workers as alienated from the nation or from society. Since they *are* society, alienation in this sense is considered to be a tendency of the intelligentsia; moreover, there is a natural overlap between struggles for national liberation and social justice.[50] In America, on the other hand, where "nation" and "small-propertied class" were for a long time virtually synonymous, the intelligentsia was never as alienated as the underclass from society itself. (Indeed, for a long time the American underclass was officially "invisible" and "society" was assumed to consist of a mass of independent property-owners.) As a result, militant leaders of poor and outcast groups, emerging during rare periods of underclass visibility, have played a domestic role equivalent to that of the alienated intelligentsia in European society. That is, they see the existing political system as "strangers in the land," and judge it, prophetically, as a whole. They know through experience that the system is based on domination and exclusion, and this knowledge enables them to pierce the facile ideological façades, the sentimental self-images of bourgeois liberalism. Sorrow and anger combine, on occasion, with the detachment of the excluded to create a prophetic style — the style of the slave Sojourner Truth and Chief Joseph of the Nez Percé, Mother Jones of the Populist movement and the Haymarket Square anarchists, Malcolm X, and Martin Luther King, Jr.

In 1963, Malcolm X greeted the news of John F. Kennedy's assassination with the remark that America's violent "chickens" were "coming home to roost." Although the proposition was documented in full by the Report of the National Commission on the Causes and Prevention of Violence, issued six years later,[51] the official "nation" was horrified by this bitter detachment. It had been equally horrified eighty years previously when a German immigrant unjustly convicted and sentenced to death in connection with the Haymarket Square bombing calmly remarked,

I found, long ago, that the workingman has no more rights here than anywhere else in the world. The States Attorney has stated that we were not citizens. I have been a citizen this long time; but it does not occur to me to appeal for my rights as a citizen, knowing as well as I do that this does not make a particle of difference.[52]

Compare the more recent, no less "shocking" remarks of Black Panther Huey P. Newton:

Many people have spoken of violence or of our advocating violence. Well, we're not advocating violence. We're advocating that we defend ourselves from aggression. If America is armed, and if it's right for America to arm herself and even commit violence throughout the world, then it's right for black people to arm themselves.[53]

What links these comments is their distance from "America," an accurate reflection of the isolation and alienation of the underclass. But the descriptive power of this thought has not been sufficient to overcome the situation it describes. Each of the three primary styles of underclass leadership — the revolutionary, the nationalist, and the integrationist — sets out to solve the related problems of isolation and powerlessness, but each depends for practical realization on an *absence* of isolation, a connection with the outside society which, until recently, did not exist. Revolutionaries from Big Bill Haywood to Huey Newton were unable to answer the question of how isolated, relatively powerless minorities can make a national revolution (as opposed to a coup). Nationalists from Jefferson Davis to Stokely Carmichael have discovered that secession cannot take place without civil war or the consent of the original nation, and that extreme nationalism may isolate even underclass groups from each other. Integrationists like Walter White and Whitney Young were frustrated by the hard fact that the bourgeois alliance *requires* the existence of an underclass. Moreover, the process of "bourgeoisification," which was painfully slow even for white groups during the heyday of industrial expansion and political opportunity, has become a vain hope for masses of poor people living under modern conditions of economic stagnation and political rigidity. For these reasons, despite their analytical power and emotional force, all three styles have in the past been utopian.

I am suggesting that the theoretical power of underclass political thought, and its practical weakness, derive from the same source: an economic and political isolation so profound as to make alliance-formation a virtual impossibility. Revolutionary theory, for example, ordinarily assumes the existence of a coherent mass peasantry or proletariat which can be mobilized to overthrow the established order and whose interests will be represented by the revolutionary leadership after the old ruling class has been defeated. What is a revolutionary to do in the context of a *three*-class system in which the underclass and the industrial working force are often at war — a system in which the lowest stratum of the proletariat is allied as often with the business elite as with bourgeoisified labor? The traditional exhortations to the powerless to "get it together" with the working class are correctly described by Harold Cruse as a radical form of integrationism, sharing the same fundamental defect as conservative integrationism — that is, the assumption that time, patience, hard work, and good will will convert the street hustler of today into the business hustler (or labor organizer) of tomorrow.[54] The truth, made even more poignant by the advent of the technological age, is that time, patience, etc., no longer serve (if they ever did) to raise underclass groups into the small-propertied class. For one thing, the small-propertied class itself is disappearing under the pressures of technological change. For another, even where sub-groups manage somehow to climb into the petty bourgeoisie, this merely increases the necessity to maintain the rest of the underclass in isolation and subjection, or to reduce new groups to that status. For, as we have seen, the precarious status of the lower middle class, and hence its very identity, depend on the continued existence of an out-caste at the bottom of the social ladder. Ironically, therefore, what would make integration possible would also make revolution possible; the simultaneous *proletarianization* of the old underclass and small-propertied class. I will have more to say about this very real possibility in the next part of this book.

Group nationalism, or some combination of revolutionary theory and nationalism, might seem to be the most logical way out of the dilemma. As stated earlier, the underclass is constantly being shattered or atomized by the need for individual self-preservation, thus inhibiting the development of communal politics. Nationalism is one way of attempting to create a collective life in which the individual, with his need to compete against his brother or sister for survival, is submerged. It is a method of trying to terminate the state of nature, or "war of each man against every other man," which the system imposes on the underclass. In fact, as the underclass becomes proletarianized, revolutionary nationalism takes on a new cogency. The rhetoric of Black Power, for example, is translated into the call for an independent black political party; dreams of returning to Africa are replaced by a program for black control of black communities. But it is important to understand that the underclass is not a social supernumerary, as reactionary nationalist analyses often declare; it cannot be "released" by the bourgeoisie to emigrate or to found an independent or quasi-independent state within the United States. It is a *necessary* element of the liberal-capitalist order: a captive market, a source of surplus labor, and a political weapon with which to divide the potential working class. The demand for real autonomy is not viewed by those in power as a neutral act. As United States history demonstrates only too graphically, it is viewed (correctly) as revolutionary in effect, if not in intention. Oppressed nationalities within the United States will therefore be liberated in the context of a general revolution, or not at all.

Scarcity cannot be wished away, nor can isolation be overcome by calling it a virtue. It is impossible to remain forever a nationalist without a nation, a revolutionary without a working class, or an integrationist without equality. The tragedy of underclass groups in political terms has been precisely this: that having developed the intense, clear-sighted perspectives of the alienated intelligentsia, they have been prevented by continuing isolation and threats to their survival from putting theory into practice. Under such circumstances, ideology eventually becomes a pose; even dying for one's beliefs can be a pose; and after the heroics are over, the people on the street return to the old game of *sauve qui peut*. For a long time, this is the way it has been in America: the underclass suffers and strikes poses; the small-propertied class struggles and deludes itself; and the great bourgeoisie rules.

Can it be otherwise? In succeeding chapters, analysis of the present political crisis in America leads us to answer, yes — yes, profound changes are now taking place both in the coalition system we have described and in the three-class structure which supports it. Ultimately, reality triumphs over ideology. A coalition system based upon an alliance of two bourgeois classes and exclusion of the underclass can survive only so long as the three-class structure is rooted in economic and social reality — or, to put it the other way around, the three-class system *has* survived in the past because it reflected socio-economic realities, and not merely the "false consciousness" of the system's dupes. We will see, in what follows, that the present period of dissent and disorder in America does *not* represent merely another turn of the coalitional wheel — that it prefigures a radically reordered polity — precisely because those underlying realities are shifting. Feeling the top of a building sway in a windstorm, one may not know whether it is swaying because of the wind, because the foundation is settling, or because an earthquake has begun. In my view, the disorders of contemporary American political life are surface tremors indicating that profound shifts are taking place underfoot — the end of an economic order, the disintegration of the three-class system, and the demise of the American system of coalition government. In coming years, some will mourn the wreck of old structures, and some rejoice at the opportunity to build anew. But it is not just the wind we feel. It is the earthquake.

PART 3

THE EMERGENCE OF
NEW ALTERNATIVES

. . . the alternative to the established semi-democratic process is *not* a dictatorship or elite, no matter how intellectual and intelligent, but the struggle for a real democracy.

— HERBERT MARCUSE,
"Repressive Tolerance," 1968

1

Bob Dylan sings, "You know something's happening, but you don't know what it is / Do you Mr. Jones?"[1] It is best to begin with a confession: In analyzing contemporary political change, we are *all* Mr. Jones. Notwithstanding government research grants and presidential commissions, institutes for the study of change and computerized data banks, the "experts" are little wiser than ordinary citizens when it comes to understanding the nature and direction of political development in the United States. Virtually all authorities agree that the years since 1960 have seen a significant rise in levels of political violence (including "official violence"), social disorder, political activism on the part of previously quiescent groups, and polarization among conflicting groups. Disagreement begins with attempts to give these developments shape and form by relating them to other changes taking place within American society.

Hypotheses, of course, are never wanting. Depending upon one's perspective and methodology, facts can be adduced to support any number of theories purporting to explain modern social disorder and political conflict. Choose one: Political instability is the result of (*a*) revolutionary agitation, (*b*) a decline in traditional morality, (*c*) the breakdown of the nuclear family, (*d*) mass education and rising expectations, (*e*) inflation and high taxes, (*f*) the Indochina war, (*g*) the collapse of capitalism, (*h*) discontinuities inherent in modernization, (*i*) decay of the two-party system, (*j*) congressional default, (*k*) bureaucratic rigidity, (*l*) generational conflict, (*m*) the rise of a new consciousness, or, for that matter, (*n*) the imminence of the Second Coming. The list could be extended almost indefinitely. Reading it, one becomes aware of a vast confusion; as Henry Bienen has remarked, the analysts of the social change cannot agree, to begin with, on a definition of "change"![2] Some scholars view the American political system as a well-constructed piece of machinery which occasionally needs oil, or, at the most, a few new parts. They tend to view political instability as the end-product of temporarily dislocating factors such as generational conflict, overinflated mass expectations, inflation, or the Indochina war. (By implication, when the temporary dislocation ends, stability will be restored.) To others, however, the political order is not a machine (unless, perhaps, it is "self-destruction"). It is an aspect of our social life which, together with all other aspects, is presently undergoing very rapid transformation.

According to this perspective (which I share), economic and social relationships in America are changing rapidly. So are political attitudes and patterns of behavior, particularly at the communal or "grass roots" level. But established political institutions, which reflect an older set of social relationships, resist change which threatens the power of vested interests. Specifically, the American ruling class attempts to channel change into familiar coalitional forms, perhaps endangering certain interest groups, but rescuing the great bourgeoisie from the threat of a lower-class alliance. Therefore, America experiences political turmoil and disorder — products of this collision between new social reality and old political structure. Moreover, where the changes taking place in society are rapid and profound enough to threaten those holding power under the old system with loss of their economic and political preeminence, the turmoil may be rightfully called "revolutionary." It was Marx and Engels, of course, who gave definitive expression to the idea that revolution was the body politic's response to socio-economic transformation. Where the rate of social and economic change was greatest, they argued, there political obsolescence would be most marked, and the incidence of revolution highest. Therefore, most revolutions prior to the twentieth century occurred in the western nations, which were experiencing the unprecedented changes associated with the transitions from feudalism to capitalism. Further-more, since the rate of social change clearly tended to rise even faster in the advanced industrial societies, the next wave of revolution would also take place in the West, where the development of industrial technology was visibly shattering the economic and social relationships character-istic of early capitalism.

Marx's scenario for advanced industrial capitalism proph-esied the elimination of all the old classes (petty bour-geoisie, independent farmers, craft workers, etc.) and the division of society into two monolithic, hostile classes: on one side, the bourgeois owners of the means of production — by now a small group of powerful monopolists and their allies; on the other, the wage-earning proletariat — by now an angry mass of workers threatened with extermination by the system's insatiable need for profits, its substitution of machines for human labor, and its tendency to experience increasingly severe depressions and increasingly destructive wars. Under these conditions, Marx predicted, the ruling class would be progressively weakened and the working class steadily strengthened. While the bourgeoisie was ripped apart, first by increasingly savage internal competition, then by international competition and war, the workers would be driven together by the industrial system itself, which forced men to work and live together cooperatively if they wished to survive. Inevitably, as real power gravitated into the hands of organized workers, while formal power and its attendant privileges were monopolized by the capitalist ruling class, there would be a revolution of the vast, suffering majority against the small privileged minority. The revolution would be followed by a brief period of continued class rule — that is, domination of the bourgeoisie by the proletariat (a "dictatorship of the majority"). However, elimination of the bourgeoisie as a viable economic and political force would introduce the age of communism and true democracy — self-government by workers sharing equally in industrial abundance.[3]

One of the great commonplaces of American scholarship after World War II was that Marx's scenario had been proved wrong. Socialist revolutions did not erupt in advanced industrial societies like Germany and the United States, but in relatively backward nations like Russia, China, Vietnam, and Cuba. Moreover, according to most analysts, such revolutions *could not* take place in the advanced industrial countries, because capitalism, by changing its nature in certain significant respects, had saved itself from the doom predicted by the Marxists. What accounted for this self-salvation? Although they disagreed about specifics, the anti-Marxists agreed generally that a combination of factors, summarized economically under the heading "technological revolution" and politically under the heading "welfare state," had operated to save industrial capitalism from itself. The machine did not condemn labor to lower wages and unemployment; it generated increases in productivity so enormous as to permit increases both in profits *and* in real wages, that is, a rise in standard of living for all classes. Workers organized, receiving further recognition and protection under the modified social democracy of the New Deal and Fair Deal. Government intervention also helped to stabilize the positions of key middle-class groups like farmers, white-collar workers, and small-scale businessmen, while federal regulation and fiscal and monetary policies were employed in an effort to moderate the business cycle. Meanwhile, under the impact of new technology, business itself changed. Stock ownership became more diffuse, and ownership of large industrial enterprises was separated from control. White-collar and service employees became the fastest-growing occupational group in the nation, and a new class of managers and technical experts assumed important roles in big business. Following World War II, the renewed depression predicted by many economists failed to occur, in part because the new industrialists had learned how to create demand through the medium of advertising, in part because the government had learned how to create demand through the medium of military expenditures. But even when the postwar boom seemed finally to be ending in a wave of inflation and unemployment, capitalism again demonstrated its flexibility — a Republican President imposed peacetime price and wage controls on a relatively docile nation.

The result of all these changes, according to anti-Marxist analysis, was that in nations like the United States, the two-class system envisioned by Marx — the basis for all his subsequent predictions — never materialized.[4] For one thing, the great middle class emerged from World War II stronger, not weaker, than before; workers with jobs and job security, fatter paychecks, new consumer goods, and high hopes for the future were thinking and acting like members of the bourgeoisie — and so, obviously, were the "new class" of white-collar workers and technical and service employees. Moreover, while Marx had defined social classes by reference to their relationship to the means of *production,* most Americans were more inclined to define their class position, if at all, by reference to their status as *consumers.* By 1965, most American families owned a home, and, very likely, an automobile, a telephone, and a television set; the majority were decently clothed and fed; and a rapidly increasing number was sending one or more children to college. Thus, where Marx had predicted a radical separation between workers and owners, there was apparent equalization, at least in life styles. Despite an unpopular war and a rise in civil disorder, an economic slowdown and a decline in delivery of public services, most American wage earners did not seem in any sense to be potential candidates for revolution.

Hence, few viewed America's troubles of the 1960's as a vindication of earlier Marxian predictions. Instead, ghetto rioting, minority group militance, violence on the campuses, the development of a hippie counterculture, and other manifestations of protest seemed to *confirm* the anti-Marxist analysis. In general, protest was characterized as group-conscious, not class-conscious; anarchist, not socialist; concerned with spiritual quality, not economic quantity.[5] Blacks were promoting Black Power and Black Studies, growing Afro haircuts, listening to soul music, advocating community control, and dreaming of an independent black republic. Whites were promoting Student Power and Radical Studies, growing long hair, listening to rock music, advocating world peace and dreaming of a republic of communes. The former had been left behind by the new abundance; what they really wanted was admission to the middle class. The latter had left abundance behind; what they really wanted were lives of personal significance. Other groups "politicized" in the 1960's and early 1970's — for example, policemen and schoolteachers — were described as participants in a conservative "backlash" against disorder and protest, or as a liberal "frontlash" against the "backlash." The politics of "backlash-frontlash" were interpreted as providing the coup de grace to Marxian theory; for it was the working class — rural folk and blue-collar workers, clerks and cops — which was most vehement in defending "law and order" while the affluent middle class, from its havens in suburbia, provided most of the advocates for a "new politics."[6] What refutation of Marxist predictions could be more devastating? If working-class Americans are not the shock troops of socialism but of fascism, leadership in the cause of liberalizing democracy *must* be provided by the liberal bourgeoisie.[7]

At this point, the reader may begin to experience strong feelings of *déjà vu*: despite the modernistic tone of the analysis, both its claims and the evidence adduced to support them are quite traditional. Labor "conservatism" is not new to American politics; we know that when a governing coalition begins to lose authority, the ambivalent discontent of small-propertied workers is often directed towards punishing the underclass and preserving the status quo. Neither is business "liberalism" new, for under these same conditions, advanced elements of the great bourgeoisie have always challenged the legitimacy of the old business elite. Similarly, as the crisis of authority deepens, one is not surprised to see "conservative" workers responding to antibusiness rhetoric, or "liberal" businessmen and their captive politicians moving away from support for the underclass (e.g., civil rights for blacks) in order to capture the small-propertied majority. Least surprising of all in this period of flux are attempts by both liberals and conservatives to suppress and destroy forces calling for a radical alliance of the two lower classes. Therefore, insofar as anti-Marxist analysis stresses elements of novelty, modernity, and the uniqueness of the present, it is suspect. Insofar as it suggests that technological development and political reform have eliminated classes and class conflict from American life, it is wrong. For, as has been shown, America was neither a classless society nor a two-class society, pitting peasantry against landowners or proletariat against bourgeoisie. It was a *three*-class system which could be made to appear "classless" by ignoring the existence of the underclass and focusing one's vision unwaveringly upon the "alliance of the whole bourgeoisie."

Ironically, the modernistic perspectives of conventional social science do not advance our understanding of what is new or "modern" in contemporary politics; they explain why the American political system has changed so *little* during the past forty years. The classless, affluent society proclaimed by theorists of modernization is little more than a souped-up version of the all-bourgeois alliance, implying the continued existence of our traditional three-class structure. (And the social scientists who have announced the dawn of this utopia are not so much its analysts as its ideologues.) The workers' identification with the bourgeoisie or participation in populist-style protest movements; big business leadership of liberal coalitions or manipulation of the underclass; underclass group nationalism or practice of the politics of survival — all these phenomena reflect the persistence of class consciousness within a three-class system. Anti-Marxist analysis implies that changes taking place deep within an advanced industrial society have somehow operated to preserve this structure; that, as a result, no unbridgeable gap between social reality and political form has opened, and that revolution is therefore unnecessary.

The significant question, then, is whether the three-class system *is* alive and well in America, or whether it is decaying. For if it is a permanent feature of American life, we can predict a continuation of the system of coalition government described earlier in this book and redescribed by the anti-Marxists. If, on the other hand, America is to be polarized between a mass working class and a small monopoly-capitalist elite, a new system of politics, bearing new hopes and new dangers for democracy, is bound to emerge. In my view, the overwhelming preponderance of the evidence supports the conclusion that modernization in

America is *destroying* the three-class system and substituting for it a two-class structure. The political consequences of this fundamental social change are of immense importance; but let us first try to comprehend the change itself.

▌▌

In order to sustain a three-class social system, it is axiomatic that *every class must be preserved*. This was the conclusion of both Aristotle and the authors of *The Federalist*, and is the principle followed in practice by all politicians who seek to govern on a coalitional basis. From the point of view of the ruling class in such a system, it is absolutely essential to preserve the separate identities of the two lower classes, for fusion of these classes could produce an American version of the Marxian proletariat — and would certainly generate new political movements dangerous to those in power.

But a principle feature of modernization, recognized by virtually all theorists, is the tendency of advanced industrial economies to centralize economic power in the hands of a relatively small number of large-scale enterprises, thus destroying the material basis for a small-propertied class.[8] Little by little, but inexorably, small businesses are driven to the wall by large, efficient corporations; individual entrepreneurs become functionaries in corporate bureaucracies; family farmers abandon the land, or become employees of "agribusiness" corporations; independent retailers become corporate franchise-holders; unorganized semiprofessional workers become organized "industrial" workers; homeowners become home-renters; even private colleges close their doors or else "go public." We are told that the number of families whose income level entitles them to be called lower middle class continues to increase — but in the context of centralization, lower middle class is a misleading, even irrelevant, term. An income at $12,000 per annum no longer guarantees the American family access to the sources of economic or political power in a monopoly-capitalist society; indeed, the $12,000-per-year man is more likely than ever to be an employee of some giant bureaucracy, private or public. Regardless of income level shifts, small property is liquidated, and with it the productive nexus which bound the monopolist together with the "little man" in an all-bourgeois alliance.

The traditional liberal response to this challenge (at least since the days of Teddy Roosevelt) is to *strengthen government*, to confer sufficient power on federal agencies to enable them to function as independent sources of protection for the small-propertied class, bastions of countervailing power capable of resisting the assaults of Great Property. Alas, the dream has proved hopelessly utopian, for the costs of resisting modernization prove, in the last analysis, to be unbearable. Forced to choose between the increases in productivity associated with large-scale capital and protecting less efficient small-propertied enterprises, the liberal always ends by declaring, with Woodrow Wilson, "I am for big business, and I am against the Trusts." Theoretically, this result is not necessary; government could nationalize the monopolies or (where efficiency does not depend upon size) break them up. But a government strong enough to control or reverse the related trends towards monopoly enterprise and mass consumerism would have to be the master, not the "partner," of the great bourgeoisie. Such mastery, in turn, could not be based upon an alliance between the industrial elite and small-propertied groups with votes. It could arise only if the lower classes, *united as a working class*, were prepared to oust the corporations from power and manage the economy themselves. This was the reformers' dilemma: so long as they remained committed to the private enterprise system, they undermined their own efforts to protect small private property from extinction; but if they moved seriously to break the power of large-scale private enterprise, they would be driven towards socialism — that is, towards elimination of concentrated private property and class distinctions based on wealth. In fact, the reformers chose to impale themselves on the first horn of the dilemma, proclaiming all the while that government intervention would save the small-propertied class from both the monopolists and the socialists.

Sooner or later, reality was bound to break through this ideological smokescreen. Consciousness would finally reflect the fact that, notwithstanding Wilson's Progressivism, Roosevelt's New Deal, Johnson's Great Society, and Nixon's New Federalism, the condition of the small-propertied class continued to deteriorate. Even the staunchest defenders of New Deal politics are now compelled to admit that virtually every program of government intervention on behalf of the "little man" has accelerated rather than blocked the trend towards economic concentration, rationalization of production and marketing, and elimination of small property.[9] The logic of this process, however, escapes those who view the counterproductivity of liberal programs as a paradox. We have seen that aid to multiclass interest groups and regulation of industries favor the most powerful (i.e., monopoly) elements within each interest group or industry. Federal antitrust policies benefit oligopolistic corporations and agricultural policies agribusiness; regulation of the private power, transportation, and communications industries strengthens the position of monopolies in these industries; and legislation aimed at protecting labor increases the power of the industrial giants. This is not a mystery; it is the logical and necessary result of the elite's attempt to save itself from destruction. Left to itself, without government intervention, free market capitalism would quickly follow the path described by Marx: large, efficient, mechanized enterprises would eliminate the petty bourgeoisie, economic depression would become endemic to the system, and the industrial elite would soon find itself confronted by a huge, angry working class. Government action, liberals believed, could avert this fate. But how? By attempting to salvage the small, inefficient businessman or farmer? Surely not! Measures might be adopted to prolong the period of annihilation of small property, but protection of inefficient enterprises would bring on the socialist apocalypse even earlier than predicted.

What would save the private property system (although at the cost of transforming the idea of "private property") was increased demand, supported by a mass of consumers and taxpayers *whose standard of living was rising*. Mass living standards could be raised, in turn, not by protecting small property, but by aiding great corporations to achieve productivity breakthroughs. In other words, the industrial elite found it necessary to seek to lower the production costs of goods and services *without* decreasing wage levels proportionately. In general, the only enterprises in a position to attempt this were large corporations or government agencies able to afford the costs of technological modernization, or powerful enough to command direct or indirect subsidies for this purpose. In fact, no corporation can afford all the infrastructural costs associated with modernization, as a result of which the public is required to bear an increasing share of these costs. Therefore, although government may set out to protect the interests of small-propertied Americans against controllers of great wealth, it invariably ends by favoring those corporations powerful enough to participate in the struggle to raise living standards through modernization.

For example, the New Deal set out to protect the interests of family farmers, but necessarily stopped short at the point at which subsidizing inefficient farm producers generated unacceptably high taxes and food prices. When it became clear that aid to farmers might threaten the living standards of nonfarmers, farm depopulation had to be accepted as a "fact of life." Similarly, small business interests could be protected only insofar as such protection was compatible with the public interest in high wages and low prices — which meant that the federal government might force General Motors to divest itself of Du Pont stock, but would not dream of protecting less efficient domestic auto manufacturers against Detroit's "Big Three." On the contrary, the automobile oligopoly's ability to modernize permitted it to offer its United Auto Workers employees generous increases in wages and fringe benefits without pricing itself out of the auto market. In theory, these workers could use their increased wages to buy automobiles and other consumer goods, homes and even investment property or corporation stock. Increased productivity would secure their membership in the small-propertied class and preserve their bourgeois consciousness. But for three reasons, this strategy must be accounted a failure.

First, the existence of an economic system based on private property and profit-making makes a *continuous* technological revolution impossible. Investments must, after all, be recovered before a new wave of modernization can begin — and, meanwhile, more modern economies (like the Japanese) outsell American companies and undermine the dollar. Domestic companies are unable to remodernize without squeezing (and therefore "debourgeoisifying") American workers or (by demanding tax subsidies of various kinds) American taxpayers.

Second, and equally important, since "progress" depends upon sacrificing the small-propertied class on the altar of increased productivity, what is the worker to do with his wealth? When wage levels increase he may buy consumer goods (on installment), a mortgaged house, or a few shares of General Motors and *believe* himself to be bourgeois, but this property no longer confers power on the holder. Indeed, as small property continues to be undermined, and as power continues to flow towards the monopolies, the economic and political gap between workers and their giant employers widens. The American consumer may enjoy luxuries unknown to the laboring classes of other eras; still, he is increasingly isolated from control over the productive process. The auto worker may own a car and a television set: even so, he has less influence over General Motors's investment policy and his country's foreign policy (the two are related!) than his father did in the days of the old CIO.

Third, the "standard of living" can not be measured merely by one's ability to buy goods or services on the private market. It depends increasingly on the quality and quantity of available *public* services. As we shall see a bit later, public services in the United States are in a state of near collapse because of the crisis of our private property system.

A basic contradiction, it seems to me, arises out of the elite's attempt to keep a small-propertied class consciousness alive while destroying the economic basis for a small-propertied class. The full irony of this situation can be seen in the activities of reformers like Ralph Nader, who demand, on the one hand, that automobiles be made safer to drive (essentially a "standard of living" demand), and call, on the other hand, for the breaking up of oligopolies like the auto industry (a "small property" demand).[10] The problem is that consumer protection, environmental protection, and other standard of living programs which fall short of nationalizing industry invariably improve the position of those industries and companies able to afford the additional costs of protecting the public. That is, they strengthen the monopolies, which are thus better able to resist new demands by groups representing the public! This is more than irony, however: it is the sort of contradiction which ends by exploding established political orders. For as the small-propertied class collapses, skilled workers must inevitably lose both the opportunity to climb the bourgeois ladder and their middle-class identification. We have been given to understand that American workers are incurably bourgeois in their thinking, that no matter what their objective position relative to the ruling class, they have been "hooked" on consumer goods, and will not awaken to the reality of their powerlessness. This I categorically deny. The bourgeois consciousness of American workers was based on the *reality* of a small-propertied class, and cannot long survive destruction of that class.

An example: the fastest-growing sector of the American economy is the service sector (including government services); more Americans now work for local, state, and federal government agencies than are employed in manufacturing.[11] Traditionally, many skilled service occupations — private secretary, teacher, nurse, accountant, civil servant — were considered "middle-class" jobs which conferred professional or quasi-professional status upon their holders. Skilled service workers identified with their employers rather than with unskilled fellow employees; therefore, although stock clerks, school custodians, or hospital maintenance personnel might organize industrial-style unions to engage in collective bargaining, secretaries, teachers, and nurses would not. Government work, of course, was considered a privilege, and organizing or striking against "the public" was (and is) generally banned. It is enough to mention this traditional "class" distinction to recognize the extent to which it has disappeared. Of course, service workers, like all workers, attempt to keep the labor supply short by professionalizing their occupations (that is, multiplying apprenticeship requirements for entry, codifying standards of performance, etc.); but they have in practice surrendered their claim to be superior to "ordinary" workers. Professionalization has become a cover for industrialization; the electricians and steelworkers also have stiff apprenticeship requirements and codified standards of performance. Twenty years ago, most teachers, nurses, interns, policemen, and bureaucrats would not have dreamed of joining a union. Today, militant labor organizations of skilled service workers are flourishing in all these occupations, some combining skilled and unskilled workers, others frequently acting in concert with organizations of the less skilled. Bourgeois pretensions still exist, of course, but lower-level white-collar and blue-collar workers no longer inhabit separate worlds. The consciousness that they are all workers is growing.

Again, one is aware of the all-pervasive contradiction: in order to preserve the middle-class outlook of skilled workers (that is, to keep them in the small-propertied class), it is necessary to satisfy the growing demand for public and private services. But satisfying this demand requires the creation of immense bureaucracies whose employees, whether skilled or unskilled, must finally act collectively to defend their economic position. As a result, even where general living standards are rising, one witnesses a progressive erosion of traditional distinctions between service and manufacturing employees, skilled and unskilled workers. White-collar workers are driven by the annihilation of small property into the ranks of an enlarged, increasingly restive working class. Simultaneously, corporations and government agencies seek to contain labor militancy and to control wage levels by incorporating formerly out-caste groups, like blacks and women, into the work force. Once incorporated, however, these underclass groupings tend irresistably to organize, first independently in imitation of more advanced workers, then in concert with them. Despite persistent friction between old small-propertied and old underclass groups, the *economic* basis for conflict tends to disappear over time, leaving a residue of racial or ethnic hostility which is the final barrier to collective organization. Finally, as living standards cease to rise, the objective situation is embodied in mass consciousness. A working class comes into existence — neither because leftist agitators have succeeded in convincing American petty bourgeois that they are workers, nor because the majority of workers are facing starvation — but because *modernization itself erases traditional status differentiations between types of labor and reduces all to a common condition*. It lowers the old small-propertied class and raises the old underclass to the uniform level of a modern proletariat.

This development, it seems to me, accounts for much of the malaise now afflicting unionized industrial workers, that relatively small segment of the working class commonly known as "organized labor." The disaggregation of organized labor provides compelling proof that the proletarianization of America — the creation of a mass working class comprising the vast majority of her people — is finally taking place. During the Depression of 1929–1939, proletarianization seemed inevitable, especially after the CIO broke away from the AFL and began to open its doors to blacks and other members of the underclass. Responding to the threat of a lower-class alliance, the New Deal produced a battery of laws and decisions of government agencies which guaranteed workers in major national industries the rights to organize, to bargain collectively, to engage in strikes, and to receive federally guaranteed minimum wages, overtime pay, maximum hours, unemployment compensation, accident insurance, and other benefits. The labor programs of the New Deal and Fair Deal, combined with government attempts to stimulate the economy, were intended to render the workers' "small property" — their individual labor power — defensible by aggregating it through the medium of collective agreements, while raising their standard of living to the point that they would think and act like members of the middle class. For a time the strategy worked. A proletarian consciousness did not develop — or, rather, its expression was limited to brief bursts of antimanagement militancy during hard-fought strikes. Away from the job, living in ethnically or racially identifiable communities, workers "thought" middle class, and attempted to lead middle-class lives. Nevertheless, the evidence now suggests that this *embourgeoisement* was neither as profound nor as permanent as had been thought. The New Deal reforms did *not* transform industrial workers into members of the ruling class. It would be more accurate to say that the Roosevelt reforms did for some unions (the so-called "labor aristocracy") what they did for some farmers; that is, raised them to the status of wards of the ruling class, specially favored children temporarily entitled to privileges and protections which were shared only in part (if at all) by the unorganized three-fourths of the American work force.

For the same legislation which gave the great unions a voice in determining wages and working conditions strengthened the commanding position of the great corporations in the nation's economy. Like the consumer-protective legislation mentioned earlier, labor legislation raised the cost of doing business, helping to insure the survival of those companies able to absorb high labor costs either by administering prices or replacing men with machines. Technologically advanced monopolies — the capitalist vanguard — therefore brought into existence a "labor aristocracy" whose security was inextricably bound up with the fortunes of the great corporations. But this was a marriage of convenience only; labor's interest would

be sacrificed (like the farmer's) as soon as its privileges
conflicted with demands for increased productivity. The
corporations could not survive as profit-making institutions
without creating mass markets with the capacity to absorb
their production. The system's potential for overproduction and underconsumption, which had plunged it into
the Great Depression, could be vitiated for a time by stimulating private demand through advertising, encouraging
installment buying, and adopting other techniques of "consumerism," but the success of such tactics hinged upon a
favorable wage-price ratio: high wages and fringe benefits
could not be permitted to drive prices out of reach of the
mass of American wage earners. Alternatively, demand
could be supplied by government in the form of vastly
increased military expenditures, but (as the Indochina war
demonstrated) this meant either increased taxation and
rationing, or price inflation and decreased purchasing
power — further trouble either way. After a twenty-year
binge, it was becoming apparent to businessmen that new
increments of privilege to organized labor not matched
by new increments of productivity could wreck even the
strongest company.

Unless the great unions are willing to move against the
profit system itself, they must recognize that the need to
maintain a favorable wage-price ratio takes precedence
over their members' "special privileges." To maintain
consumer demand, lower labor costs, and keep the peace
in the cities, blacks and other members of the underclass
must either be given employment (implying desegregation
of unions) or paid by the taxpayers in the form of increased welfare costs (organized labor's other *bête noire*).
To increase overall industrial efficiency, long nationwide
strikes must be outlawed in practice, if not in law (but
this is labor's trump card!) and "featherbedded" contracts
eliminated (but every contract in which men are paid for

doing work which machines might do more efficiently is really "featherbedded"). To make United States industry competitive with highly automated foreign industry, union resistance to automation must be lowered (but this means loss of job security, the prime goal of the labor movement since World War II). To hold the wage-price ratio in line, wage increases must be controlled and price increases held down either by "jawboning" or by outright price control. (But this destroys labor's "sweetheart" relationship with the monopolies, which has shielded many workers from economic reality since the 1930's.)

In short, labor's "special privileges" are threatened all along the line, just like farmers' and small business's privileges, by the necessity to save the profit system from self-created inefficiencies. The logical solution (given a commitment to preserve capitalism) is President Nixon's new economic policy of 1971. Led by the United Auto Workers, the great unions demand labor contracts tying future wage increases to increases in the cost of living; but such contracts, severing the relationship between wage and productivity levels, are held to be inflationary. What organized labor receives instead (with the acquiescence of the AFL–CIO leadership) is government-declared, employer-enforced wage control, and the threat of further legislation to ban "costly" interstate strikes! Under these circumstances, a revolt of the rank and file is hardly surprising.

Slowly but certainly, as all workers below the top management levels in business, the professions, and government are amalgamated into a new whole, the lines of status and power separating the small-propertied class from the underclass become indistinct. This happens not only because the underclass moves into the work force, but because white workers who are laid off or retired on a "social insecurity" pittance, women who cannot find jobs or who are compelled to work for substandard wages, elderly people living in retirement-death camps, who will work at any price — these and other "small-propertied" citizens can no longer distinguish their position from that of the underclass except by resort to obsolescent forms of racial and sexual prejudice. As Marx said, the imperatives of efficiency finally drive real wages towards the level of subsistence; all who live above that level are, in fact, wards of the corporate state. At the other extreme, economic concentration converts even professionals and skilled administrators into workers; they know that only a handful will be selected to join those at the apex of the hierarchical power pyramid. Disenchanted members of the middle class recognize that, for most of them, not even $30,000 per year, not even a hundred shares of AT&T, will purchase a voice in determining their nation's destiny, or their own. They, too, are wards of the state, and their position is not truly secure.

Breakaway movements of young professionals — doctors, lawyers, teachers and technicians who insist on working for poorer people and sharing their lot — reflect a similar consciousness: not so much a new idealism, really, as a new realism about the nature of monopoly power. Similarly, the persistent refusal (even during a recession) of large numbers of recent college graduates to join the great corporations or their governmental, military, and professional auxiliaries seems to me a kind of anticipatory strike by those who recognize that service to the monopolies will not produce either the status or the power to which ambitious men and women normally aspire. The recognition by the young that they are workers, and are fated to remain workers no matter what the title on an office door, demoralizes some, who "drop out." Others, less able to surrender worldly ambition, it angers. These people become revolutionaries. During the student uprisings of the

1960's, many analysts characterized student protest as a rebellion of affluent children against bureaucratized, workaday society, predicting that a strong dose of postgraduate reality would cure their malaise. In fact those "children of affluence" are now overflowing the colleges and graduate schools to join the ranks of the unemployed and marginally employed working class. Their "dose of reality" produces angry workers, not happy corporate drones.

Therefore, as the three-class system which had supported the American system of coalition government disintegrates, a dual division between monopolists and workers gradually emerges to take its place. I am aware that this is not, at present, a fashionable perception. Race, ethnicity, and the "counterculture" were discovered in the 1960's, and are still the "in" subjects among historians and social scientists. The scholars seek to explain working-class discontent on the basis of ethnic-racial factors, "frontlash," "backlash," and so forth. But I have attempted to show that racial and ethnic divisions do not exist in a vacuum, or simply because of the tenacity of racial-ethnic prejudices and loyalties. Their political potency was *functional* for a three-class system in which skin color, sex, religion, or country of origin reinforced one's membership in one of the classes. As an American proletariat develops, therefore, one would expect the politics of ethnicity to give way to a politics of class, with racial conflict intensifying for a time as a last-ditch effort by the disappearing small-propertied class to halt its amalgamation with the underclass. In fact, this combination of weakening ethnic identity, strengthening class identity, and last-ditch racism can be clearly observed in the new working class suburbs now proliferating outside every large American city. A recent study of these neighborhoods in the Chicago area points out that they are ethnically heterogeneous (representing the breakdown of the old "ethnic neighborhood") but extremely uniform as to class and income level. This is the combination which produces a "white power" reaction against working-class blacks — intensified racial conflict generated by the disappearance of other distinctions which formerly separated elements of the working class. Perhaps — and we will discuss this a bit later — this betokens the development of an American fascism. It signals, in any event, the end of the old political order.

III

Some might object to my thesis as follows: assuming that I am correct in describing the breakdown of the three-class system and the emergence of a two-class polarity in its stead, I am still not entitled to call this process "proletarianization," or to discuss on that basis a significant change in political consciousness. All I have succeeded in doing is confirming the existence of a "mass society," a familiar sociological concept which affirms that society has become more or less homogeneous at the mass level, and that effective governing power is in the hands of a relatively small elite. "Mass society" theorists insist that this mass is a collection of individuals, anomic or pacified, not a proletariat with revolutionary potential. It is generally understood that a proletariat, or working class capable of supporting a socialist revolution, must (1) occupy a common relationship to the means of production; (2) identify itself as the working class; (3) develop cooperative or communal forms of association and organization; and (to some theorists, most important of all) (4) become immiserated and compelled to seize power by the necessity to survive. Obviously, it is maintained, the mass of Americans do not fit this description, and probably never will.

Americans, we are told, do *not* identify themselves as old-fashioned workers or producers, and rightly so, since most of them are technologically obsolescent if not obsolete. Their true function as producers is to participate in bureaucracies which improve the quality of life by delivering services. As consumers, their task is to maintain a high level of demand for the cornucopia of goods, services, and life styles which a few producers are now capable of delivering. Therefore, according to mass society theory, they do not move towards new forms of cooperative organization but new forms of bureaucratic subordination and individual consumption. Rather than demonstrating increased solidarity and militancy, they display marked tendencies towards submissiveness, political disaggregation, self-isolation, competitiveness, and manipulability.[12] (Hence Americans rely on the mass media to prepackage ideas like TV dinners, and to "sell" presidential candidates like brands of toothpaste.) Moreover, they are *not* being pauperized or immiserated. Notwithstanding periodic recessions and an official unemployment rate ranging from four to seven percent, workers are being enriched, overall, by the continuing revolution in technology.[13] There is a strong suggestion in all this that utopia (or antiutopia) has arrived. Survival, it is said, has been permanently eliminated as a problem for most Americans since the system is productive enough to provide well-paid work for most people and conscientious enough to take care of those who cannot work. Economically, the "problem" now is how to produce further abundance without despoiling the environment, and how to use the surplus to best advantage. Politically, it is how to contain the demands of impatient or misguided groups until the entire society has been peacefully transformed. For the era of "quantitative" demands by working people has ended, and a new era of qualitative, "postindustrial" demands has begun.

Does this development, then, betoken the rise of a new sort of class consciousness even more threatening to the elite than the old? Although a few theorists (for example, Herbert Marcuse[14]) think so, most assume that the individuals who comprise the American "mass" remain, for the most part, thoroughly middle class in their thinking and behavior. Hence they continue to join interest groups which coalesce on a cross-class basis to form governing coalitions. Although distinctions between lower-level management employees and white-collar workers, white-collar workers and blue-collar workers, blue-collar workers and the marginally employed are disappearing, this process does not produce a Marxian proletariat but a *middle-class mass* whose political attitudes are essentially those of the historical small-propertied class. Therefore, mass society theory leads one to predict the *continuation* of fundamental patterns of coalitional change described earlier. No general attack on capitalism or the great bourgeoisie is to be anticipated in domestic politics. The bourgeois political parties will continue to hold the field. Those interests dissatisfied with the quality of life under the present governing coalition will eventually form a new cross-class alliance and attempt to take power (as always) on behalf of a political party representing the "whole bourgeoisie."

This line of thinking has a deceptive appeal: it appears to explain certain notorious "facts," such as the conservatism of the American worker and his fixation on consumer products, the flexibility of American capitalism and its power to "coopt" or buy off dissidents, the durability of interest-group politics and the hold of the two cross-class parties on the American political imagination. Its weakness lies in the projection of these "facts" indefinitely into the future — in the failure to recognize that revolutionary changes in social structure will produce revolutionary changes in politics no matter how clever the tactics of the governing elite, or how seemingly backward the consciousness of the masses. In order to break the link between social and political revolution, theories of the mass society

place heavy emphasis upon the *manipulability* of ordinary
people. They are assumed to be consumer-robots pro-
grammed to choose among whatever products (economic,
political, ethical, or aesthetic) are offered by the system's
managers, or consumer-addicts so hooked on goods that
they can no longer distinguish between pleasure and pain.
Like junkies, they dream happy dreams of success while
their bodies deteriorate.

These assumptions we may reject, for the moment, simply by affirming that men cannot be manipulated indefinitely nor consciousness long sundered from reality — that
there is at the core of human personality even when under
hypnosis or in a death camp a will to truth, freedom and
power (really a will to live) which social theorists ignore
at their peril. The heroes of George Orwell's *1984* and
Aldous Huxley's *Brave New World* are lonely rebels who
refuse to accept the false consciousness of their "brain-
washed" brethren. We ought to ask the learned cynics how
such heroes can arise in a supertotalitarian state, and why
if some can, millions or tens of millions can not arise with
them. The notion that most Americans have become docile
units of consumption strikes one as wishful thinking on the
part of the elite's ideologues, whose doctrines of infinite
manipulability betray a thinly disguised contempt for "the
mob." They might reflect that, before the Revolution, the
last message given every tyrant by his advisers is "All is
well. They are pacified."

Two related assumptions require more detailed analysis: first, that the American economic system is capable
of continuing to deliver goods and services in such abundance as to keep the masses contented (or to dispose them
at most to some sort of "qualitative," "postindustrial" discontent); second, that if economic disaster is avoided, no
political movement can hope to inspire the mass of workers to struggle against the industrial elite. These assump-

tions are closely linked, and in my view, they are both plainly false. We will consider in this section the matter of "delivery of the goods," and in the next, the question of political organization.

Earlier socialists, influenced by Marx's quasi-religious eschatology, believed that capitalism would collapse amid scenes of fire and devastation. Czarist Russia's wartorn finale strongly reinforced the notion that the old order would end with a bang as a result of a cataclysmic war and socio-economic chaos. In my view, this denouement is possible, but not necessary, in order to produce a revolutionary upheaval in the United States. The question is: what *is* a "breakdown" or "collapse"? If the unemployment rate rises above 10 percent, has the system "collapsed"? If the crime rate doubles, has the system lost its ability to maintain order? I believe that as a working class comes into existence in America, the incapacity of the profit system to satisfy mass demand becomes evident, and we are able to recognize the existence of economic crisis and social breakdown without the necessity for dramatization of the situation in the form, say, of nuclear war or mass starvation.

Initially, consumer demand reflects the yearnings of members of the disappearing small-propertied class for bourgeois status. The emphasis is on acquiring individual or family property (or claims on property and services) in the form of private homes, automobiles, appliances, bank accounts, education, "our family doctor," "our cleaning woman," "our congressman," etc. (all servants amenable to personal influence). But this type of demand for private property and services, which some view as a final, permanent feature of advanced capitalism, represents only the first stage in a movement of mass demand towards *social* property and services. As the small-propertied class and underclass disappear, members of the emerging working class discover that, collectively, they *are* being immiserated by the capitalist system's inability to convert increasingly useless private property into desperately needed social property. The system's incapacities are recognized fairly easily once it is understood that the distinction between quantitative "consumer" demands and qualitative "human" aspirations is invalid — or, rather, that it is, in fact, a distinction between means and ends.

For example, one purchases an automobile in order to increase one's personal mobility, to broaden economic opportunities, to bring distant friends within reach, to make travel within the community more pleasant and convenient. (The purchase is directly related to human aspirations, among which are life, liberty, and the pursuit of happiness.) What happens, however, when the nexus between "goods" and "good" is broken — for example, when my automobile and that of my neighbors become death-traps, spewers of pollution, contributors to an endless traffic jam, sources of increasing taxation, expense, and worry? What happens when my co-workers and I recognize that our commitment to the private car and highway system has wrecked public transportation, increased our taxes, despoiled cities and rural areas, murdered approximately one million of our brethren since 1950, and, in the end, has made us *less* mobile than if we had supported public transportation? According to anti-Marxist theorists, two things happen. First, the government shifts some public resources into mass transportation. Second, the automobile industry becomes the nation's largest advertiser in order to convince Americans that private cars will still make them happy. This task, as we know, involves attempts by motivational research experts and advertising agencies to convince consumers that the product is an end in itself — that the good is equivalent to the Good — by promising that its ownership will satisfy profound, unfulfilled psychological needs. (Therefore, the automobile is a sex symbol, a status symbol, a power symbol — anything *but* a safe, efficient means of getting from place to place.) What both the advocates of manipulatory advertising and its muckracking opponents neglect to point out, however, is that *consumers refuse, over the long run, to be manipulated in this manner.* The true function of this sort of advertising is to buy time for companies compelled to respond to the inexorable pressures of changing demand. Although some hold that the major consumer industries and their advertising agencies are in complete control of this process — that it is they who create and modify demand to begin with — this grandiose notion is hardly ever supported by hard data, for the simple reason that it is unsupportable. If it were true, for example, in the auto industry, Americans would still be driving block-long, gas-eating cars with tail fins. There would have been no demand for small, economical, foreign cars, no American "compact cars," no auto safety legislation, and no pressure for public transportation as an alternative to the private car.

On the contrary, it strikes me that apolitical consumer demand moves towards political working-class demand through stages which correspond roughly to the stages of proletarianization of the American wage earner. The drift of this process, which is towards social planning and social control of industry, is resisted at each stage by the industries and their "hidden persuaders" but continues nonetheless. The process begins when technologies of mass production bring commodities which were formerly luxury items for the rich within range of small-propertied workers. They are desired both as symbols of the purchaser's would-be middle-class status *and because their possession confers genuine advantages upon the owner.* With a car, for example, an assembly-line worker can become a trav-

eling salesman, or a city dweller can become a suburban-
ite. The auto, at this stage, is a badge of middle-class
membership, and its design — individualistic, wasteful,
and ostentatious — reflects its function. Rapidly, however
(and coincident with the leveling down of the small-
propertied class into the growing working class), the product becomes a necessity — not just a psychological
"necessity" created by advertising manipulators, but a sine
qua non for economic survival in a complex industrial
society. Without the product, or its equivalent, immiseration is inevitable and rapid. If the assembly-line worker
wishes to remain a worker, he had better own an automobile capable of following the movement of industry out to
the suburbs. If he and his family are to live economically
— to shop at the shopping centers, for example, or to take
vacations without going into debt — at least one automobile is a necessity.

Now, however, the product begins to reflect its altered
social function (Volkswagen, in German means "people's
car"). The need for motorized transportation becomes a
recognized social need which overpowers individual desires
for status differentiations. "Never mind the tail fins, just
give us a cheap, safe car that works!" The telephone company may offer status-conscious consumers new styles of
telephones for the home or office, but with the telephone
now another necessity for life in modern society, the basic
demand (which is reflected in unprecedented pressure to
control AT&T's rates) is for cheap, reliable telephone
service for all workers. In this second stage of demand,
working-class consumers call upon private industries, in
effect, to renew the technological revolution by producing
larger quantities of cheaper, safer, more efficient products.
And, as we saw earlier, this insistence upon efficient production of socially necessary goods and services has the
effect of undermining small property, strengthening mo-

nopolies, and enlarging the proletariat. Rather then creating such demand, industry is compelled to satisfy it if it can, for as proletarianization progresses, commodities which were first deemed prerogatives of the middle class are seen as necessities to which all workers are entitled *as a right*.

Health services, for example, are now entering this category; that is, the mass demand for decent health care does not decline as medical costs increase, but calls into existence a health insurance industry to protect wage earners against ruination by the costly illnesses characteristic of industrial society. Still, demand is not satisfied. As private health insurance companies prove incapable of providing decent health care at reasonable cost, individual consumers become a *political constituency*: the bourgeois demand for medical security turns into a working-class demand for some form of "socialized medicine." The psychological basis for this process is a surrender of middle-class pretensions by the proletariat, a recognition that since all are "in the same boat" together, it is better to give up meaningless individual perquisites (such as the right to choose among twelve brands of expensive toothpaste) for the good of all (the right to low-cost public dental service). The economic basis relates the dissatisfaction of Americans as consumers of health services to their common position as producers who have nothing but their labor to sell. Nothing could illustrate better the nexus between private property and worker immiseration, public property and mass survival. International statistics show that the private health care system in the United States (like the private transportation system mentioned earlier) is becoming relatively *less* efficient with the passage of time; it is literally inconsistent with the survival of the mass of American workers. Is the demand for health care, then, a "qualitative" or "postindustrial" consumer demand? Nonsense! It is as intimately related to worker survival in the

1970's as was the demand for labor unions in the 1870's.

Nevertheless, in this second stage of demand, the worker-consumer believes that he can "have his cake and eat it too." Choices between public and private services are deferred as long as possible: the public demands efficient public transportation *and* highway system giveaways, free health care *and* drug companies with huge advertising budgets, "law and order" in the cities *and* a private enterprise system which generates unemployment. "Quasi-public" solutions to social problems — for example, government subsidies to private health insurance companies — correspond to the consciousness of workers who have not entirely accepted their working-class position. The quasi-public solution (e.g., AMTRAK for the railroads, COMSAT for the communications industry, subsidies for airlines and defense contractors, giveaways of the public domain to the oil and timber industries) is an exercise in working-class masochism, for it is worker-taxpayers who pay the bills while monopolists reap the profits and maintain their elite position. The result of failure to choose among incompatible alternatives is worse than illogical; it means that the worker must tax himself so that others may profit from the business of providing him with essential goods and services. To illustrate: what is the true "price" paid by Americans for medical care? To compute it, we would have to add to obvious out-of-pocket costs (like doctors' fees, hospital fees, drug bills, and health insurance premiums) the not-so-obvious public costs of education of medical personnel in tax-supported institutions, government payments under the Medicare program to doctors and medical institutions, payments to group health insurance programs by employers who pass them on to employees and consumers in the form of lower wages and higher prices, medical research and development performed by government agencies and exploited for profit by drug companies and medical equipment manufacturers, free medical care for armed forces and other government personnel, government subsidies to hospitals, medical schools, insurance companies and others — and this is just a partial list.

This "price" Americans pay for a deteriorating health care system, while drug companies' stock rises and doctors' incomes average about $40,000 per year!

Please note, however, that the same analysis could be made of the "price" Americans pay for other necessary goods and services: direct out-of-pocket costs are only the tip of the economic iceberg.[15] Of course, the costs of necessary social programs do not have to be taken from workers' paychecks and taxes; they could be subtracted from the profits, capital gains, rents, dividends, interest, tax breaks, subsidies, and executive salaries collected by those who control private capital. An alternative to self-taxation by workers is taxation of the great bourgeoisie. (Taxation to the point of eliminating private profit altogether would, of course, renew the necessity for worker self-taxation — but at this point, the people, not the industrial elite, would be in control of their own economy and polity.) The position of industry, however, is that any significant diminution in private profit would be ruinous to private enterprise in a "mature economy" in which rates of industrial growth, investment, and profit are already "dangerously" low. Industry recognizes, on the other hand, that it is equally dangerous for those in power to increase the burden of self-taxation to the point that workers become conscious of what George Meany of the AFL–CIO (speaking of President Nixon's wage control plan) has called "inequality of sacrifices." Therefore, the ruling class responds to the rising demand for social property and services by proclaiming the *elimination of waste* in public and private enterprise, and the necessity for new breakthroughs in industrial productivity. Belt-tightening is the answer. New sources of wealth must be found to permit the financing of social necessities without either ruining the capitalist or impoverishing the worker. This means, of course, that labor must make sacrifices, accept discipline, speed up production, call off strikes, yield to automation — all in order to preserve the capitalist system. The call for elimination of waste sets the stage for the third stage of worker-consumer demand, which is the demand for socialism.

When the bourgeoisie cries for belt-tightening and sacrifice, we know that a crisis of capitalism is at hand. This has happened before, at least twice within living memory. Early in this century, with socialist movements sweeping through the ranks of industrial labor, "progressives" of both political parties attempted to deintensify class conflict by preaching the virtues of efficiency, conservation, and scientific management of industry. (Their hero was Frederick Winslow Taylor, the father of scientific management, who believed that scientific methods of production would make labor unions unnecessary).[16] In the latter days of the New Deal, with class conflict again threatening to rend the political fabric, efficiency and productivity were again promoted as America's saviors, first by the National Reconstruction Administration, then in relation to the war effort. It should not surprise us, therefore, to see latter-day progressives of all political persuasions proposing drastic measures to eliminate waste (for example, in defense spending) and to increase industrial productivity (for example, by freezing wages and granting investment tax credits to business). Both the liberal effort to achieve a transfer of resources from defense spending to social services and the conservative effort to subsidize industrial modernization are responses to the threat of renewed class warfare. With the help of foreign wars and government aid to business, such tactics have worked before to raise the system's economic floor (thus mollifying the workers) while preserving existing inequalities of income and privilege (thus mollifying the great bourgeois). Why should they not work again to freeze consumer demand at stage two?

The answer, implicit in our previous discussion, is that such tactics "work" only in the short run and under conditions of incomplete proletarianization. In fact, the very bursts of industrialization which serve temporarily to "bourgeoisify" workers — like the postwar booms following the two world wars — actually help to destroy the small-propertied class, raise up the underclass, and bring the American proletariat objectively into existence. Thus, during each of the booms of the 1880's, 1920's and 1950's, government spokesmen, industrialists, and intellectuals proclaimed the pacification of labor and the "final solution" to the problem of class conflict. But in each instance, after the smoke had cleared, a larger, better-organized, more class-conscious working class emerged, threatening renewed class warfare and stimulating industry to undertake new prodigies of production. The "final solution," in other words, ends by producing exactly those conditions which it is intended to avoid. As the industrial system advances, the mass proletariat therefore enters the third stage of demand, which is the demand that large-scale private enterprise be converted to public ownership, use, and control.

This occurs for several related reasons:

(1) In order to supply the mass demand for even the most basic goods and services — for example, food, clothing and housing — private enterprise must continue to modernize. But on their own, private companies simply cannot afford the costs of modernization, which are there-

fore borne to a greater and greater extent by the public — which is to say, the working-class majority. The public bears the costs of educating the highly skilled employees whose brainpower provides the great corporations' principal asset. The public pays (through government agencies like the Defense Department) for an increasing share of corporate research and development. The public (again through government agencies) licenses private use of the public domain. The public provides tax breaks to producers and government aid to consumers on which whole industries depend (for example, government-insured mortgage loans). The public furnishes virtually the entire infrastructure, from highways to skyways, without which private industry could not operate for a day, and, in a pinch, the public even bails out failing corporations like the Lockheed Aircraft Corporation and the Penn-Central Railroad Company. This means, in effect, that the effort to escape worker self-taxation through increasing productivity must fail, for *it is the working class which now bears the principal costs of industrial expansion.* The American worker is an investor without stock in private industry; he is the "silent partner" who pays the piper, but does not yet get to call the tune. So long as proletarianization was incomplete, a collective consciousness of this reality — "we pay the cost but they take the profit" — could not develop. (Members of the small-propertied class consider themselves neither "we" nor "they.") The creation of a mass proletariat makes it highly likely, if not inevitable, that the silent partners will soon end their silence. The financing of industry by the working class *must* produce a mass demand for collective ownership of public "investments" and control over the surplus which they generate.

(2) Generally speaking, increasing industrial productivity means replacing men with machines in the industrial sector. Simultaneously, as the demand for necessary social

services increases, jobs are created in the service sector of the economy (particularly in "public" occupations like government service). Nevertheless, expansion of the public sector is limited. The public's "investment," as we have seen, is diverted into private enterprise; private enterprise similarly diverts the lion's share of surplus thus produced into a relatively few pockets. In 1968, the top 5 percent on the American income ladder received more personal income than the bottom 40 percent. In 1962, some 1.77 percent of the people owned 67.8 percent of the individually owned stock.[17] Senator Harris of Oklahoma has pointed out that the top 20 percent of our people receive 41 percent of the income, while the bottom 20 percent receive 5 percent,[18] and Ferdinand Lundberg has shown that about 200,000 households in the United States control 22 percent of all wealth and, more critically, 60 to 70 percent of our corporate wealth.[19] Therefore, despite deficit financing by governments, the public service job market does not expand fast enough to absorb unemployed and marginally employed workers, and not nearly fast enough to satisfy the increasing demand for social services. Indeed, when it comes to consumption of public services, as opposed to private enterprise's goods, industrial and government elites reverse the process of "creating" consumer demand. They attempt to *hold back* the demand for universal health care, guaranteed nutrition levels, free legal aid, day-care centers, decent jobs for minorities and women, adequate public housing and education, universal higher education, cheap mass transportation, noncommercial television, public vacation centers, and so on. *As a result, we experience a manufactured job shortage,* for while there may be job scarcities in private industry, existing and yet-to-be created public service jobs which could fulfill social needs remain vacant or uncreated.

The effect of this incongruity is often grotesque: for example, seven small hospitals serve South Chicago, an area inhabited by some 850,000 people who ordinarily suffer unemployment at more than double the national average rate. In 1971, four hospitals announced their intention to leave the area for financial reasons. Yet the people of this area need double the existing number of hospital beds just to reach the national average per capita, and they are desperately short of outpatient medical personnel and facilities (not to mention the endemic shortages in this "lower middle class" area in housing, education, day-care centers, transportation, recreational facilities, and the like). Therefore, because ten of thousands of workers in South Chicago cannot find employment in an industry which yields someone a profit, they must work at marginal jobs, turn to crime, or go on welfare — which compels hospitals in the area to close for lack of paying customers![20] This sort of problem was formerly thought to be limited to the poor "ghetto." Now, with public service demands skyrocketing while industry becomes less labor-intensive, it has become a typical problem of the working-class community. In short, the job shortage in the private sector creates an artificial "job shortage" in the public sector. The diversion of the economic surplus into great-bourgeois pockets impoverishes not just the outcast poor, but all who work for wages. Consciously or unconsciously, driven by the need for productive work and for satisfaction of social consumption needs, the working class feels its way towards the solution: amalgamation of the public and private economies, planned use of the industrial surplus, worker control over the economy.

(3) In making a virtue of efficiency and a vice of waste, the bourgeoisie sows the wind. It reaps the whirlwind when workers recognize that their demands cannot be satisfied merely by taking the waste out of private enterprise, *since to take the waste out of private enterprise is to destroy it.* Economists generally agree that without planned obsoles-

cence of consumer goods, "creation" of new consumer needs through advertising, costly campaigns to obtain customer differentiation of substantially similar products, wartime-level defense spending by government, environmental pollution, payments to agribusiness for nonproduction of farm commodities — that is, without systematized waste production — the private economy would not survive. But without elimination of *social* waste, working people will not survive. When the businessman or government offical speaks of "eliminating waste," he does not mean that industry will stop producing shoddy, useless, destructive goods, or that government will terminate arms production, foreign aid to dictators, corrupt practices, or giveaways of the public domain. "Waste" in the bourgeois lexicon refers to the methods, not the purposes, of production. Workers, on the other hand, are driven by the need to live together as human beings to embrace a broader definition: waste is the failure, because of greed, to provide for human needs.

This progress in working-class consciousness can be comprehended as a synthesis, a resolution of the contradiction between consumerism and proletarianization. After World War II, industry invested enormous quantities of effort and money to insure the disappearance of the old "capitalist ethic," which emphasized the virtues of hard work, frugality, self-reliance, and self-denial. It advocated instead a hedonistic consumer ethic intended to induce workers to live for the moment, to spend without guilt, and to incur debts in optimistic reliance upon their future earning capacity. (In fact, consumerism was closer than the so-called puritan virtues to the genuine capitalist ethic of risk-taking; in effect, the consumer was invited to become a "plunger.") On the other hand, workers undergoing proletarianization in the real world do *not* enter the middle class, because the industrial revolution's advance continues to eliminate the small-propertied basis for a middle class. Lacking economic security, they are unable to embrace consumerism fully without abandoning responsibility for the future welfare of their communities, their families and themselves. Reality, in the form of rising inflation and rising taxes, the inevitable family emergency, the possibility of a layoff or long illness, the need for new streets and schoolhouses, the imminence of early retirement, the potential expenses of children in college — inescapable reality requires that working-class families continue to practice the ascetic, puritan virtues of self-sacrifice and self-restraint even while they are deluged with propaganda urging them to liberate their libidos and their checkbooks. Not surprisingly, the contradictory commands of consumerism and reality tend to produce a kind of social schizophrenia. Workers fighting for the four-day week condemn welfare recipients and youngsters who "refuse to work"; the alcohol-and-tranquilizer generation attacks the wine-and-marijuana generation; boosters of "old-fashioned Americanism" condone unconstitutional wars and government attacks on the Bill of Rights; advocates of traditional morality contribute to a skyrocketing divorce rate. The contradiction cannot persist, however; it demands resolution. Already hedonistic thesis and ascetic antithesis have begun to generate the synthesis which I call third-stage consumer demand.

In this stage, working people move actively into politics. Political organizations of all sorts flourish. Protest groups bloom on the Left, Right, and Center. With regard to specific political issues, parties, and candidates there is confusion and irresolution. Nevertheless, worker protest has a common core: rejection of the values both of individual consumerism and individual puritanism, affirmation of the willingness to make collective sacrifices to satisfy collective needs. Working people compelled to eliminate waste in their own communities and households refuse to bear the costs of useless wars and useless products, government corruption and business profiteering, political programs which don't function and household goods which don't work. All "middlemen" — those who stand between social sacrifice and social reward — are subject to attack. Mayors are defeated and union leaders turned out of office; clergymen and bankers alike lose their immunity from criticism. Working people turn to reformers to make the system work, but the liberal programs, always too little and too late, prove to be just another form of waste. They turn to conservatives and neo-fascists, but the "law and order" hardliners can not even lower the crime rate, much less deal with the causes of social disorder— still more waste. Gradually, despite false starts, dead ends, and confusion, despite efforts to confuse and divide them, American wage earners adopt a social definition of efficiency which renders the private business corporation as obsolete as the spinning jenny. As capitalism's crisis deepens, the stage is set for a revolution in American politics.

IV

It may seem odd to speak of revolution in the early 1970's, when, according to most analysts, previously "revolutionary" groups like urban blacks, radical students, and the women's liberation movement are returning to more traditional forms of interest-group and electoral politics. The prospect of revolution recedes, in their view, because Abbie Hoffman has cut his hair and the Black Panthers are quiescent! But this sort of analysis duplicates the errors made by radicals who believed that consciousness could be severed from history, that an American revolution could be based solely on altruistic identification with the black–Third World struggles for national liberation. Students for a Democratic Society and the Black Panther Party could not "make the revolution" by deciding to make it; by the same token, their successors cannot prevent a revolution by deciding to "work within the system." If, as I maintain, profound social changes have rendered the system of coalition government obsolescent, it will not be resurrected, any more than it could be prematurely buried, by acts of faith and will.

Political scientists, unfortunately, have converted interest-group theory into a principle of methodology. They attempt to answer the question "Is the situation revolutionary?" by posing the further question "What interest-groups or political parties favor or oppose revolution?" Obviously, the inquiry produces a preprogrammed answer: since most young "revolutionaries" of 1968 are now either in jail, graduate school, or the Democratic Party, the turmoil of the 1960's must be at an end. But traditional interest-group analysis will not tell us what we want to know, which is whether American political institutions have been so undermined by social change that they now function as forms without content, giving the illusion of capacity to govern without in fact possessing that capacity. The practice of "politics as usual" is sometimes a sign that interest groups, party organizations, bureaucratic structures, and other institutions of government are vital and functioning well. In the 1970's it is a sign of exhaustion, indicating only that, in the face of uncomprehended change, people will cling for a time to outmoded political habits.

Legitimacy — the lifeblood of any political system — may drain away so quietly and persistently that, when least expected, the "patient" suddenly ceases to function. Indeed this is one of the apparent paradoxes of revolution: that States which seem perfectly healthy (even all-powerful) to contemporaries unexpectedly collapse, *after* which political analysts declare, with the advantage of hindsight, that the weakness of the State prior to the revolution was the "obvious" cause of its downfall! (As Crane Brinton has remarked, everyone expects the revolution to occur in his grandchildren's lifetime, never his own.[21]) What makes prediction in this area particularly difficult is the question of too much versus too little power. Are political systems overthrown because they are too forceful, because they abuse their power and become oppressors of the people? Or are they overthrown because they are not forceful enough, because they cease to govern, forcing the masses to choose between revolutionary order and anarchy? The answer, which seems paradoxical, is "Both." Hannah Arendt has pointed out that States which lose *authority* — the ability to get people to work together for common goals — tend to substitute violence for their lost authority.[22] Coercion replaces voluntary compliance, and the State thus becomes more forceful as it becomes less powerful.

Government institutions lose legitimacy and authority when the power relationships which they enshrine no longer correspond to social reality. The major social reality in the United States not reflected in government institutions is the development of a working class composed of former members of the small-propertied class and the underclass, and their children — the emerging mass proletariat described earlier in this book. The decline of these old classes and the emergence of a proletariat naturally worries members of the great bourgeoisie, who sense that they are being isolated, morally and politically, from their "subjects." They feel the growing hostility of a mass of workers, black and white, poor and near-poor, increasingly conscious of their collective identity and interests, and inclined to make "irresponsible" demands (for peace, jobs, education, health, housing) which are incompatible with the system of monopoly capitalism. Business and government spokesmen therefore begin to make angry speeches defending big business's "image" and equating attacks on the corporations with attacks on America. This is not the first time the great bourgeoisie has felt itself so threatened: we saw earlier that the threat of a lower-class amalgamation has driven it before to excesses of self-defense. But — and this is the critical point — the proletarianization process is now so far advanced that hallowed techniques formerly employed to shatter working-class consciousness no longer serve their purpose. We can survey these techniques briefly:

(1) *Recognition of dissidents as ethnic interest groups.* When class conflict threatens to erupt in the United States, big business and its government allies respond in much the same way as colonial powers threatened by a revolt of native tribes. They "adopt" key protest groups, insuring

their loyalty by according them special privileges and making them "feel" like members of the ruling class. The tribal analogy has special meaning for the United States, a nation of nations in which recognition is often accorded on the basis of ethnicity or race. Once a group accepts such definition for political purposes, benefits accorded to elite members of the group are experienced vicariously as benefits accorded to the entire group. For example, so long as all Irish-Americans, from millionaires to unemployed longshoremen, identified themselves politically as "the Irish," favors to the Irish elite would seem to accrue to Irish workers. (Franklin Roosevelt's appointment of millionaire Joseph P. Kennedy to the Court of St. James was perceived as a boon to "the Irish," not just to the great bourgeoisie.) What more and more workers now recognize, however, is that recognition of ethnic or racial elites does *not* inure to the benefit of the whole group. (We can thank the black community for popularizing the notion of the Uncle Tom.) Of the Irish, Italian-American, Polish-American, or Afro-American communities, a few individuals achieve entry into the ruling class while the many are either stranded in the disappearing small-propertied class or incorporated into the growing proletariat. Members of white ethnic groups therefore display a well-merited and growing hostility towards their bourgeois "leaders," while in sprawling working-class suburbs ethnicity becomes a sentiment, not an ideology. Although by no means vanished as a political force, ethnic divisions are steadily losing potency; Edmund Muskie's failure to capture the Polish working-class vote in the 1972 Democratic presidential primaries is a case in point.

(2) *Recognition of dissidents as economic interest groups.* As we saw earlier, this technique was used during the New Deal to incorporate successful farmers, organized workers in interstate industries, and other privileged sections of the working class into the Roosevelt coalition as "junior

partners." Again, however, proletarianization undercuts its present effectiveness, since, with labor organizations of all kinds proliferating, a majority of the working class opposes the creation of any "labor aristocracy." As in the case of ethnic groups, the viability of this strategy depended upon less fortunate members of the group accepting as their own status gains made by the more fortunate. Formerly, all workers, even the unorganized, might have considered a victory for the Steelworkers' Union, say, to be a triumph for "labor." Currently, on the other hand, a steel strike which increases the price of automobiles is resented by workers struggling to earn the price of a new car, while steelworkers with children in school may be infuriated by the demands and strikes of the Teachers' Union. Ironically, this increased competitiveness among organized elements of the working class does *not* work for the benefit of the ruling class, whose every beneficence (for example, wage increases granted by President Nixon's Wage Board) is greeted with deafening cries of "Me, too" from newly organized and even unorganized sections of the proletariat. This chorus of demands, superficially dissonant, represents a vast refusal by workers to live vicariously on the successes of a favored few, or to accept status gratuities in exchange for power. It poses a desperate difficulty for the ruling class, which now finds itself compelled, willy-nilly, to deal with wage earners *as a class* (for example, by freezing *all* wages), thus intensifying class consciousness even more. The disappearance of a sentimental labor "solidarity" based on inequalities among workers sets the stage for development of a genuine solidarity based upon opposition to monopoly power. For the first time since the 1930's, one now hears trade unionists utter the two words best calculated to deprive big businessmen and bureaucrats of their sleep: "General Strike!"

(3) *Racism.* With the working class refusing to divide as

of old along ethnic or economic interest-group lines, the great bourgeoisie and its public servants attempt to drive a wedge between white and black workers by fanning the flames of racism. This ancient stratagem admits of two variants: either the government can appeal directly to white racial prejudice by blaming nonwhites for all the ills which afflict the small-propertied class (e.g., "lazy" welfare recipients, the "criminal element," "immoral youth," etc.), or it can sponsor provocative *pro*minority programs which will arouse white opposition and be defeated (e.g., programs to eliminate de facto segregation in housing and public education). In either case, black and white communities are invited to fight it out, to forget that in the world's richest nation it should not be necessary for racial groups to compete for jobs, living space, or public resources. Under President Nixon's regime, for example, the Department of Justice conducts "law and order" campaigns which intensify white fear of black criminals, while at the same time it brings symbolic lawsuits to compel white suburbs to accept racially integrated public housing projects! Even so, notwithstanding the persistence of hostility between the races, it proves impossible for the government to satisfy either side without running the risk of social chaos and revolutionary upheaval.

In order genuinely to solve the "crime problem," for example, it is necessary either to put lower-class neighborhoods under military occupation, which would surely produce new uprisings in the cities, or to eliminate poverty within the United States. Seeking to avoid extremes of fascism and socialism, the ruling class tries a little of each — on the one hand, a half-hearted "crackdown" on crime; on the other, half-hearted proposals for economic reform. Obviously, this satisfies no one. Meanwhile, as proletarianization continues, the underclass and small-propertied class continue to merge. Blacks and whites find themselves working at the same mind-destroying jobs and teaching in the same bankrupt schools, fighting the same useless wars and breathing the same fouled air. Living side by side in uninhabitable city neighborhoods and decaying suburbs, they are equally powerless, relative to the ruling elite, to reestablish control over their environment or their government. In this context, although racism does not vanish, many recognize it to be a sentimental luxury which neither class can really afford. There is an increasing tendency on both sides to blame business and government, rather than the traditional racial enemy, for the deteriorating socio-political landscape: hence, the failure of the Republican appeal to working-class racism during the elections of 1970, and George Wallace's tendency to substitute populist for racist rhetoric in his presidential campaign of 1972.

(4) *War.* Along with racism, war has been the ruling class's trump card in the struggle to prevent unification of the working class. As pointed out earlier, war has worked effectively in the past to unite all classes in holy crusades against the foreign enemy, while during postwar periods, mass hostility has been successfully directed against the "subversive" enemy within. The domestic history of the Indochina conflict, however, provides the clearest indication that social change in America has already altered the rules of the political game. Patriotism, in the sense of unquestioning obedience to governmental decisions on questions of war and peace, has become another sentimental luxury for the hard-pressed worker. What is most impressive about the antiwar movement in America is the extent to which it has gained the support of industrial and white-collar workers, blacks, rural folk, soldiers, and other American wage earners, despite the obvious distaste felt by many of them for the political style of the student-dominated "movement." Clearly, "movement" activities initiated and catalyzed dissent: students played a significant role in the New

Hampshire primary of 1968, at the Democratic Convention of that year, during the invasion of Cambodia, and elsewhere in generating an atmosphere of moral and political crisis which kept the issue in the forefront of the national consciousness. But the "alarming" development (from the point of view of the ruling class) has been the rise of antiwar sentiment among traditionally reliable segments of the working class — among "establishment" labor unions, for example, and in the U.S. Army itself, which literally had to be withdrawn from Indochina lest rebellion and demoralization, drug addiction and desertion, destroy it from within.

But if working people will not fall obediently into line to support colonial wars, will they still support domestic "anticommunist" crusades? Following World War I, World War II, and the Korean War, radical movements were destroyed by "Red scare" tactics which succeeded in equating dissent with treason. This could happen again after withdrawal from Indochina, but, again, proletarianization militates against such historical repetition. The same working class resistance to "one-way patriotism" (sacrifices by workers which benefit only the ruling class) which helped frustrate ruling-class designs on Indochina should stifle postwar attempts to whip up hatred against the "enemy within." In previous periods of postwar reaction, organizations of returning veterans actively supported government-sponsored witch-hunts for so-called subversives. By contrast, veterans returning from Vietnam seem more inclined to lead the antiwar movement than to oppose it. Similarly, working-class juries show a marked disinclination to convict domestic dissenters charged with conspiracy to commit political crimes, and proposals of amnesty for draft evaders do not evoke the degree of patriotic hysteria one would have expected in times past. It may therefore be doubted whether attempts by the elite to promote a "stab in the back" explanation for defeat will be any more successful than the war itself. Nationalism, like racism, seems inversely proportional to acceptance of proletarian reality.

To summarize. As the old three-class system continues to decay, a mass working class highly resistant to traditional ruling-class techniques of fragmentation and manipulation comes into being. American wage earners fail to respond reflexively to stimuli which in the past have operated to drive small-propertied or lower-middle-class people into the arms of the great bourgeoisie: cooptation of ethnic and economic interest groups, incitement to racial conflict, war against the foreign enemy, repression of "treasonous" dissent. The consciousness which tends more and more to resist both cooption and repression does *not* result from the conversion of workers to socialism, nor is it a product of affluent, postindustrial, or countercultural ideology. On the contrary, formation of the class precedes class consciousness; the pressure cooker of social change compels American wage earners to seek new solutions to their common problems. Working people therefore turn against the rich and the State which reflects the interests of wealth on the basis of relatively narrow perceptions of self-interest and "gut" perceptions of injustice. Their demands are reformist in intention, not revolutionary—but at certain historical turning points which we call "revolutionary eras," it becomes clear that reform cannot be implemented without revolution —that peace cannot be obtained, for example, without the overthrow of a war-making elite, nor individual property protected without the expropriation of corporate property.

This is not yet clear to the majority of American workers. Most working people are not now prepared to support a conscious movement aimed at overthrowing the great bourgeoisie and instituting a workers' state. Still, it seems to me that this is the direction in which working people will move as the logic of their position is made manifest. Already, one senses a powerful disenchantment with politics-as-usual — a marked (and measurable) inclination to distrust all "leaders," including the leaders of the two major political parties.[23] Equally important, given the American tendency to substitute technocratic for political authority in a crisis, is the growing recognition that what is wrong in our nation is not merely a technical matter for solution by experts and planners, but a "political" problem in the classical, ethical sense of the word. (Indeed, the inability of technocrats to solve political problems, dramatized by the military failure in Vietnam, has also undermined the authority of the computer wizards.) It is not just a matter of redistributing income equitably, but of redistributing power and reorienting purpose — of rediscovering a *polis*, or political community, which will give our common life meaning. Lack of community and of justice is experienced as a spiritual sickness; the "malaise," "anomie," "alienation," or "despair" afflicting American society is the correlative of powerlessness, isolation, absence of social purpose. What will cure us? While many intellectuals and most politicians propose palliatives, many begin to understand that such a disease requires strong medicine. It requires nothing less than reconstitution of American community on a new political basis.

On what principles will such a reconstitution proceed? How will American workers satisfy the self-interest and sense of justice which they now begin to experience as a class? There are no prepackaged answers to such questions; the answers will be discovered, as the questions have been discovered, through struggle. Nevertheless, working people in the United States seem to be moving, slowly and painfully, towards solutions which are expressed, albeit imperfectly, in the concept of "socialist democracy." (I say imperfectly because no state presently calling itself a socialist democracy possesses both the technological potential and democratic traditions of the United States.) Thus in response to economic chaos, inequality, and starvation of the public sector, the ideas of social ownership of industry and the planned economy take root. At the same time, however, political powerlessness generates a strong interest in decentralization of political power and the construction of new political institutions through which the popular will can be expressed. Alienation and anomie demand for their cure new forms of community and meaningful work, which, together with the mass demand for peace, suggest that the solution to America's problems will involve reintegrating the nation into the world community of workers. American wage earners are not interested in utopias, but in making a better life for themselves and their children. A socialist democracy is not the Kingdom of God; it is simply a more just and humane political system than the one we have at present. What I am suggesting here may startle some and disappoint others, but it is no less than this: *even in the absence of socialist traditions, ideology, and effective leadership, American working people are now feeling their way towards a unique fusion of socialism with democracy.*

V

In his provocative essay, "The End of American Party Politics," Walter Dean Burnham discusses "periodic critical realignments in our electoral politics." He states:

As a whole and across time, the reality of American politics appears quite different from a simple version of pluralist democracy. It is shot through with escalating tensions, periodic electoral convulsions and repeated redefinitions of the rules and general outcomes of the political game. It has also been marked repeatedly by redefinitions — by no means always broadening ones — of those who are permitted to play. And one other very basic characteristic of American politics that emerges from an historical overview is the profound incapacity of established political leadership to adapt itself to the political demands produced by the losers in America's stormy socio-economic life.[24]

Specifically, Burnham notes that in periods of political stress, when the socio-economic "losers" are raising new and disturbing political issues like the slavery issue, the subordination of agrarian West to industrial East, or labor's right to organize, both major parties tend to rally to the defense of the status quo, driving protestors into third party movements, intensifying political instability, and setting the stage for "critical realignments" accomplished against the background of "overwhelming external force."[25] Burnham adds that the last such realignment took place with the election of Roosevelt in 1932, and that we have entered a new period of instability and "electoral disaggregation" which may end either in a new realignment or in the end of party politics. In the latter case, he concludes pessimistically, the political system will be characterized by "oligarchy at the top, inertia and spasms of self-defense in the middle, and fragmentation at the base."[26]

It can easily be seen that, up to a point, Burnham's analysis correlates with the theory of coalition government presented earlier. A "critical realignment" within the two-party system reflects the rise to power of a new governing coalition constructed on the matrix of one of the major political parties. (Later on, it will establish a consensus which eliminates or coopts the opposition, permitting control of both major parties by the same governing coalition.) Nevertheless, Burnham's conclusion is wrong: "the end of American party politics" does not mean that oligarchy must triumph. A false dichotomy is presented: either there will be another "critical realignment" (presumably a new New Deal of some sort) or we will have "nonrule," featuring an elitist oligarchy, a defensive middle and a fragmented base. Burnham correctly intuits that the first alternative no longer exists, but he does not recognize that, since the three-class system is obsolescent, the second alternative does not exist either. The same factors which militate against establishment of a stable liberal coalition preclude the "nonrule" described by Burnham: each year the middle becomes less defensive, the base less fragmented, and the elite less secure. The emergence of a mass working class in place of "middle" and "base" classes suggests that the next critical realignment will be of a new type: it will align Left against Right in a historic struggle to determine the direction of American political development.

As the three-class system decays, the process of *political disaggregation* accelerates. Recognized political groupings lose coherence (they disintegrate); the old collective loyalties no longer bind; linkages connecting leaders with followers are broken; and groupings whose socio-political reality was unquestioned (for example, farmers, organized labor, the Irish) become, in a sense, unreal. New organizations compete for the loyalty of the disaffiliated, struggling to discover the secret of reaggregation or reaffiliation: what do the people need and want? What groups are becoming "real"? As competition intensifies, answers begin to emerge; political activists of all stripes discover that a working class including most American wage earners and would-be workers, and extending far beyond the boundaries of the old organized labor grouping, is becoming real. The Left therefore moves towards reaggregation by mobilizing class-conscious working people against the corporate elite, while the Right attempts to organize mass resistance to proletarianization. The Indochina war, it seems to me, has proven so divisive precisely because it accelerates separation of Americans who have accepted their working-class membership from those who have not. Proletarianized workers identify the national interest with their class interest in wresting control of the nation's resources away from big business and its military-professional allies, while workers resisting proletarianization interpret national interest in the traditional, bourgeois sense of extending "American power" abroad and upholding the "national honor." In short, as small-propertied class and underclass political groups disaggregate, reaggregation takes place on the Left and Right, expressing workers' acceptance or rejection of the proletarian condition.

Burnham and others present impressive evidence demonstrating that electoral disaggregation is a long-term trend, reversed only temporarily by the New Deal, which "has resumed in many measurable dimensions, and with redoubled force" since 1952.[27] At the present time, the number of voting-age Americans declaring themselves "independent" of the two major parties is comparable to the number declaring adherence to either party, and among younger voters, party identification is becoming almost a rarity. In recent years, disaggregation has meant increased ticket-switching and intensive use of the mass media to "sell" political candidates to those without strong party affiliation, while preliminary reaggregation (for this process takes some time) creates political formations to the Right and Left of the center parties. Meanwhile, the two major parties attempt to capture and control the forces which are tearing them and their constituent interest groups apart. Liberal Democrats return to the antibusiness, anti-military, social welfare rhetoric of the mid-1930's, promising to "redefine priorities" and to bring the giant corporations under control (but not to put them out of business). Conservative Republicans attempt to resuscitate an even earlier brand of populism which pictures government bureaucrats, intellectuals, and the eastern "establishment" as the enemy, promising to liberate individuals from bureaucratic restraints.[28] Nevertheless, neither party is able to control or coopt the forces of social change. Dominated by the great bourgeoisie, both parties aim at eventual restoration of the all-bourgeois alliance, which is now an impossibility.

Thus, although polarization tends to drive liberals to the Left and conservatives to the Right, the major parties' area of agreement remains very broad. Both favor ending the Indochina war (but some Democrats would end it more quickly). Both deplore crime in the streets (but some Republicans would support urban police forces more vigorously). Both favor equality of opportunity for non-whites in principle, but not to the extent of alienating the white working class. Both approve scaling down the arms race in principle, but not to the extent of impairing America's nuclear superiority. The Republicans support price and *wage* control, the Democrats wage and *price* control — and so it goes. Such agreement between the two major parties was once thought to reflect a profound national consensus. Now, with the major parties either ducking the real issues (corporate imperialism, the defense economy, the collapse of the city, etc.) or posing them in a manner which precludes solution (for example, ending street crime without abolishing poverty and unemployment), "consensus" becomes another word for paralysis — a symptom of the elite's inability to deal with the demands of a mass working class. Reformers cannot realize these demands without attacking monopoly capitalism at its roots; reactionaries can no longer divert attention from them by stimulating social and nationalistic conflict. One can therefore predict a continuation of electoral disaggregation in the 1970's, with workers leaving the Democratic-Republican club to form or to strengthen independent organizations of the Left and Right.

Were the three-class system still functioning, one could also predict the sequel — an electoral reaggregation, or realignment, based on absorption of these independent movements and adoption of some of their principles by the major parties. (Examples: The Republican Party's absorption of Abolitionists after 1856, the Democrats' absorption of Populists after 1892, the New Deal's absorption of Socialists after 1936.) Indeed, both major parties now behave as though disaggregation can be anticipated and aborted. Thus, in 1972, the Republicans moved to absorb the Wallace movement in the South, while the Democrats attempted a liberal reorganization around the candidacy of Senator George McGovern. Temporarily — that is, while remnants of a three-class system still exist — Republicans may continue to attract conservative votes and Democrats liberal votes. To the extent that ultraconservative and ultra-liberal movements represent the old class consciousness, they can be manipulated, undercut, and absorbed by the major parties. Their rhetoric aside, George Wallace and Richard Nixon promise to protect *small-propertied Ameri-*

cans (e.g., "the silent majority") against the excesses of the underclass. Similarly, George McGovern and Ralph Nader pledge to protect *small-propertied Americans* (e.g., "consumers") against the excesses of the monopolists. In both cases, the assumption is that a small-propertied class exists and that it can be secured either by restoring law and order or by reviving business competition. In both cases, the goal is reconstruction of the all-bourgeois alliance (which is why so many affluent Americans find it possible to support "populist" conservatives and "social-democratic" liberals). The major parties will shortly learn, however, that a subtle but profound change has been occurring under their very noses. Their former constituencies simply refuse to believe the old lies or to accept the old panaceas, for the class consciousness of a mass proletariat cannot be manipulated, undercut, or absorbed. It must end by destroying or utterly transforming the American party system.

This is something new in American history. The closest domestic parallel, perhaps, is presented by the history of the political parties prior to the Civil War, when new organizations constructed outside the two-party system raised questions so dangerous to party elites as to cause the collapse of both national party organizations. Then, as now, the question which the major parties were unable to encompass involved the expropriation of a ruling class — the southern slaveholder elite. Then, as now, protest movements which began among the affluent and the oppressed spread throughout the middle classes and polarized the nation. But the parallel cannot be pressed too far. The Civil War was a contest between sectional ruling classes, each with mass support, which decided that there would in future be but one nation and one ruling class. There was clear continuity between the northern elite which controlled the old Whig Party and the victorious rulers of the postwar Republican Party. By contrast, the contest which now approaches will pit the workers of a united nation against a national (really, international) monopoly bourgeoisie. Continuity of rule is possible in this case only if the bourgeoisie wins, but in such a case, continuity would probably be overshadowed by a neofascist political transformation (see the next section). The great bourgeoisie will shortly be threatened as never before by economic and political dispossession. If it wishes to remain in power, it will be compelled to oppose a genuine workers' movement by attempting to suppress and outlaw it, and by converting one or both of the major parties to neofascism. Although this suggests the possibility of a bitter contest for the loyalty of the working class, it does not point in the direction of sectional or racial civil war but of revolution.

Revolution! To Americans, the word conjures up visions of mobs attacking the White House, a small group of conspirators seizing power, dictatorship, mass execution of opponents. The commonly accepted image of revolution is the nightmarish reverse of the American political dream, in which significant reforms are always enacted by a majority expressing itself peacefully and legally through normal political channels. On the one hand, peaceful, legal evolution representing the will of the majority; on the other, violent, illegal revolution representing the will of a minority (and led, no doubt, by outside agitators) — these stereotypes are part of our "political religion" although neither describes the methods used in times past to achieve significant political change. During past eras of disorder, the nation labored painfully to give birth to *new* political forms, such as the opposition political party, the labor union, the urban political machine, and the regulatory agency. These institutions thereupon became sanctified elements of "the system," theoretically available for general use as agencies of political change, but actually methods of vesting the interests of groups controlling a governing coalition. The methods of protest and organization used to achieve such breakthroughs were neither "revolutionary" nor "evolutionary"; one would have to describe the mass demonstrations of the Jeffersonians, the early strikes and boycotts of the labor unions, the organizing techniques of the urban machines — or, for that matter, the sit-ins of modern civil rights workers and students — as *quasi*-legal, *quasi*-peaceful, and *quasi*-majoritarian. Similarly, any contemporary movement for serious political change is compelled to improvise methods of protest and organization (and, having gained power, to improvise institutions) which are partly "within" and partly "outside" the system.

What does it mean, then, to speak of a workers' revolution in the United States? Revolution refers to a fundamental redistribution of power, including the power to make further redistributions, both in the State and in Society. Specifically, it means that bourgeois monopolists and their allies are deprived of those rights, privileges, powers, and immunities which permit them to dominate the nation's economic and political life, and that the working people of the United States are empowered to rule. Because revolutions propose to dispossess some and repossess others, they generate intense social and political struggles which often spill over into violence, but, especially in the American context, worker revolution does *not* require a bloodbath, a coup by a minority "vanguard," or the imposition of totalitarian controls by a revolutionary regime. These were concomitants of revolutionary upheavals in economically and politically backward nations like czarist Russia, where the working class was a small boat floating in a peasant sea, and the crew — the politically conscious elements of the proletariat — a vanguard within a vanguard.[29] In the United States, where a high level of economic development is coupled with strong traditions of political participation and constitutional freedom, proletarian revolution has the meaning originally ascribed to it by Karl Marx: it is the "self-conscious, independent movement of the immense majority, in the interest of the immense majority."[30] In this context, socialism and democracy are not conflicting values; on the contrary, each is a necessary precondition for the other. A genuine American workers' movement will therefore commit itself not only to public ownership and control of the economy, but to decentralization of control over the work process; not only to establishing a responsible central government, but to satisfying the needs of diverse communities for local autonomy and community power; not only to destroying the basis for bourgeois rule, but to extending political democracy and preserving constitutional liberty. Are these values contradictory? On the contrary, it is only by taking possession of the monopolies that Americans can restore the degree of economic democracy which they desire. It is only by controlling political power from the center that they can establish the decentralized power structures for which so many communities yearn.[31]

All this could happen relatively peacefully if the elite would permit it to happen. The course of history up to the present time does not incline one to optimism, however; in order to keep the world safe for business, the American ruling class has already sacrificed a good many lives. In my view, the worsening economic crisis in the world capitalist community will accelerate the process of proletarianization over the next few years, increasing the appeal of an American-style socialism to working people, and inclining the great bourgeoisie towards "preemptive counterrevolution" or fascism. The principal threat to democracy in the next decade will therefore emanate not from organizations of revolutionary workers but from those forces opposed to peaceful revolution — from those big businessmen, politicians, and military men who would sacrifice the

Constitution rather than permit it to be used as a means of overthrowing the ruling class. The "violent revolutionary" is a stereotype which must be abandoned if we are to understand how serious political change can take place in a nation like the United States. The extent to which a movement for change achieves its purpose peacefully and legally is determined by a number of interrelated factors, the most important of which, I think, are (1) the movement's success in attracting mass support and (2) the resistance of those in power to organized activities which threaten their supremacy. The interplay of these factors helps to explain the incidence of violence during a struggle for revolutionary change.

Consider the following diagram:

	Low	High
(1) Mass support for change	A	C
(2) Official resistance to change	B	D

Situation A–B (low mass support, low resistance) defines the politics of stability during periods like the 1950's; political violence at such times is at a minimum, and some change (generally reforms emanating "from the top") may take place. A–D, on the other hand, describes the situation which exists early in the development of a mass movement for change, when public support is low and resistance is high. At such times (for example, during much of the 1960's), the use of repression by the authorities combines with desperation on the part of relatively small out-groups to produce spontaneous or adventurist violence, from riots and riotous demonstrations to sporadic acts of terrorism and political martyrdom. Assuming that the forces of change weather this period, and that new groups disaffected with the existing regime further weaken authority's mass support and increase that of the movement, two alternatives remain: C–B (high mass support, low resistance) and C–D (high mass support, high resistance). In the former situation, political change — even change of a revolutionary nature — can be implemented without a holocaust of violence. In fact, before World War I, revolutions were not generally as violent as counterrevolutionary propaganda pretended. France's "reign of terror," for example, took fewer lives than are lost in a few months on the American highways! This was because the situation C–D — high mass support and high resistance — was virtually inconceivable in the absence of modern means of technological warfare. When mass support spread to the armed forces of the State, that was the sign that victory for the revolution was inevitable, although foreign intervention might trigger large-scale violence, as in France after 1796 or in Russia after 1918. Today, however, C–D *does* exist — as in Indochina, where a movement with mass support wages a protracted revolutionary war against a foreign elite with access to technological death machines. "High resistance," under these circumstances, may be a euphemism for genocide. In the domestic context, then, the question of violence may hinge on the willingness of America's rulers to use against their own people the techniques employed against the people of Vietnam.

Of course, one can construct any number of scenarios describing how a new American revolution might take place; the subject is obviously speculative. Nevertheless, on the basis of what has been said thus far, the following seems persuasive to me:

(1) *Political disaggregation continues; reaggregation begins.* Electoral disaggregation continues to weaken the two-party system just as, more generally, political disaggregation weakens the interest groups which are the build-

ing blocks of the parties. Legitimacy, draining out of national and state institutions, is reestablished for some Americans at the level of the community organization or the union local; many find it to their advantage to support new national organizations representing worker interests (including organizations representing the interests of blacks, Chicanos, women, and other groups of oppressed workers.) Despite Democratic attempts to absorb the Left and Republican attempts to absorb the Right, most Americans become "independents," seeking solutions to their problems in the formation of diverse class-based political organizations. Independent parties proliferate, accounting for an increasing minority of votes in national elections and occasional majorities in local and state elections. The Electoral College system is altered to prevent presidential elections from being thrown into the House. Nevertheless, the Bobbsey Twin parties continue to lose coherence and legitimacy. Relatively small groups therefore wield increasing power. Both political instability and political participation continue to rise.

(2) *Political reaggregation continues; national alliances are formed.* As the center parties disintegrate, local groups and caucuses representing diverse worker interests coalesce, forming regional and national alliances capable of making a legal bid for national power. Simultaneously, the great bourgeoisie rallies to its cause groups representing upper-class interests and elements of the working class which identify with the elite (i.e., fractionated elements of the small-business, professional, white-collar, farmer, and industrial labor communities). In the late 1970's or early 1980's new national parties appear, openly representing the interests of monopoly capital and labor, perhaps using the old parties, or some combination of them, as organizational matrices. Left and Right extremists, calling either for immediate violent revolution or for immedi-

ate counterrevolution, flank the major coalitions, but remain relatively weak. As proletarianization continues, mass support drains steadily from Right to Left, confronting the Right with a fateful decision.

(3) *The Right decides.* An event of a catastrophic nature (perhaps a new war, ecological disaster or economic collapse) mobilizes the mass party of the Left. The great bourgeoisie sees that its days in power are numbered; it must therefore choose between yielding power to the revolutionary alliance or resorting to force in an attempt to destroy it. If the former course is adopted, right-wing terrorism is suppressed and the transition to socialism takes place with a minimum of disorder, constitutional liberties are respected, and legal instrumentalities of change are employed. If, on the other hand, the Right refuses to permit a socialist government to take power or lends itself to violence by right-wing terrorists, the outcome of the struggle must be determined by the armed people. Although history suggests that the elite would probably choose the latter course, I believe it could recognize the advantages to be gained through preserving the maximum possible continuity between prerevolutionary and postrevolutionary systems, and avoiding a protracted revolutionary war.

(4) *The Left decides.* As stated above, if bourgeois repression does not force the workers' movement to militarize and move underground, democratic socialism may be instituted in a relatively peaceful and orderly manner. I say "relatively" because great moments of change are not accomplished without mass mobilization, intense political conflict, excesses of revolutionary zeal and counterrevolutionary reaction. Nevertheless, there is no reason why a workers' government cannot bring the economy under public ownership and control, decentralize and extend the instruments of mass democracy, and initiate a new era of communal enterprise and cultural renewal while preserving

the right of dissenters to speak and organize. There is absolutely no reason why constitutional freedom cannot be strengthened and extended under a democratic socialist regime. It is only when the ruling class attempts to save itself by prompting counterrevolution that such freedoms may be limited by the necessity for protracted war. In this case the nation may be torn apart and the final triumph of the revolution, although predictable, appears the lesser of two tragedies.

Let me make this more specific. In the birth of a new nation, or of a new political system, there is a particularly intimate relationship between means and ends. A system born out of a war of independence, like the United States and many of the Latin American nations, often emphasizes national independence, pride, and unity above all else, deferring the struggle for social justice until much later in its history. A system born out of civil war or protracted revolutionary war, like the Soviet Union or the Peoples Republic of China, may embody the martial spirit long after the revolutionary generation has gone, ruthlessly hunting down "enemies of the State" even when they are not counterrevolutionaries, but merely dissenters.[32] At the opposite extreme, a system akin to the socialism of Scandinavia can be implemented with virtually no social struggle because it does not threaten to make permanent alterations in basic political institutions or established social relationships; in a sense, it is not a new system at all, and therefore remains vulnerable to overthrow by forces representing either revolution or reaction.[33] An American workers' State which is also democratic and libertarian is not a utopian pipe dream; it can be realized through struggle, provided that a popular movement commanding mass support is not confronted by a monopolist minority wielding the weapons of technologized, counterrevolutionary warfare. The choice between fascism or socialism is not only a decision which working people must make; it is also a choice for the bourgeoisie. During the next fifteen years, the rights of great property will come under increasingly heavy attack, but these rights do not define — in fact, they twist and subvert — our democracy, our liberty, and our social contract. In my view, American workers will not permit their nation to fall into the hands of either Nazis or Stalinists, but they *will* organize, and, one way or the other, they will win.

VI

Opponents of revolution — particularly those of liberal persuasion — have often stated that revolutionary political movements are not worth the risks they engender. According to these analysts, a serious political upheaval in the United States would more likely produce fascism than socialism; and, in any event, the institutions of democracy could not long survive even a socialist victory. This pessimism has three sources: first, a historical analogy likening American students or workers to the German petty bourgeois of the Hitler era;[34] second, an interpretation of history which holds that revolutionary regimes invariably end by imitating the worst excesses of their predecessors ("The Revolution devours its own children")[35]; and, third, a specific historical judgment linking free political institutions with the capitalist "free market," and asserting that abolition of capitalism must produce an unfree polity.[36] The first of these objections is particularly serious, since there *are* disturbing similarities between the United States in the early 1970's and Germany in the early 1930's. I have argued that a fundamental reorienting of American politics within the next decade is inevitable. What are the chances that this reordering will be in the direction of fascism rather than socialism?

Like Germany between the wars, the United States is a highly developed industrial nation experiencing, on the one hand, concentration of economic power in the hands of a relatively small number of industrialists and bureaucrats, and, on the other, proletarianization of the middle class. As in Germany, a government composed of well-meaning liberals and moderate conservatives fails to solve the fundamental economic and social problems of the nation, with the result that political polarization continues: the Left and Right gain strength at the expense of the Center. Again as in Germany, generational conflict is superimposed on political conflict; the youth play an important role in mobilization of new political formations. As socialist movements gain strength, so does the Right, whose mass support is provided by groups attempting to resist proletarianization (the petty bourgeoisie, some craft workers, disgruntled farmers and rural folk, some white-collar workers, some war veterans, etc.), while its finances, always plentiful, are provided by right-wing industrialists who seek salvation from the socialist threat. The ideology of American right-wing movements, like that of German National Socialism, combines emotional appeals to patriotism with populist denunciation of the political elite. In both cases, a powerful sense of alienation and self-hatred produces a search for national purpose; mass yearning for an end to political strife and social disorder generates pressure to restore the old morality and sense of national community. In both instances, military armaments and adventures are used to overcome the economic and political breakdown of capitalism, while internal unity is imposed by attacking the Negro-Jewish-communist "enemy within."[37]

Of course, there is a potential for fascism in the United States — how can one deny this? The point is not that domestic fascism is impossible, but that it is by no means inevitable; it can be combatted and defeated. Note the words combatted and defeated. For while American scholars often attribute the rise of nazism to "backlash," implying that a quiet, respectable American Left will avert the fascist threat in this country, it was the quiet, respectable Social Democratic Party — the largest party in Germany — which permitted the Nazis to take power legally while even the Communist Party did not awaken to the true extent of the fascist threat until too late.[38] If, instead of excoriating Red "extremists," the German liberals had gone into the streets to fight the Nazis, Germany would have experienced great disorder, perhaps a revolution — but the world would have been spared Adolf Hitler! In this respect, it is important to recognize the extent to which America is *already* moving towards fascism, for we will make a great mistake if we wait for the appearance of brown-shirted storm troopers or a homegrown *führer* to announce the arrival of the New Order.

Fascism develops not just out of mass alienation or fear of socialism, but as the result of an endemic economic crisis which threatens to topple the capitalist elite. A mass movement based on resistance to proletarianization, it combines the social mobilization and control commonly associated with socialism with preservation of private property in the hands of the great corporations. (This, for a monopolist, is the best of all possible worlds!) In the fascist state, workers are required to make great sacrifices for "the nation," but national leadership remains firmly in the hands of a monopolist-bureaucratic elite. For this reason, efforts by the American ruling class to subordinate the interests of "labor" to those of "the nation" through wage control, inhibition of the right to strike, military conscription, forced labor for welfare recipients, and similar measures are oriented towards fascism, since new increments of worker sacrifice are not matched by new increments of worker power. Formerly bourgeois elements of the population may accept this elitism as a way of maintaining their old status, at least psychologically: this was the psychosocial function of Hitler's glorification of individual work, property, the traditional family structure, and the master race.[39]

Similarly, political fascism (the attack on legislative power, subordination of liberty to order, militarization of the work force, official racism, extermination of "subversives") associates intense social control with powerful status rewards: those who obey are more than oppressed workers — they are members of a superior nation-race! Moreover, like economic fascism, political fascism develops more rapidly than the Red revolution to which it is supposedly a response. Thus, fascists find it necessary to manufacture plots and conspiracies in order to justify suppression of potential revolutionaries, while repression of the citizenry at large continues through proliferation of secret police and intelligence agencies, compiling and storing data on citizens' political activities and private lives, removal of judicial restraints on law enforcement, and erosion of constitutional protection of civil rights and liberties. An overtly fascist stance in foreign policy may develop well in advance of domestic policy, as the ruling class seeks to extricate itself from domestic crisis by turning internal conflict-energy against a foreign enemy. The hallmarks of such a policy are the creation of a permanent state of war or national emergency, the use of massive military expenditures to rescue the economy from depression, the establishment of puppet states controlled by cliques of military men or by big business, and alliances with other fascist powers.

Clearly, in certain respects, America is already leaning in the direction of fascism. I hasten to add that fascism has not yet triumphed here, and that, in my view, it will *not* succeed, as it did in Germany, in perverting the direction of American political development. Barrington Moore has pointed out that Germany never became a liberal-capitalist nation like Great Britain or the United States; her unification was accomplished late in the nineteenth century under Prussian leadership. The German industrial ruling class therefore continued and extended the power of the traditional landed aristocracy; large segments of her population, like the peasantry and army, were not imbued with capitalist values.[40] (In fact, the discontinuities in German development were so great that "Red" German workers, represented by Rosa Luxemburg and Karl Liebknecht, were considered the most advanced Communists in the world, while Prussian aristocrats and Bavarian peasants longed for the return of the Hohenzollern monarchy!) On the contrary, the United States has always been a thoroughly capitalist nation. As our analysis has shown, it is now so thoroughly and uniformly industrialized that proletarianization — the creation of a mass working class encompassing virtually the entire population — is now proceeding very rapidly along a broad front.

As a result, the movement for democratic socialism in the United States is not compelled to address itself merely to "advanced" elements of the population while more backward groups, with roots in a feudal past, conspire to restore a lost world. On the contrary, the divisions between America's lower classes, and even between elements of the working class, are disappearing. As in Germany, it is *resistance* to this process which provides rightward-leaning movements with much of their mass support— but the process has advanced much farther here than in Germany or Italy, and now seems unstoppable. Moreover, the German middle classes and those with middle-class aspirations were subjected to the twin shocks of a lost war and a desperate economic depression, while in the United States proletarianization proceeds more slowly and evenly, giving militant resistance less of a chance to build. Of course, some privileged workers would still like to maintain a wide separation between themselves and the "niggers" lest they be compelled to recognize that, in terms of political and economic power, they are becoming "niggers" too. One can even predict an increase in this sort of sentiment as some make last-ditch efforts to deny social reality. But it is too late, I believe, for the German "solution." Barring some early catastrophe like a racial civil war in the United States or nuclear war internationally, the potential mass support for fascism should continue to erode as proletarianization is accepted and, finally, welcomed.

In this context, it is worth remembering that, during the early and mid-1930's, what one might call protofascist tendencies among farmers, the petty bourgeoisie, and some workers were pronounced. The conservative labor movement accepted the cartelization of private industry under the National Recovery Administration. Middle America and the South responded to the demagoguery of Huey Long, William Lemke, and Father Coughlin, whose attacks on the power structure were soon directed against the "hidden government" of Negroes, Jews, and Communists. Admirers of Hitler and Mussolini were not limited to corporate boardrooms, although they tended to concentrate there; the pro-Nazi Bund and the Silver Shirts were organizations to be reckoned with. Nevertheless, as the economic crisis deepened, economic issues tended to overwhelm racial-nationalistic irrelevancies. The mid- to late 1930's saw workers and farmers moving into the CIO, the Farmer-Labor movement, the Communist Party, and a host of other moderate-to-extreme left-wing organizations, a process aborted only by the rise of international fascism and World War II. The coming years, in my view, will witness a similar deepening of economic crisis and a similar movement of worker support from right- to left-wing political movements. Again, this does not mean that fascism cannot succeed in America. It *can* succeed here if masses of working people embrace either the vicious panaceas of militarists and racists or the weak-kneed reformism of a crumbling Center. The only conclusive answer to the fascist threat is a militant mass organization of workers dedicated to smashing monopoly power and implementing the rights of working people to control their own national resources, political institutions, and personal lives.

Even if counterrevolution does not triumph in America however, will not a socialist revolution end, as some have, by turning over control of the nation to a new bureaucratic elite? Is it possible to eliminate the free market without eliminating freedom, as we understand it in the West? These are questions more properly answered in another book, but the argument already made with respect to avoiding fascism in America implies an answer to those as well. America is not Germany; and neither is she the Soviet Union. Socialist revolutions ending in rule by bureaucratic elites have occurred in nations in which the masses of people have been peasant farmers and the politically conscious elements of the proletariat so small as to constitute, in effect, counterelites. In nations like the Soviet Union and China, socialists have been compelled by the economic backwardness of their peoples to serve as modernizers — and, as we know from European history, modernization is not a gentle or democratic process. It was precisely for this reason that Marx and Engels saw the most advanced industrial nations (those which had already undergone modernization) as the arenas for revolutions which would be both socialist *and* democratic. For Marx, "dictatorship of the proletariat" meant rule by a worker majority dedicated to eliminating private property in the hands of a capitalist minority, not rule by a bureaucratic elite over a subject majority. The Chinese communists, very much aware of this difficulty, apparently carried out their Great Proletarian Cultural Revolution in an effort to compel *their* bureaucracies to subordinate their interests to those of the majority of peasants.[41] In any event, we are not concerned with determining whether Soviet or Chinese communism, or some other form of socialism, is the best possible system for Third World people. For the American people, socialism is not antithetical to democracy, but a logical continuation of it. Given the tendency of political and economic authority to concentrate *under captialism* in the hands of a bureaucratic elite, socialism represents our last, best hope for truly popular government.

An American socialist movement would not, and under conditions of mass mobilization could not, transfer the power of the great bourgeoisie to a totalitarian clique. The myth of an irresistible tendency towards elitist, bureaucratic rule, formulated by apologists for monopoly capitalism, assumes the existence of a passive mass or "mob" subject to periodic convulsions of mindless violence and fit only to obey. On the contrary, once mobilized, America's urbanized, educated mass working class will defend its interests against any totalitarian threat. Our people will insist that a socialist government begin — and only begin — by eliminating the power of the great bourgeoisie over the national life (for example, by nationalizing large-scale private enterprises, taxing the rich out of existence, and controlling the accumulation of private property). Even establishment of new social welfare programs, even guaranteeing all Americans a decent job and dwelling place, an adequate income, nutritional and health care, an education through college, and a fruitful, secure old age will be but a beginning. For American workers will not sell their birthright for the sake of social welfare programs. I believe that they will *demand* that power to control the nation's economic and political life be returned to *them*:

(1) through creation of new units of local government and the decentralization of decision-making power, as far as possible, to the level of the plant, the city or suburban neighborhood, and the rural district;

(2) through establishment of intermediary units of government representing their interests as rural residents and city dwellers, blue-collar and white-collar workers, men and

women, black people and members of other national minorities;

(3) through enforcement of guarantees permitting all workers to speak freely, to form political organizations and parties, to establish and maintain voluntary associations, to worship as they please, and to be accorded due process of law.

The American people would insist on this, would they not? Of course, the matter is speculative; I do not know what the people would decide, once liberated from the dictatorship of the bourgeoisie. But I do know that fears of a totalitarian coup or a Stalinist administration in the United States stem from profound feelings of paranoia and impotence which are bred into us by our present system. *Paranoia*: We fear that someone, or some group, is "out to get us." A band of fanatical revolutionaries will seize control of the nation, compelling obedience to their will by the use of terror. When I speak of revolution, I am talking about a people's revolution, one made by you and me, but you think that I am talking about "them." *Impotence*: We do not think that we are capable of making decisions or of controlling representatives whom we choose to make decisions; we fear that we will fall helplessly into the hand of rulers cleverer and more cruel than those who oppress us now. Obviously, these sets of feelings are related, and they run deep. Perhaps we are projecting onto the fantasy of an American socialist dictatorship feelings which we have about our *present* leadership, which is in fact becoming dictatorial, but which many feel powerless to oppose. Perhaps, at some level of consciousness, we *want* to fall into the arms of some *führer* who will promise to solve all our problems, and who can then be blamed for failing to solve them.

I don't know; I am not a social psychologist. But as a student of politics, I can say with some confidence that no government is maintained for long by terror. It is a truism, but true nevertheless, that people get the kind of government they want, whether it be a Nazi or Stalinist regime, a corporate state, or a socialist democracy. It is also true that the only way a people learn to wield power intelligently, humanely, and responsibly is by wielding it; the only education for government is governing. Therefore, when we fear a "communist takeover" of our government, we are really saying that we are impotent to overthrow a repressive regime and to control a new one, that we do not trust the people — which is to say, we distrust ourselves. Thus, the revolution begins with an act of faith, a decision to trust the people, which means to trust oneself.

POSTSCRIPT

While this book was in press, President Richard Nixon was reelected for a second term, defeating the Democratic candidate, Senator George McGovern, by a wide margin. The results of this election, it seems to me, help to validate the analysis just presented. Still, some may ask how it is possible to speak of a "left turn" in American politics when the nation seems so clearly to be turning right. What is the significance of the Nixon landslide of November 1972?

It is important to note that the Nixon victory did not reverse but may have even accelerated the process of political disaggregation referred to earlier. The landslide was entirely personal; it did not help to advance the Republican Party's position either in the Senate, the House of Representatives, or in state and local governments. (In fact, the disparity between Nixon's presidential triumph and his party's faltering fortunes elsewhere was considered "incredible" by newscasters and commentators not familiar with the process of disaggregation.) Similarly, although the titular majority party retained control of Congress and most state governments, increasing incoherence was evident on the Democratic side as well. McGovern-style progressivism, an only slightly updated version of the middle-class progressivism of 1910–1920, seemed irrelevant or threatening to most working people. Nevertheless, a vote for Nixon was not a vote to strengthen the party of Big Business; in the throes of proletarianization, the majority remained restless, discontented, and confused. The McGovernites' failure to capture working class support might throw control of the Democratic Party back to the big money men, labor bureaucrats, and Dixiecrats who had supported Johnson and Humphrey — but to what avail, if young workers, blacks and liberals were thereby alienated? Although papered over by electoral success, the Republicans' dilemma was similar: how to capture the loyalty of an emerging proletariat while retaining the devotion of the Big Money? Contradictions, contradictions!

The percentage of eligible voters that cast ballots in the 1972 presidential election reached a modern low, well below the usual norm of 60 percent. As stated earlier, political apathy signifies either a high level of contentment with the status quo or something akin to a mass state of shock caused by rapid and uncomprehended change — by the absence, as it were, of a stable status quo. Under these circumstances (for it is surely the latter apathy which we now experience), one may vote for the presidential candidate who appears most stable, sound, old-fashioned, and authoritative while undergoing the most ferocious radicalization at the job site, in the local community, or in the home. If my analysis is correct, Nixon's victory at the polls does not represent a "right turn" in American politics, but a wish to escape the arena of political choice altogether. (The President's New Federalism, for example, is an escapist fantasy which promises to solve national problems by turning them over to the states!)

But again, if I am right, there will be no respite for us in fantasyland. The inability of either major party to form a stable and effective governing coalition derives from their more profound incapacity to "manage" the forces now proletarianizing both the old small-propertied class and the underclass. Naturally, as the mass proletariat emerges, leaders of both parties issue frantic calls for the elimination of waste, a renewal of the spirit of work (production speedups), and a restoration of national unity. I have already commented on the inability of such policies to prevent the dreaded two-class polarization.

The 1970's, I continue to believe, will be an era of class struggle in America. In the course of this struggle, which has already begun in earnest, working people will recall that government was instituted to serve human beings, not vice versa; that the question is not what they can do for their nation, or unaided for themselves, but what they *could* do for each other were the economy and the State not controlled by a small, violent minority. Nixonian escapism — the latest version of the liberal capitalist myth — will not avert the choice which confronts America in the coming decades. Business oligarchy or workers' democracy: it must be one or the other.

NOTES

PART ONE

1. Winthrop Jordan, *White over Black* (Chapel Hill, University of North Carolina Press, 1968).
2. Grant Foreman, *Indian Removal* (Norman, University of Oklahoma Press, 1932); see also John W. Ward, *Andrew Jackson, Symbol for an Age* (New York, Oxford University Press, 1955).
3. E.g., "I will say, then, that I am not, nor have ever been, in favor of bringing about the social and political equality of the white and black races [applause]: that I am not, nor have ever been, in favor of making voters or jurors of Negroes, nor of qualifying them to hold office, nor to intermarry with white people" (speech in Charleston, South Carolina, September 18, 1858). Quoted in Richard Hofstadter, *The American Political Tradition* (New York, Vintage Books, 1954), p. 116.
4. John Hope Franklin, *From Slavery to Freedom: A History of American Negroes* (New York, Knopf, 1956), pp. 445–446.
5. Frank Freidel, *F.D.R. and the South* (Baton Rouge, Louisiana State University Press, 1965); see also Howard Zinn, *The Politics of History* (Boston, Beacon Press, 1971), pp. 173–178.
6. Julius W. Pratt, *Expansionists of 1812* (Gloucester, Mass., Peter Smith, 1957); Richard Hofstadter, *American Political Tradition*, pp. 39–44.
7. Albert K. Weinberg, *Manifest Destiny: A Study of Nationalist Expansionism in American History* (Chicago, Quadrangle Press, 1963).
8. Wood Gray, *The Hidden Civil War: The Story of the Copperheads* (New York, Viking Press, 1942); see also Rich-

ard Hofstadter, *American Political Tradition*, pp. 126–133; David Donald, *Lincoln Reconsidered* (New York, Knopf, 1965).

9. Richard Hofstadter, *The Age of Reform, From Bryan to F.D.R.* (New York, Knopf, 1956), pp. 270–281.

10. Allan R. Bosworth, *America's Concentration Camps* (New York, Bantam Books, 1968). See also Barton J. Bernstein, "America in War and Peace: The Test of Liberalism," in Bernstein, ed., *Towards a New Past: Dissenting Essays in American History* (New York, Vintage Books, 1969), pp. 289–299.

11. Richard Hofstadter, *American Political Tradition*, p. 42, see pp. 32–44.

12. Lee Benson, *The Concept of Jacksonian Democracy: New York as a Test Case* (Princeton, Princeton University Press, 1961); Marvin Myers, *The Jacksonian Persuasion: Politics and Belief* (Stanford, Stanford University Press, 1957). Cf. Michael A. Lebowitz, "The Jacksonians: Paradox Lost?" in Bernstein, ed., *Towards a New Past*, p. 65.

13. On Wilson's economic policies, see Gabriel Kolko, *The Triumph of Conservatism. A Reinterpretation of American History, 1900–1916* (New York, Free Press, 1963), and Hofstadter, *The Age of Reform*, pp. 213–254. On those of the New Deal see William A. Williams, *The Contours of American History* (Chicago, Quadrangle Press, 1966), and Barton J. Bernstein, "The New Deal: The Conservative Achievements of Liberal Reform," in Bernstein, ed., *Towards a New Past*, pp. 263–288.

14. Hannah Arendt, *On Revolution* (New York, Viking Press, 1963), pp. 91–101.

15. Materials on revolts in the colonial period are just now becoming available. See, for example, Richard E. Rubenstein, *Rebels in Eden: Mass Political Violence in the United States* (Boston, Little, Brown, 1970), pp. 48–56, and Bibliography at pp. 198–199; Richard Hofstadter and Michael Wallace, eds., *American Violence: A Documentary History* (New York, Knopf, 1970). Jesse Lemisch's massive work in this area is to be published shortly.

16. See Edmund S. Morgan, *The Birth of the Republic, 1763–1789* (Chicago, University of Chicago Press, 1956). Herbert Aptheker, *The American Revolution, 1763–1783* (New York, International Publishers, 1960).

17. See Oscar Handlin, *Race and Nationality in American Life* (Boston, Little, Brown, 1957).

18. Charles A. Beard, *An Economic Interpretation of the Constitution of the United States* (New York, Macmillan, 1935), discussed in Richard Hofstadter, *The Progressive Historians, Turner, Beard, Parrington* (New York, Knopf, 1968), pp. 207–284. Hannah Arendt discusses the idea of "mixed" or "balanced" government in *On Revolution*, Ch. 4.

19. See, e.g., H. M. Brackenridge, *History of the Western Insurrection, 1794* (Pittsburgh, 1859), reprinted in Robert M. Fogelson and Richard E. Rubenstein, eds., *Mass Violence in America* (New York, Arno Press–N.Y. Times, 1969).

20. Sanctification extends only to the two major parties, of course. Other parties are not considered legitimate and may, for example, be kept off the ballot, especially when they are "ideological."

21. See, for example, Louis Hartz, *The Liberal Tradition in America* (New York, Harcourt, Brace, 1955).

22. In fact, this combination of general advance and relative decline is now considered a major cause of revolution: James C. Davies, "Toward a Theory of Revolution," in Davies, ed., *When Men Revolt and Why: A Reader in Political Violence and Revolution* (New York, Free Press, 1971), pp. 134–147; Ted Gurr, *Why Men Rebel* (Princeton, Princeton University Press, 1971).

23. This was the insight of some "radical Republicans." See James M. McPherson, *The Struggle for Equality: Abolitionists and the Negro in the Civil War and Reconstruction* (Princeton, Princeton University Press, 1964). John Hope Franklin, *Reconstruction after the Civil War* (Chicago, University of Chicago Press, 1961), pp. 54 ff.

24. A useful anthology is Perry Miller, *The American Transcendentalists* (New York, Anchor Books, 1957).

25. Gilbert Hobbs Barnes, *The Antislavery Impulse, 1830–1844* (New York, Harcourt, Brace, 1964); Eric Foner, *Free Soil, Free Labor, Free Men: The Ideology of the Republican Party before the Civil War* (New York, Oxford University Press, 1970); Milton Viorst, *Fall from Grace: The Republican Party and the Puritan Ethic* (New York, New American Library, 1968), pp. 31–40.

26. Rayford W. Logan, *The Betrayal of the Negro, From Rutherford B. Hayes to Woodrow Wilson* (New York, Collier Books, 1965).

27. C. Vann Woodward, *Reunion and Reaction* (New York, Anchor Books, 1956).

28. See, for example, John Higham, *Strangers in the Land: Patterns of American Nativism, 1860–1925* (New Brunswick, N.J., Rutgers University Press, 1955).

29. William R. Taylor, *Cavalier and Yankee: The Old South and American National Character* (New York, Harper & Row, 1969).

30. For example, see Louis Adamic, *Dynamite! The Story of Class Violence in America*, rev. ed. (Gloucester, Mass., Peter Smith, 1963); Robert V. Bruce, *1877: Year of Violence* (Indianapolis, Bobbs-Merrill, 1959); John W. Caughey, ed., *Their Majesties the Mob* (Chicago, University of Chicago Press, 1960); Arthur F. Raper, *The Tragedy of Lynching* (New York, Arno Press–N.Y. Times, 1969 [1933]).

31. See Frederick W. Taylor, *The Principles of Scientific Management* (New York, Norton Library, 1967 [1911]).

32. Samuel Yellen, *American Labor Struggles* (New York, S. A. Russell, 1956 [1936]), and other narratives make this quite clear.

33. The story of the iron workers' bombing of the *Los Angeles Times*, for example, is told (from the business point of view) in William J. Burns, *The Masked War* (New York, Arno Press–N.Y. Times, 1969 [1913]). See also Louis Adamic, *Dynamite!*

34. On the relative weakness of the American radical tradition see Christopher Lasch, *The Agony of the American Left* (New York, Vintage Books, 1969).

35. For example, the attempted assassination of Henry Clay Frick: Alexander Berkman, *Prison Memoirs of an Anarchist* (New York, Mother Earth Publishing Society, 1912). IWW leaders were tried for the assassination of former Governor Steunenberg of Idaho: see William D. Haywood, *Bill Haywood's Book: The Autobiography of William D. Haywood* (New York, International Publishers, 1929).

36. Richard Hofstadter, *The Age of Reform*; Gabriel Kolko, *The Triumph of Conservatism*.

37. Morton G. White, *Social Thought in America: The Revolt against Formalism* (Boston, Beacon Press, 1957).

38. Marc Karson, *American Labor Unions and Politics, 1900–1918* (Boston, Beacon Press, 1965), pp. 136–138.

39. C. Vann Woodward, *The Strange Career of Jim Crow* (New York, Oxford University Press, 1966).

40. For example, Counselor Robert Lansing (later secretary of state) stated that loss of allied markets would produce "restriction of outputs, industrial depression, idle capital and idle labor, numerous failures, financial demoralization and general unrest and suffering among the laboring classes." Quoted in Richard Hofstadter, *American Political Tradition*, pp. 264–265.

41. See, for example, Emerson Hough, *The Web* (1919), and R. G. Brown, Zechariah Chafee, Jr., et al., *Illegal Practices of the Department of Justice* (1920), both reprinted by Arno Press–N.Y. Times, New York, 1969.

42. William A. Williams, *The Roots of the Modern American Empire* (New York, Random House, 1969).

43. See Rexford G. Tugwell, "The Experimental Roosevelt," in William E. Leuchtenburg, ed., *Franklin D. Roosevelt: A Profile* (New York, Hill and Wang, 1967), pp. 84–85.

44. Rita James Simon, ed., *As We Saw the Thirties: Essays on Social and Political Movements of a Decade* (Urbana, University of Illinois Press, 1967).

45. Cf. Howard Zinn, *The Politics of History*, pp. 118–136.

46. Art Preis, *Labor's Giant Step: Twenty Years of the C.I.O.* (New York, Pathfinder Press, n.d.).

47. C. Wright Mills, *The Power Elite* (New York, Oxford University Press, 1956); see also Milton Friedman, *Capitalism and Freedom* (Chicago, University of Chicago Press, 1962), Chapters VIII and IX. It is still not well recognized that federal agencies established to regulate access to truck, rail, and air routes, radio and television frequencies, power supplies, government markets, etc., are in the business of carving up the public domain among competing corporate giants. The effect is to "attach" them to the federal establishment much as Hamilton "attached" the creditor class via his funding program.

48. Ferdinand Lundberg, *The Rich and the Super-Rich* (New York, Lyle Stuart, 1968); Gabriel Kolko, *Wealth and Power in America: An Analysis of Social Class and Income Distribution* (New York, Praeger, 1962), pp. 9–45.

49. "Dr. Win-The-War," he said, had replaced "Dr. New Deal."

50. In Samuel Lubell, *The Future of American Politics* (New York, Harper & Row, 1951).

51. Christopher Lasch, *Agony of the American Left.*

52. Judd Polk, "The New International Production" (Chicago, Adlai Stevenson Institute, Working Paper 2, 1972), p. 4. See also Richard J. Barnet, *Intervention and Revolution: America's Confrontation with Insurgent Movements around the World* (New York, World Publishing Company, 1968), p. 15. Barnet's more detailed study of the multinational corporation is to be published shortly.

53. "Multinational Companies," *Business Week*, April 20, 1963, quoted in Paul A. Baran and Paul M. Sweezy, *Monopoly Capital*, New York, Monthly Review Press, 1966, pp. 196–197, see pp. 192–202; see also Harry Magdoff, *The Age of Imperialism* (New York, Monthly Review Press, 1969).

54. By 1953, the U.S. defense budget exceeded the highest annual war budget of the Second World War.

55. Seymour Melman, *Pentagon Capitalism: The Political Economy of War* (New York, McGraw-Hill, 1970); see also David Horowitz, ed., *Corporations and the Cold War* (New York, Monthly Review Press, 1969).

56. For example, by John Kenneth Galbraith, *The New Industrial State* (Boston, Houghton Mifflin Co., 1967); Baran and Sweezy, *Monopoly Capital.*

57. See Herbert Marcuse, *One-Dimensional Man* (Boston, Beacon Press, 1959).

58. Karl Marx, "The Eighteenth Brumaire of Louis Bonaparte," Karl Marx and Friedrich Engels, *Selected Works* (New York, International Publishers, 1968), p. 170; V. I. Lenin, *State and Revolution* (New York, International Publishers, 1932), pp. 21–31.

59. See, for example, Fred Branfman, "Air War: The New Totalitarianism," *Liberation*, February–April 1971; *Project Air War Handbook* (Washington, D.C., Project Air War, 1972).

60. John Kenneth Galbraith, *The Affluent Society* (Boston, Houghton Mifflin Co., 1958); Daniel J. Boorstin, *The Genius of American Politics* (Chicago, University of Chicago Press, 1953).

61. Seymour Martin Lipset, *Political Man: The Social Basis of Politics* (New York: Doubleday and Co., 1960); Daniel

Bell, *The End of Ideology: On the Exhaustion of Political Ideas in the Fifties* (New York, Free Press, 1960).

62. See Morris Janowitz, *Social Control of Escalated Riots* (Chicago, University of Chicago Center for Policy Studies, 1967).

63. The application of technocratic method in pursuing the Indochina war is discussed in Richard M. Pfeffer, ed., *No More Vietnams? The War and the Future of American Foreign Policy* (New York, Harper & Row, 1968).

64. *Report of the National Advisory Commission on Civil Disorders* (Kerner Report) (New York, Bantam Books, 1968).

65. Theodore Roszak, *The Making of a Counter Culture* (Garden City, N.Y., Doubleday, 1969).

66. For an excellent discussion of this and related points, see John McDermott, "Technology: The Opiate of The Intellectuals," *New York Review of Books*, March 13, 1970.

67. See Peter Schrag, *Out of Place in America: Essays for the End of an Age* (New York, Random House, 1970); Michael Novak, *The Rise of the Unmeltable Ethnics: Politics and Culture in the Seventies* (New York, Macmillan, 1972).

68. Dramatized in Daniel Berrigan, *The Trial of the Catonsville Nine* (Boston, Beacon Press, 1970); see also Francine Du Plessix Gray, *Divine Disobedience: Profiles in Catholic Radicalism* (New York, Knopf, 1970).

69. Civil disobedience among the guardians of law and order often assumes strange forms. Policemen, for example, have conducted "job actions" involving the ticketing of every automobile arguably in violation of a parking or traffic law (*Chicago Sun-Times*, October 2, 1972), which one is tempted to call "civil overobedience."

70. Hannah Arendt, *On Violence* (Boston, Beacon Press, 1971).

PART TWO

1. James G. Wilson, *Varieties of Police Behavior* (Cambridge, Harvard University Press, 1968), p. 290.

2. Robert A. Dahl, *A Preface to Democratic Theory* (Chicago, University of Chicago Press, 1956), p. 24.

3. Discussed in Henri Lefebvre, *The Sociology of Marx* (New York, Vintage Books, 1969), pp. 89–122, especially p. 120.
4. Karl Marx and Frederick Engels, "Manifesto of the Communist Party," in *Selected Works* (New York: International Publishers, 1968), pp. 40–46.
5. Aristotle, "Politics" (Jowett translation), in William Ebenstein, *Great Political Thinkers, Plato to the Present*, 4th ed. (New York, Holt, Rinehart and Winston, 1969), pp. 104–109.
6. C. Wright Mills, *The Power Elite* (New York: Oxford University Press, 1956); G. William Domhoff, *Who Rules America?* (Englewood Cliffs, N.J., Prentice-Hall, 1967), *The Higher Circles: The Governing Class in America* (New York, Vintage Books, 1971); Ferdinand Lundberg, *The Rich and the Super-Rich* (New York, Lyle Stuart, 1968).
7. Marx and Engels, "Manifesto," pp. 42, 44.
8. See, for example, Hannah Arendt, *On Revolution* (New York, Viking Press, 1963), pp. 63–64. Louis Hartz, *The Liberal Tradition in America* (New York, Harcourt, Brace, 1955).
9. Ted Gurr, *Why Men Rebel* (Princeton, Princeton University Press, 1970).
10. See, for example, Jerome H. Skolnick, *The Politics of Protest* (New York, Simon & Schuster, 1969), pp. 210–240.
11. Marx and Engels, "Manifesto," p. 44.
12. Marx, "The Eighteenth Brumaire of Louis Bonaparte," in *Selected Works*, p. 138.
13. William V. Shannon, *The American Irish* (New York, Macmillan, 1963).
14. See Hugh D. Graham and Ted R. Gurr, eds., *Violence in America: Historical and Comparative Perspectives* (New York, Bantam Books, 1969).
15. Richard Hofstadter and Michael Wallace, eds., *American Violence: A Documentary History* (New York, Knopf, 1970).
16. Quoted in Richard Hofstadter, *The American Political Tradition* (New York, Vintage Books, 1954), p. 256.
17. Frances Perkins, "A Little Left of Center," in William E. Leuchtenberg, ed., *Franklin D. Roosevelt: A Profile* (New York, Hill and Wang, 1967), p. 227.

18. Max Weber, *Max Weber on Charisma and Institution-Building: Selected Papers*, S. N. Eisenstadt, ed. (Chicago, University of Chicago Press, 1968).

19. For an interesting example of liberal antipluralist criticism, see Theodore Lowi, *The End of Liberalism* (Chicago, University of Chicago Press, 1970).

20. Note, however, that Irish immigrants, who arrived in the United States in very large numbers between 1830 and 1860, did not succeed in capturing control of city governments until the period 1890–1920, and did not become part of a national governing coalition until the 1930's. This has been a much longer process than is generally realized. Cf. William Shannon, *The American Irish*.

21. The demand for compensation recently raised by certain black leaders has been greeted with the usual shocked disbelief by most American liberals. Cf. Robert S. Lecky and H. Elliott Wright, eds., *Black Manifesto: Religion, Racism and Reparations* (New York, Sheed & Ward, 1969).

22. Useful materials on the history of American business are contained in Alfred D. Chandler, Jr., *Strategy and Structure — Chapters in the History of American Industrial Enterprise* (Garden City, N.Y., Doubleday, 1962).

23. See Michael A. Lebowitz, "The Jacksonians: Paradox Lost?" in Barton J. Bernstein, ed., *Towards a New Past: Dissenting Essays in American History* (New York, Vintage Books, 1969), pp. 65–89.

24. Albert K. Weinberg, *Manifest Destiny: A Study of Nationalist Expansion in American History* (Chicago, Quadrangle Books, 1963).

25. See William A. Williams's important study, *The Roots of the Modern American Empire: A Study of the Growth and Shaping of Social Consciousness in a Marketplace Society* (New York, Random House, 1960).

26. *The Pentagon Papers: The Defense Department History of United States Decision Making on Vietnam* ("Senator Gravel Edition") (Boston, Beacon Press, 1971).

27. Robert Sherrill, *The Accidental President* (New York, Grossman, 1967).

28. Seymour Melman, *Pentagon Capitalism: The Political Economy of War* (New York, McGraw-Hill, 1970).

29. A recent example is the sponsorship of legislation creating a Federal Consumer Protection Agency by liberal Repub-

lican Senators Percy and Javits, the same senators who
advocate a "productivity revolution" for American business. The legislation has been opposed by most old-line industrialists, and is supported by elements of the new
business vanguard, e.g., the department store oligopolists.
MARCOR (Montgomery Ward), which supports Senator
Percy's bill, formerly employed as general counsel one
Daniel Walker, who at this writing is the liberal-Democratic candidate for governor of Illinois, and an exponent
of consumer protection, antipollution, the "productivity
revolution," etc.

30. See, for example, Grant McConnell, *Private Power and
American Democracy* (New York, Knopf, 1967).

31. William A. Williams, *Roots of the Modern American Empire*; Seymour Melman, *Pentagon Capitalism*; Gabriel
Kolko, *The Roots of American Foreign Policy* (Boston,
Beacon Press, 1969); David Horowitz, ed., *Corporations
and the Cold War* (New York, Monthly Review Press,
1969).

32. Henry D. Thoreau, "Walden," in *Walden* and *Civil Disobedience* (New York, Rinehart and Company, 1949),
p. 43.

33. See, for example, C. E. Black, *The Dynamics of Modernization: A Study in Comparative History* (New York,
Harper & Row, 1967).

34. G. William Domhoff, *The Higher Circles: The Governing
Class in America* (New York, Vintage Books, 1971), p.
109.

35. See footnote 6 above.

36. G. William Domhoff, *The Higher Circles*, p. 106.

37. Marx and Engels, "Manifesto," in *Selected Works*, p. 106.

38. Cf. Arthur M. Schlesinger, Jr., *The Bitter Heritage: Vietnam and American Democracy* (Boston, Houghton Mifflin,
1967); Roger Hilsman, *To Move a Nation* (Garden City,
N.Y., Doubleday, 1967).

39. In addition to the works cited, see Noam Chomsky, *Ameri-
can Power and the New Mandarins* (New York, Vintage
Books, 1969). See also G. William Domhoff, *The Higher
Circles*, pp. 111–275.

40. Herbert Marcuse, *One-Dimensional Man* (Boston, Beacon
Press, 1959), p. 56.

41. See William A. Williams, *The United States, Cuba and*

Castro (New York, Monthly Review Press, 1962); Theodore Draper, *Castro's Revolution: Myths and Realities* (New York, Praeger, 1962); Robert Scheer and Maurice Zeitlin, *Cuba: Tragedy in Our Hemisphere* (New York, Grove Press, 1963).

42. William R. Polk, *The United States and the Arab World*, 2nd ed. (Cambridge, Harvard University Press, 1970); Robert Engler, *The Politics of Oil* (New York, Macmillan, 1961); Richard J. Barnet, *Intervention and Revolution: The United States in the Third World* (New York, World Publishing Co., 1968).

43. See Terence Cook and Patrick Morgan, eds., *Participatory Democracy* (San Francisco, Cornfield Press, 1971). Cf. Ernest Mandel, *The Revolutionary Student Movement: Theory and Practice* (New York, Pathfinder Press, n.d.).

44. See Richard E. Rubenstein, *Rebels in Eden: Mass Political Violence in the United States* (Boston, Little, Brown, 1970), pp. 30–32, 117–119.

45. Cf. W. J. Cash, *The Mind of the South* (New York, Vintage Books, 1954).

46. President's Commission on Law Enforcement and the Administration of Justice, *The Challenge of Crime in a Free Society* (Washington, D.C., U.S. Government Printing Office, 1967); Ramsey Clark, *Crime in America* (New York, Simon & Schuster, 1971), pp. 1–50.

47. See *Handbook on Women Workers, 1969* (Washington, D.C., Women's Bureau, U.S. Department of Labor).

48. UCLA Institute of Government and Public Affairs, *Los Angeles Riot Study* (Los Angeles, 1967); Robert M. Fogelson, *Violence as Protest: A Study of Riots and Ghettos* (Garden City, N.Y., Doubleday, 1971).

49. Malcolm X, *Autobiography* (New York, Grove Press, 1966), p. 373.

50. See, for example, the essays collected in Norman Miller and Roderick Aya, eds., *National Liberation* (New York, Free Press, 1971).

51. National Commission on the Causes and Prevention of Violence, *Report* (Washington, D.C., U.S. Government Printing Office, 1969); see also Task Force Reports, especially Jerome H. Skolnick, *The Politics of Protest* (New York, Ballantine Books, 1969).

52. Address of George Engel, in L. Parsons, *The Famous*

Speeches of the Eight Chicago Anarchists in Court (New York, Arno Press–N.Y. Times, 1969 [1910]), p. 38.

53. "An Interview with Huey P. Newton," in Bracey, Meier and Rudwick, *Black Nationalism in America* (Indianapolis, Bobbs-Merrill, 1970), p. 535.

54. Harold Cruse, *The Crisis of the Negro Intellectual* (New York, William Morrow, 1967), esp. pp. 115–181.

PART THREE

1. Bob Dylan, "Ballad of a Thin Man," *Highway 61 Revisited* (M. Witmark and Sons [ASCAP], 1965).
2. Henry Bienen, *Violence and Social Change: A Review of Current Literature* (Chicago, University of Chicago Press, 1968), pp. 2–3.
3. Karl Marx and Frederick Engels, *Selected Works* (New York, International Publishers, 1968); V. I. Lenin, *State and Revolution* (New York, International Publishers, 1932); Leon Trotsky, *The Permanent Revolution and Results and Prospects* (New York, Pathfinder Press, 1970); see also Henri Lefebvre, *The Sociology of Marx* (New York, Vintage Books, 1969); C. Wright Mills, *The Marxists* (New York, Dell, 1962).
4. John Kenneth Galbraith, *The New Industrial State* (Boston, Houghton Mifflin Co., 1967); Arnold M. Rose, *The Power Structure* (New York, Oxford University Press, 1967); Ralf Dahrendorf, *Class and Class Conflict in Industrial Society* (Stanford, Stanford University Press, 1959); Daniel Bell, *The End of Ideology: On the Exhaustion of Political Ideas in the Fifties* (New York, The Free Press, 1960).
5. See, e.g., Theodore Roszak, *The Making of a Counter Culture* (Garden City, N.Y., Doubleday, 1969); Charles Reich, *The Greening of America* (New York, Random House, 1970); Harold Cruse, *Rebellion or Revolution?* (New York, William Morrow, 1968).
6. See essays collected in Burkhart and Kendrick, *The New Politics: Mood or Movement?* (Englewood Cliffs, N.J., Prentice-Hall, 1971).

7. Or by some sort of "new proletariat": See Norman Birn-baum, *The Crisis of Industrial Society* (New York, Ox-ford University Press, 1965); Herbert Marcuse, *An Essay on Liberation* (Boston, Beacon Press, 1969). Abandon-ment of belief in the revolutionary potential of the working class produces either a liberal or an apocalyptic attitude towards change — or both simultaneously: see Abbie Hoffman, Jerry Rubin and Ed Saunders, *Vote!* (New York, Grove Press, 1972).

8. C. E. Black, *The Dynamics of Modernization* (New York, Harper & Row, 1966); Paul A. Baran and Paul M. Sweezy, *Monopoly Capital: An Essay on the American Economic and Social Order* (New York, Monthly Review Press, 1968), pp. 218 ff.; P. S. Labini, *Oligopoly and Technical Progress* (Cambridge, Harvard University Press, 1962). Cf. Karl Marx, *Capital, Volume 1: A Critical Analysis of Capitalist Production* (New York, International Publishers, 1967), pp. 626–628.

9. See, for example, Grant McConnell, *Private Power and American Democracy* (New York, Knopf, 1967).

10. Mark J. Green, *The Closed Enterprise System: Ralph Nader's Study Group Report on Antitrust Enforcement* (New York, Grossman Publishers, 1972).

11. See Franz Schurmann, "System, Contradictions, and Revo-lution in America," in Roderick Aya and Norman Miller, eds., *The New American Revolution* (New York, Free Press, 1971), p. 27, citing *Handbook of Labor Statistics*.

12. See, for example, the subtle variations on this theme de-veloped in William Kornhauser, *The Politics of Mass So-ciety* (New York, Free Press, 1959); and Herbert Marcuse, *One-Dimensional Man* (Boston, Beacon Press, 1959). See also Vance Packard, *The Hidden Persuaders* (New York, McKay, 1957).

13. John Kenneth Galbraith, *The Affluent Society* (Boston, Houghton Mifflin Co., 1958).

14. In the *Essay on Liberation*. See also Norman Birnbaum, *Crisis of Industrial Society*, pp. 143 ff., for a suggestion that student revolt may be related to the rise of a new technocratic elite.

15. A research project of major importance, which, to my knowledge, has not yet been undertaken, is the construc-tion of a *true budget* for the American workingman or

woman. Over the course of a year, what is a typical worker's true "income" from all sources, direct and imputed?
What does he "spend," and how much does he "invest" in
the industrial infrastructure?

16. Frederick W. Taylor, *Principles of Scientific Management*
(New York, Norton Library, 1967 [1911]); Richard E.
Rubenstein, "The Technological Utopia of Frederick Winslow Taylor" (unpublished A.B. thesis, History and Literature Department Library, Harvard College, 1957).

17. Letitia Upton and Nancy Lyons, "Basic Facts: Distribution
of Personal Wealth and Income" (Cambridge, Mass., Cambridge Institute, 1971).

18. *Chicago Sun-Times*, September 7, 1971.

19. Ferdinand Lundberg, *The Rich and the Super-Rich* (New
York, Lyle Stuart, 1968), p. 23.

20. Interview with Edward T. Palmer, executive director,
COMPRAND (South Chicago Health Planning Organization), May 5, 1972, in Chicago.

21. Crane Brinton, *The Anatomy of Revolution* (Englewood
Cliffs, N.J., Prentice-Hall, 1962), p. 66. Brinton's book,
which examines the causes of revolution without reference
to the United States, now reads like a description of
America in the 1960's and 1970's.

22. Hannah Arendt, *On Violence* (New York, Harcourt,
Brace, 1970), pp. 59–87.

23. See, for example, Jim Clark, "Senate Power Base Shifting,"
Chicago Sun-Times, October 14, 1972: "Counting primary
results and retirements announced this year, 36 [Senate]
seats have changed hands since 1968. . . . No single event
or issue can explain the Senate's instability. . . ." Labor
union officials report a similar increase in turnover of local
union officers covering the same period. See also discussion
of Walter Dean Burnham's work on disaggregation, note
24 below.

24. Walter Dean Burnham, "The End of American Party
Politics," in Joyce Gelb and Marian Lief Palley, eds.,
American Politics and Social Change (New York, Holt,
Rinehart & Winston, 1971), p. 124.

25. *Ibid.*, p. 125.

26. *Ibid.*, p. 128.

27. *Ibid.*, p. 126.

28. See Richard Hofstadter, *The Paranoid Style in American Politics* (New York, Vintage Books, 1967).

29. Cf. Leon Trotsky, *The Revolution Betrayed* (New York, Pathfinder Press, 1969); Isaac Deutscher, *Stalin: A Political Biography* (New York, Vintage Books, 1960).

30. Marx and Engels, "Manifesto," in *Selected Works*, p. 45.

31. The decentralizers and *Whole Earth Catalog* utopians among us might ponder Marx's bitter criticism of leaders who "renounce the revolutionizing of the old world by means of the latter's own great, combined resources and seek, rather, to achieve salvation behind society's back. . . ." In "The Eighteenth Brumaire of Louis Bonaparte," in *Selected Works*, p. 103.

32. See the analysis of the military spirit in Stuart Schram's introduction to *The Political Thought of Mao Tse-tung* (Baltimore, Johns Hopkins University Press, 1967).

33. See Susan Sontag, *Styles of Radical Will* (New York, Farrar, Straus & Giroux, 1969).

34. Cf. Nathan Glazer, *Remembering the Answers: Essays on the American Student Revolt* (New York, Basic Books, 1970). The New Left–New Fascism equation is a favorite theme of *Commentary* magazine's establishment liberals.

35. E.g., Albert Camus, *The Rebel* (New York, Vintage Books, 1954); Hannah Arendt, *On Revolution* (New York, Viking Press, 1963).

36. Milton Friedman, *Capitalism and Freedom* (Chicago, University of Chicago Press, 1962); Friedrich A. Hayek, *The Road to Serfdom* (Chicago, University of Chicago Press, 1956).

37. On the development of German fascism, see Franz Neumann, *Behemoth: The Structure and Practice of National Socialism, 1933–1944* (New York, 1944); F. L. Carsten, *The Rise of Fascism* (Berkeley, University of California Press, 1967); Hannah Arendt, *The Origins of Totalitarianism* (New York, Meridian Books, 1958); Leon Trotsky, *Fascism: What It Is, How to Fight It* (New York, Pathfinder Press, n.d.).

38. Trotsky, *Fascism*.

39. Wilhelm Reich, *The Mass Psychology of Fascism* (New York, Farrar, Straus & Giroux, 1970).

40. Barrington Moore, *The Social Origins of Dictatorship and*

Democracy: Lord and Peasant in the Modern World (Boston, Beacon Press, 1966).

41. See Richard M. Pfeffer, "Mao Tse-tung and the Cultural Revolution," in Norman Miller and Roderick Aya, eds., *National Liberation* (New York, Free Press, 1971), pp. 249–296.

INDEX

Calhoun, John C., 104, 135
capitalism: capacities of, 196;
and consumerism, 188; contradictions of, and liberalism,
9; flexibility of, 195; free-
market, 180–181; and im-
perialism, 130–131; and
liberty, 238, 244; monopoly,
65–66, 121; and planned
waste, 208–209; preservation
of, 172–173, 181–182, 188–
189, 203–205; and progress,
120–121; and revolution, 172
Carmichael, Stokely, 162
Castro, Fidel, 143, 151
Catholics, violence against, 40
Catonsville Nine, 75
centralization, 102–104, 127,
178–180, 190, 245; see also
modernization
centrism, 87
change, dream of, 107–108
charisma, 102–103
Chavez, Cesar, 157
Chicago, 77, 157, 207–208
Chile, 151
China. See People's Republic of
China
CIO, 243; and AFL, 118, 186;
creation of, 50; militancy of,
60; and underclass, 52
civil disobedience, spread of,
75–76
Civilian Conservation Corps, 53
Civil War: and big business,
126; and coalitions, 106; and
consensus, 30; and conservative nationalism, 32; effects
of, 26–27; Lincoln's role in,
6; and myth of democracy's
progress, 3; and national
unity, 99; and ruling class,
228; and two-party system,
228
Clark, Mark, 157n
class: anti-Marxist analysis of,
173–174; and coalition, 14;

consciousness of, 39–40, 122,
216; and Constitution, 16, 87;
and democracy, 93; and interest groups, 86–88, 91, 92,
118; and nationalism, 21–22;
and polarity, 87; and political
power, 86
class conflict, 38–39; and affluence, 21, 70, 88–89; between
1877–1937, 36; and corporate
control of State, 67–68; "final
solutions" to, 205; see also
three-class system
class struggle, in 1970's, 250
Cleveland, Grover, 31
coalitions: and all-bourgeois
alliance, 44–45, 51; in American Revolution, 17–19; and
big business, 122, 129–130,
135; and blacks, 95; change-
overs of, 27, 29, 33, 107, 108,
109–110, 125–126; and class,
13, 14; and class conflict, 90;
and consensus, 69–70, 93, 94,
97, 98–99, 109, 111–112; and
conservatism, 101, 108–109;
cycle of, 113–116, 125, 175;
disbelief in, 80; displacement
of, 96, 111; and dissent and
repression, 29; dissolution of,
96–97, 107, 113, 114–115;
and elections, 94, 98, 109–
110; and extra-constitutional
action, 115; financing of, 114;
and flux, 113–114; forma-
tion of, 13–14, 17–19, 96,
106–115; and interest groups,
92–94, 132; "Jacobin" phase
of, 115, 117–118; Jeffersonian,
19; and leadership, 106–112;
and liberalism, 24; and local
power, 103–104; and mass
society, 195; and monopoly,
128; movement of from
liberalism to conservatism, 26,
33, 44–46, 48–49; and na-
tional principle, 14–15, 109–